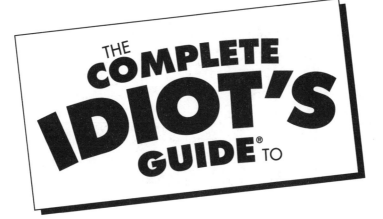

THE COMPLETE IDIOT'S GUIDE® TO

Private Investigating

by Steven Kerry Brown

ALPHA

A member of Penguin Group (USA) Inc.

To Frank Green, Jacksonville, Fla., who taught me everything I know about writing and also to the fine Special Agent Instructors at the FBI Academy, Quantico, Va., whose lessons have proven their worth for 30 years of investigative activity.

Copyright © 2003 by Steven Kerry Brown

International Standard Book Number: 0-02-864399-2
Library of Congress Catalog Card Number: 2002110187

05   04   8   7   6

Interpretation of the printing code: The rightmost number of the first series of numbers is the year of the book's printing; the rightmost number of the second series of numbers is the number of the book's printing. For example, a printing code of 02-1 shows that the first printing occurred in 2002.

Printed in the United States of America

Publisher: *Marie Butler-Knight*
Product Manager: *Phil Kitchel*
Managing Editor: *Jennifer Chisholm*
Acquisitions Editor: *Randy Ladenheim-Gil*
Development Editor: *Nancy D. Lewis*
Production Editor: *Billy Fields*
Copy Editor: *Amy Borrelli*
Illustrator: *Chris Eliopoulos*
Cover/Book Designer: *Trina Wurst*
Indexer: *Angie Bess*
Layout/Proofreading: *Angela Calvert, Mary Hunt, Kimberly Tucker, Sherry Taggart*

Contents at a Glance

Appendixes

Contents

Appendixes

Foreword

Do you want to be a private investigator? Or do you want to be just as smart as some of the best of them? Then this is the perfect book for you. Between the covers of this guide, you will find the "tricks of trade" of one of the best PI's in the business, one who knows the PI trade from the inside out and has seen it all from A to Z.

Steve Brown has the background and training of a federal agent and the experience of a private eye. His 30 years of dealing with the personal and business issues of thousands of clients gives him a unique insight into the good, the bad, and the ugly of the investigative trade, which he shares with you in the pages of this book.

When I needed an investigation done in Florida, Steve was the man I found for the job.

Throughout this book, I see many of the things that make up our daily business and some of the cases that we worked together. Steve is one of the "old pros" of the business, because he, like me, got into the business BC (before computers) back in the days when we really were gumshoes. Here you will find both the old manual methods of sifting through the big red books in the courthouse to the new technological, computerized techniques accessible instantly through the Internet.

With the advent of the telephone, fax machine, and computer, you can have access to as much information as the biggest government agency. This book reveals the little known secrets learned only through trial and error, from sitting in cars all night long, watching lovers do the horizontal rumba, following white collar weasels as they slide under the carpet without making a ripple and digging through the courthouse records to find that Mr. Wonderful is still married to someone else.

The private investigation industry is one of the most interesting and fastest growing trades in the country. The people who can locate others, determine their true background and employability and discover their hidden assets has the opportunity to make a good living with little overhead and expenses. The keys to being successful are the desire to succeed and the knowledge found through the experience of people like Steve Brown.

Is this the new career path for you? Read this book, consider the words of wisdom found within and get out there and do it! You may find yourself to have the natural talent for this profitable, fun, and interesting business. You don't need a badge, or a gun, or to have been a cop in a previous life. If you really want to do this, then find a mentor to teach you the ropes just like we did, many years ago.

Good Luck and good hunting.

Edmund J. Pankau, CLI, CPP, DABFE

Edmund J. Pankau, rated one of the nations top 10 private investigators, is a world-renowned professional speaker and author of numerous articles and several award-winning books on privacy and investigation.

His published books include *CHECK IT OUT!: Everyone's Guide to Investigation* (Contemporary, 1992), *HOW TO MAKE $100,000 a YEAR AS A PRIVATE INVESTIGATOR* (Paladin, 1993) and *The PI Portfolio* (Inphomation, 1994). His newest book, *Hide Your Assets and Disappear* is a New York Times bestseller (HarperCollins 1999).

He is the associate editor of *PI Magazine* and a contributing writer to "EscapeArtist" and numerous professional financial and investigative trade journals.

His experiences and cases have been featured in such publications as *Time, Business Week, People, USA Today,* and *The New York Times.* He has appeared as a guest on radio and television on *ABC 20/20, Larry King Live, BBC London, Geraldo Rivera, CNBC,* the *Today Show, CNN Moneyline,* and *America's Most Wanted* as an authority on privacy and investigation issues.

Ed is a graduate of Florida State University and is the director of Pankau Consulting, an investigative agency headquartered in Houston, Texas. If you really want to find him, it has been rumored that he was last sighted on the island of Roatan off the coast of Honduras.

To reach Mr. Pankau for an interview, call 713-224-3777 or visit his websites at www.pankau.com or www.hideyourassets.com (e-mail ejp@pankau.com).

Introduction

I had a college friend whose father was president of a company that made cans for vegetables and other food items. The company felt business was stagnating and wanted to expand. It hired a consultant to originate ideas on increasing business. The board of directors met with the consultant after he'd done his research. When they were all seated, he said to the board, "Okay, what kind of business do you think this company is in?"

"That's simple, we're in the can business," the board told him.

"No, you aren't," the consultant said. "Your company is not in the can business, it's in the packaging business."

With that concept in mind, the company went on to greatly expand into all areas of packaging.

Likewise, the private investigator is not in the surveillance business, or the electronic countermeasure business, or the background investigative business. Well, if it's not any of those businesses, what kind of business is it?

The private investigative agency is in the information business. The PI's client needs to know something. The PI gets the information. The unusual techniques that a PI uses are the fun part of the business and are what separates it from other information businesses, but nonetheless, information is what a PI sells.

How to get the information using tricks of the trade is what I'm teaching you in this book. Whether you're a professional PI or doing it for yourself, the techniques are the same and they're all here.

Nearly everybody has helped a friend through a divorce, or has been suspicious of an overheard telephone call their own spouse has made. Ever wondered who your daughter was dating, or have you had a teenager stay out over night, or even run away?

Did your husband repeat something to you that you only said once—to your best friend during a telephone conversation? Have you ever thought about checking the background on a babysitter, a day-care center, or a potential new boyfriend? Then this book is for you.

We all have things in our life that we'd like to check out. Suspicions we'd like confirmed. Old boyfriends or girlfriends we'd like to find. We'd like to know who our ex is dating and who's influencing our children.

You have two choices: Do it yourself, or hire it out. I've tried to put everything in this book, all the basics, to help you do it yourself or find the right PI for the job.

If you're already a professional PI, I think you'll find some "tricks and treats" in each chapter that'll help you build your business, be more professional, get more clients, and make more money.

Every chapter is woven through with real stories from the case files of my PI practice. The names and locations have been changed to protect my clients' identity, but the pertinent facts are there and the situations are real. The solutions are real, too. Real people, real facts, real life.

Now look through the table of contents to find your specific problem, and I'll show you how to get the information you need.

How This Book Is Organized

This book is presented in five sections:

Part 1, "Private Investigation, Business or Fun?" teaches a little history of the PI industry, how to find a professional PI, the legal requirements to obtaining your own PI license, the skills and equipment you'll need, and how to get hired by a PI agency.

Part 2, "Getting the Scoop," offers the basics of skip tracing. These chapters will teach you where to find information, how to dig up the dirt at the courthouse, where to access the public record databases, and how to log on to the secret "pay sites" that professional PIs use. Then you'll put it all together by learning how to do a comprehensive background investigation.

Part 3, "Learning the Basics," teaches all the basic investigative techniques. You're taught how to do interrogations, how to run stationary and moving surveillances, and how to get information from the phone company you didn't think they'd give.

Part 4, "Working the Cases," offers step-by-step instructional information on a variety of different types of cases. You're taught in detail how to do a crime scene investigation, how to sift the evidence of marital infidelity, and how to evaluate closed-circuit television cameras and set one up in your home, business, or on the go.

Part 5, "Advanced Techniques," teaches you how to perform more serious investigations, such as finding the runaway teenager or checking your phones for taps. It shows you how to morph from victim to aggressor if you've been robbed, and how a professional should gather all the evidence, report it, and present it in court.

Things to Help You Out Along the Way

Some of the great features of the *Complete Idiot's Guides* are the boxes placed through out the chapters with additional information. In these boxes I've tried to explain some extra facets of investigation. There are also tips and warnings about using investigative techniques mentioned in the chapter. At the end of each chapter, "The Least You Need to Know" sections are handy references.

Sherlock's Secrets

Sherlock knows what he's doing. He's full of tips and tricks to help you through the case you're working on.

Sammy the Snitch

When Sammy the Snitch speaks, you'd better take note. He'll warn you about dangers and legal traps that can snare you.

Crime Scene Clues

PIs speak their own language. Here are definitions of terms, slang, and jargon of the industry that you might not know.

Elementary, My Dear Watson

Watson is full of interesting facts, sidelights, and procedures relating to private investigation. He'll share all he knows with you.

Acknowledgments

So many people to thank. Where do you start? First, my agent Jessica Faust, BookEnds literary agency. Without Jessica the book wouldn't have happened. Next, thanks to Lee Owen for editing all of the chapters. What a good friend, literary critic, and writer. Special thanks to Cathy, my wife, for all those nights sleeping with the pillow over her head muffling the tapping of the keyboard. A bouquet of flowers to everyone in my writing workshop in Jacksonville, Fla.—Jeffrey Philips, Beth Cappotto, Ellen Mcanany, Tom Slade, Bettye Griffin, Larry Barnes, Margee Bugbee, Marjorie Oliver, Randy Regan, Heidi Tillotson, Julian Moss, and Clyde Rogers (deceased)—for critiquing my writing.

Also thanks to Bob Bailey, Jean Adair, and Dave Poyer, for their encouragement and advice; to James N. Frey for his great instruction in the craft of fiction; and the ReFrey group of the Oregon Writers' Colony. An especial thanks to Dr. Charles

Connor and the organizers of the Harriette Austin Writers Conference, where I met Jessica, my agent, and where the idea of this book was conceived; and to the incubators of fiction, the First Coast Writers' Conference, Florida International University and the Seaside Writers' Conference, Suncoast Writers' Conference, and the Truckee Meadows Community College Writers' Conference.

Trademarks

Part 1

Private Investigation, Business or Fun?

Need some information? Trying to solve a crime? Looking for an old boyfriend or girlfriend? Do you want to check out a potential tenant or a new employee?

In this section you learn the ins and outs of doing PI work. You'll discover how to find the information yourself, just like the pro PIs do it. If you want to become a professional PI, this section will hold your hand, show you the vision, and help you pursue that dream.

The Making of a PI

In This Chapter

- Taking lessons from the original PI
- No PI license necessary: related fields
- Solving crimes with intuitive leaps
- Carrying weapons: necessity or fatal mistake?
- The making of a good private investigator

The private investigative business is the search for truth. A PI must be impartial in this pursuit. The irony is that, many times, a private investigator's clients won't want the truth. They only want to win. It's the job of the PI to dig up the facts and help them win.

It's a dual-edged sword, because the investigator can't withhold facts that might injure his client's chances. The PI's client needs to know the "bad" stuff that is out there as well as the "good" stuff. There is nothing worse for an attorney than to go into court and be blindsided by some derogatory or hurtful piece of information that he didn't know about and should have. He needs to be aware of all the facts beforehand, and that's the private investigator's side of the business. Win, lose, or draw, we as PIs get the information, and then let the chips fall where they may.

If the other side of a lawsuit prevails, it doesn't mean the PI didn't do his job. If the PI has completed his work to the highest standards of his profession and to the best of his abilities, that is all anybody can ask.

In this book, you'll see we use the male and female pronouns, *he* and *she*, interchangeably. There are many, many good female private investigators. Also, every work-related story used as an example in this book is true and originates from the author's case files. The names and sometimes the locations or other facts that would identify the person have been changed, but the story's principle and its major accompanying facts are true.

Later in this book, you'll see why PI work is even more of a challenge than are police or FBI investigations. I know that may sound incredible, but you'll see why I make that statement as you get into Chapters 14, 15, and 16. First, though, let's see how the private investigative business originated, and why we're called "private eyes."

The First U.S. Private Investigative Agency

Allan Pinkerton, who was born in Glasgow, Scotland, in 1819, is the father of private investigation in the United States. He began his career in law enforcement as a deputy sheriff for Kane County, Ill. Do you want to abbreviate this IL or ILL?, in 1846. Four years later, he opened his detective agency in Chicago.

Pinkerton played a significant role in the history of nineteenth-century America. Documented facts are hard to come by, but it is alleged that Pinkerton became aware of a plot to assassinate President Lincoln while Lincoln was en route to his inauguration in Washington, D.C. Pinkerton overtook Lincoln's entourage and persuaded him to change his itinerary, thereby thwarting the attempted assassination.

In 1866, Pinkerton was hired by the railroads to put an end to the great train-robbery gangs, including the Jesse James gang, (also called the James-Younger gang). Early on, Pinkerton's agency didn't fair so well with the James-Younger gang. At least two Pinkerton operatives were killed in their attempts to arrest the Younger brothers. John Younger was also killed in one of those gunfights, a fierce shootout in St. Clair County, Mo., in March 1874.

> **Elementary, My Dear Watson**
>
> Some claim that Pinkerton's private detective agency with its "all-seeing eye" is the origin of the term *private eye* that we use today.

By the early 1900s, the railroad robbery gangs were out of business, thanks primarily to Pinkerton's aggressive pursuit. It is alleged that a number of innocent men were sent to jail in this gang cleanup, and hence the term came into use whenever an innocent person was "railroaded" to prison.

As his company logo, Pinkerton used the "all-seeing eye."

The "all-seeing eye" used by Pinkerton as the logo for Pinkerton Detective Agency.

This logo is also on the Great Seal of the United States.

The Great Seal of the United States.

Pinkerton's agency has now merged with Burns Security, a conglomerate listed on the Swiss stock exchange.

You can see that, even today, the "eye" has a place in the Pinkerton-Burns' logo.

The all-seeing eye is still part of the new Pinkerton-Burns' logo.

Pick a Niche

Entry into the PI field is usually gained through one of two doors: either by gaining on-the-job experience as an intern for an established private investigative agency, or else leaving an investigative position with law enforcement or the military.

Chapter 3 will take you through the twists and turns of beginning a career in this exciting field. It's not an easy line of work to enter, but once in it, you'll find it's a lot more fun than a real job.

Notice that even Mr. Pinkerton did his turn as a deputy sheriff before starting his agency. Does this mean you must have previous law enforcement experience? No, there are lots of niches in the PI field that most people never think about in which previous law enforcement training has no bearing on the work at all.

Public Record Retrieval

In Chapter 8, you'll learn what records are available at your local county and federal courthouses. An entire career can be made retrieving courthouse documents. There is a national association of document retrievers, and they earn very good incomes by circulating through the local courthouses, pulling documents requested by clients, and searching civil and criminal histories.

Information on the Public Record Retriever Network can be found at www.brbpub.com/PRRN. This is a great resource for private investigators, and you can become a member of this network yourself. Download the application from the PRRN website. The fee is only $10 per year for each county that you service. You'll receive a 32-page manual of instructions.

In most states, you probably don't have to have a private investigative license to begin this line of business. Many states have a specific exemption from their PI licensing requirements for public record and database retrievers.

In-House Investigators

If you're only interested in conducting background investigations for yourself, maybe on your new boyfriend, then check out Chapter 10 and learn how to do it yourself, no license needed. Or, if you are an in-house investigator for a business, most states allow you to do the background investigations and internal-theft investigations without a license. If you're good at investigations and have picked up a little experience along the way, then consider becoming an in-house investigator. It's a good way to get the additional experience you need to qualify for your PI license. Chapter 3 clues you in to which states require a PI license and which ones don't.

Serving Subpoenas for a Living

Subpoena service is another niche that does not require a PI license, although many of the skills needed by PIs are also needed to serve subpoenas (more on subpoenas in Chapter 13). States have varying license requirements for subpoenas services. You'll need to check with your own state to see what is required. Usually, the local sheriff's office regulates the authorized servers and can educate you as to what is required.

Can you make a good living serving subpoenas? Absolutely. The keys to making money by serving subpoenas are high volume and high efficiency. In many ways, the financial aspect of a subpoena service is very similar to a PI agency. Working for someone else serving subpoenas can be financially rewarding, but you're not going to be making a six-figure income. Normally, the server gets paid by the number of "papers" he serves. Sometimes, it's as low as $5 per service. You might be serving large corporations and registered agents for corporations where the subpoenas are easy to serve, and you may have half a dozen to serve at one time. So, even though the rate is low, you make it up in volume.

The second key to making money in the subpoena business is to be more efficient than the local sheriff's office. They will charge $20–$30 dollars for a service, and frequently, they're very slow. You might charge $50 or $60 for the service, but provide a much quicker turnaround time and better reporting to the client when the process has been served. It doesn't do anybody any good if the subpoena is served after the trial is over.

By utilizing today's wireless communications to serve subpoenas, you can increase the level of service you provide to your client. Anyone not on the front of the technology envelope is going to get left in the dust, thirsty and broke. Get comfortable with wireless technology and let the competition eat your dust.

Sherlock's Secrets _____

Some process servers use their Palm Pilots or other PDAs to e-mail their clients as soon as they complete a service. Others have set up a website where a client can enter a secure area via password and see when and what subpoenas have been served, and which are still outstanding. Prompt and efficient client service is the key to building business in the investigative field or any of its related service areas.

Skip Tracing, Locates, and Deadbeat Dads

There are investigative agencies that only do skip tracing, perform locates, and hunt down deadbeat dads. These agencies would normally have a private investigator license if required by their state. I'm familiar with one agency that only works deadbeat dad cases. It has the client sign a contract where the agency collects a percentage of the child support or alimony payments after it finds the dad. It is quite successful in its locating efforts and in collecting the money owed to these moms.

Other agencies specialize in finding the birth parents of adopted children. This is a difficult area, and has as many rewarding moments and as it does disappointments.

Mary Beth, a 30-year-old woman who lived in Maryland, contacted us and asked us to find her birth mother. The mother who'd adopted her told her she was born in Florida. When her adoptive mother died, Mary Beth began sorting out her papers and came across some notes her mother had made that included the name of her birth mother. Of course, 30 years later her birth mother had probably been married at least once, and therefore, certainly had a different name. Mary Beth had no idea if she was still alive, or living in another state.

By searching state marriage records and other databases, we ascertained that her birth mother actually now resided in a very posh, gated community in the Jacksonville, Fla., area. We discreetly made contact with the birth mother, who denied ever having a daughter and certainly never giving her up for adoption.

We contacted her again, and this time she told us that she didn't want anything to do with her daughter, that the child had been from a different part of her life, and asked us to please leave her alone. Sad, but true.

On principle, we do not reunite adopted children with their birth parents unless both parties agree. Mary Beth's natural mother had her reasons, which obviously were important to her. We had to respect her desire for privacy, as much as we didn't want to. Maybe one day in the future she'll rethink the situation and change her mind, but she's not a young woman anymore. Let's hope she does so before it's too late.

Thinking Sideways and Out of the Box

Some people are gifted pianists and can play the piano by ear, never having read the tune's sheet music. Let them hear it, and they can play it. Others have a natural gift for tongues, picking up phrases and learning other languages with little or no study. For others, mathematical concepts seem to take root in their heads, while some of us labor and labor over sine and cosines and never get it right.

And then there are those who, when given a set of facts or circumstances, can make intuitive leaps of reasoning and come to an understanding of the pattern that exists where others only see chaos. It is this talent or gift that allows the investigator to catch the criminal, solve the crime, or insert the missing link that leads to the solution of the problem.

This mental talent can be developed, just like practicing a piano will improve that skill. Will a skilled pianist ever become a gifted pianist? I won't attempt to answer that question. But even the gifted pianist must be schooled and must practice his or her skill.

Successful private investigators must learn to think outside the box. I prefer the term "thinking sideways," but both phrases encompass the meaning of the needed talent. A simple example of this type of thinking is this little puzzle that many of you are familiar with. It's been around for a long time. Draw on a piece of paper the nine dots below. Then, connect the dots with no more than four straight lines, never lifting the pencil from the paper and never crossing the same dot twice.

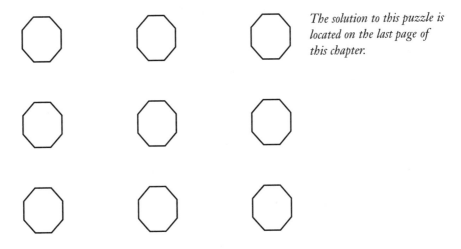

The solution to this puzzle is located on the last page of this chapter.

Surveillance Example

An attorney who represented the Jacksonville Shipyards came to my firm with a problem. The Shipyards had an employee, Richard, who was not working due to an alleged knee injury he'd received while overhauling a ship in the yard. Some of the Shipyards' employees, co-workers of Richard, told the Shipyards' manager that Richard was malingering. According to his co-workers, he was able to repair automobiles in his backyard, do household maintenance, and replace part of his roof. If he could do that, then he certainly could find useful work at the shipyard.

It irked the other employees that he seemed perfectly healthy and was collecting a full paycheck while not working, and they had to work for their paycheck.

The Shipyards hired a PI firm to put Richard under surveillance. Richard had an 8-foot privacy fence surrounding the side and back yards of his home. The firm had set surveillance vans in Richard's neighborhood, but never could catch him performing strenuous tasks. They heard metal banging on metal in the backyard, but couldn't see through the privacy fence. They even hired a helicopter to fly over, but Richard stayed in the house that day.

The Shipyards, more frustrated than ever, instructed their attorney to find another PI firm that'd maybe have better luck. This attorney recommended us because he'd previously represented a client who'd had an insurance claim. We'd had his claimant under surveillance, caught him working, and nailed him as much as anybody has ever been nailed before. His client had worked very hard laying a concrete driveway and we videotaped him for six hours straight as he worked without a break. As soon as the attorney saw our surveillance tapes, he dropped the client. For that reason, the attorney knew we could produce excellent results.

The Shipyards didn't care what it cost. They wanted Richard either back to work or fired. They needed proof that he could work. I assigned the case to one of my senior investigators. After a couple of days, the investigator told me it was impossible. Richard never came out of the house, and if he was doing anything strenuous, it had to be in the backyard. He, too, heard noises coming from the back of the house, but couldn't testify as to what was taking place back there or who was doing it.

When presented with a problem like we had with Richard, a good investigator will step back and take a look at the big problem. Creativity and innovation are required. You have to think outside the box. Think sideways. Think laterally or upside down if you have to. Attack the problem from a new angle. Let your mind roam and make that intuitive leap.

I went out to Richard's neighborhood and drove around the area up to several blocks away. Behind Richard's house was a two-story apartment complex. I approached the manager and indicated my desire to rent one of the apartments. She showed me one of the vacant second-floor units. From its back window, it had a clear view over Richard's privacy fence, and I could see the entire rear yard and one side of his house.

The problem? They had a one-year minimum lease. I didn't think the Shipyards would pay the rent on an empty apartment for an entire year. They might have. They wanted this situation resolved. But there had to be a better solution. I confided in the apartment manager the basics of my situation, but I didn't tell her who the subject was that we wanted to put under surveillance. I assured her there would be no wear and tear on the apartment. We were only going to use the apartment a few hours a day.

We struck a deal where I would pay the apartment manager $25 cash for each day that we entered the apartment. She agreed not to rent the apartment until she had no other vacancies, and then she'd give us first right of refusal on the unit.

You can guess the rest. We shot hours and hours of videotape of Richard repairing cars and working around the back of his house. We even had several days of tape of him roofing the back portion of his house. He carried stacks of shingles up a ladder and placed them around the roof so they were available when he needed them.

One of Richard's injuries was to his knee. We showed the videotape to one of his doctors, hoping she would say he was fit enough to go back to work. At one point, the doctor said that if we could show him climbing a ladder with a heavy burden, she would send him right back to work. Bingo. I pulled out the right tape and there he was on the television screen, carrying a 50-pound stack of shingles up the ladder.

From that day on, the Jacksonville Shipyards used us as their primary investigative resource until the day they closed. They spent hundreds of thousands of dollars a year with my firm. I did an analysis of all the cases we worked for them. The analysis showed we saved them several million dollars each year in wages that would have been lost and in frivolous medical bills they no longer had to pay.

Security Consulting Example

In our PI business, we also do security consulting. A client, Michael, owned a music store. He'd been broken into and called us for help.

I met with Michael and surveyed his entire building. I suggested we beef up the system he had, which we hadn't installed, to include an interior trap in the event a burglar cut a hole through the roof and entered that way. He couldn't conceive of any burglar going to the trouble to cut a hole in the roof. I tried to explain to him that it's been done before, but he didn't want to go the extra expense to cover that contingency.

Also, the store had a large ventilation fan that exhausted to the outside. I suggested the alarm system should also cover the fan in the event a burglar might push the fan into the building and enter. He pooh-poohed that idea, too.

And now you're nodding, right? About two months later, Michael called and said that burglars had cut a hole in the roof and cleaned him out. Now he wanted the interior trap. We also alarmed the fan as well.

Another couple of months later, the store's alarm goes off. It's the alarm contact on the fan. The police respond and catch the burglars still in the act of trying to push the fan into the shop.

If you're going to be successful in the private investigative and security business, you have to think sideways. Or maybe just think like a burglar. Look at a problem from a bigger perspective or the burglar's perspective. Perhaps I should have been more insistent with Michael and his music shop, but the clients have the final word, because it's their money you're spending.

The Gun Conundrum

The PI movies and television shows usually have a private investigator packing a gun. Somebody always gets shot. Whew, good thing the PI had his gun on. But of course he did—don't they all carry a sidearm?

The decision to carry a weapon is a multifaceted one. The PI must examine her feelings on these three points:

1. Is she proficient in the use of deadly force?

2. Is she prepared to take another person's life?

3. Is her judgment such that she can make life-and-death decisions in a matter of a second or two?

A concealed-weapons class, which will certify a person to carry a weapon, does not in my opinion contain enough firearms training to enable a private investigator to answer yes to question number one.

Excluding the 71 officers killed in the 9/11 attacks in New York, FBI statistics show that 60 police officers were killed in 2001 with firearms. Of these 60 officers, 45 were slain with handguns, 11 with rifles, and 4 with shotguns. Seven officers were killed with vehicles, one officer was murdered with personal weapons (hands, fists, feet, etc.), and one was killed with a blunt object.

At the time they were slain, 39 officers were wearing body armor. Sixteen officers attempted to use their weapons by unsnapping the holsters, drawing the weapons, or performing an action to indicate an attempt to use the weapons, but were unable to fire. Twelve of the officers fired their own weapons during the incident, and seven officers' weapons were stolen (taken from the scene). Three officers were killed with their own weapons.

Focus on the fact that these police officers, many of whom had gone through a rigorous training academy with several weeks of firearms and defensive-tactics training classes, still lost their firearms to felons and were shot with their own weapons. How much firearm training does a PI have to have to be considered proficient in the use of deadly force?

Only you can give the answer to question number two. If you answered yes very quickly, then I'd say you probably should not be carrying a firearm.

As to question number three: Robert Bailey, my good friend and author of the PI novel *Private Heat*, is a 20-year veteran of the PI business. Bailey says that carrying a weapon is like working a crossword puzzle with a pen full of permanent ink. Once you've written your answer, you can't go back and change it. Wearing a gun puts a serious obligation on you. It's not a place for cowboys or people who couldn't make the grade as cops.

Suppose you're a PI. You're walking down the sidewalk and hear a gunshot. As you turn the corner to head toward your bank, you hear the bank alarm ringing. A second later, a man comes running toward you carrying a bank bag and holding a gun. People are diving for cover every which way. The running man is looking over his shoulder and doesn't see you. He bumps right into you and knocks both of you flat on the ground. In a flash he's up, curses at you, and starts running again. You, the macho PI, are armed. You pull out your gun and shoot the man, figuring you've just shot yourself an armed and dangerous bank robber. Good job, right?

Not! You just shot the bank manager. While the bank was being robbed, the bank manager pulls a gun out from his desk drawer. The robber, seeing the manager's gun, runs out of the bank and continues fleeing on foot. He's in such a hurry that one of the bags of cash he's carrying slips out of his grasp and falls to the sidewalk. The manager, still holding the gun, gives chase. The manager sees the dropped bag of cash and picks it up, holding it in one hand and the gun in the other, continuing the chase.

Now you have a chance to explain to the district attorney why you shouldn't be tried for homicide and spend the rest of your life in jail.

As a private investigator, think twice before strapping on that sidearm. Every time you put a gun on your hip, you're betting 20 years of your life in a penitentiary against the fact that you can think fast enough, evaluate and process all of the information coming at you, and arrive at the right conclusion. You'll be making a decision in a split second that might later take the U.S. Supreme Court a year to decide whether it was right or wrong.

If you have the license and the liability insurance, it's your decision, but it's a serious one. Don't take it lightly.

Cop Wannabes

How many antennae are on your car? That's a crazy question, huh? This may hurt some feelings, but read it carefully and see if it applies to you. If not, then skip over it. If it does apply to you, then before you jump into the PI life, consider the years you're likely to waste trying to make a success in the PI business, because you'll surely fail. The more antennae, the higher the likelihood of failing in the PI business.

Tow truck drivers and police-beat reporters excluded, if you drive around town with a police scanner blasting on your dash, then you're not the right personality for being a successful private investigator. In addition to the police scanner, are you also driving a used police car? You know the ones—solid white, with black-wall tires and a spotlight just forward of the driver's-side window. Do you already have a concealed-weapons permit? Do you keep the gun in a little case under the front seat or hooked under the dash, where you can reach it easily? Or do you prefer the shoulder holster like James Bond and the TV cops?

If you find yourself nodding along with any of those, then I'd suggest you try out at the police academy first. Cop wannabes don't make good private investigators. They're more in love with the idea of "being like a PI" than actually doing the work that a PI has to do.

It's similar to being a writer. Many people love the idea of "being a writer." They see the romantic image of the writer slaving over a keyboard, pounding out his work. Or they see themselves sitting at the beach, writing the great American novel on a pad of paper while the gulls chatter overhead. That's the romance of being a writer. The reality is much different.

I mentioned Robert Bailey earlier in this chapter. He begins his novel *Private Heat* with PI Art Hardin this way:

> "Everybody wants to be a detective, carry a big shiny gun, and be all the rage at cocktail parties. Nobody wants to get up at o-dark-thirty and drive ninety-three miles to see if Joe Insurance Claimant—who has been collecting a total disability check for the last three years—is also working for wages on the sly, but that's the kind of work that usually pays the bills, not the flashy stuff you see on the tube."* From *Private Heat*, by Robert Bailey. Used by permission of the publisher, M. Evans and Company, New York.

If you're looking for a career that is interesting and exciting, private investigation fits that bill. I can't think of anything more interesting than being a private investigator. But it also has hour after hour of sheer tedium. The job requires a mountain of paperwork and documentation. If small details are "your thing," then the private investigative field may be for you. If you're not up for the paperwork, dotting the *i* and crossing every *t*, then you'd better think again.

If you want the flashy stuff and the red Ferrari, then you'd be better off turning on the television, pulling that bag of chips out of the cupboard, and settling in for the *Magnum PI* reruns.

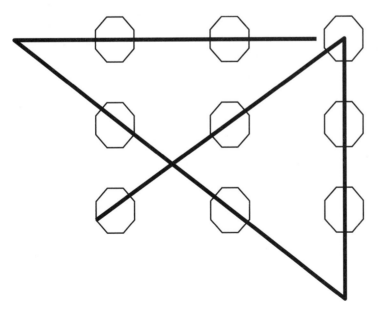

The solution to the puzzle lies in thinking sideways or outside the box. Draw two of the four lines beyond the visual box made by the nine dots.

The Least You Need to Know

- Allan Pinkerton began the private investigative business in the United States in 1850. The term *private eye* may have originated from Pinkerton's company logo, "the all-seeing eye."

- There are areas such as public record retrieval, in-house investigations, and subpoena service that don't require a PI license. Good incomes can be made in these areas. Finding birth parents and deadbeat dads are two more niche areas in the PI arena.

- Successful private investigators must be able to make intuitive leaps in reasoning. It is a talent that can be learned and practiced. Some call it thinking outside the box or thinking sideways.

- Carrying a firearm as a PI is a heavy responsibility. Carefully consider all of the ramifications of taking another person's life before deciding to carry one. Once the trigger is pulled, you can't undo it.

- Some people are more in love with the idea of being a PI than they are with actually being one. Cop wannabes do not make good private investigators.

2

Becoming Your Own PI

In This Chapter

- ◆ Deciding to perform the investigation yourself
- ◆ Having your day in court
- ◆ Do not go to jail
- ◆ Avoiding the fight-and-flight scenario
- ◆ Finding the personal protection niche
- ◆ The best method of locating a PI

You have a need for information. You want to rent your garage apartment to this gentleman who seems so nice, but maybe you should check his background first. Your husband comes home with makeup on his shoulder. He says an old lady at the office hugged him, but you're not sure. Your teenager didn't come home last night and you're worried to death that something might have happened to her. You need to find her so you can kill her yourself.

You've already thumbed through this book and read the chapter that deals with your particular problem. Now is decision time. Should you hire a PI to ferret out the facts or do it yourself? This same question arises in many different areas of our lives. Do you hire a plumber to replace the disposal in the kitchen sink, or head down to the local hardware store with the credit card? Do it yourself or hire the professional?

Why and Why Not

The why and why not of doing any project yourself usually boils down to time, money, and quality of workmanship. If you're being blackmailed, or your child has been kidnapped and is being held for ransom, then I'd suggest you hire a professional. Now. This is the only time I'll tell you it's okay to drop this book.

When your daughter tells you she's headed out to the movies with friends and you have a nagging doubt, then you may want to read the chapters in this book dealing with surveillance, and then go gas up the car.

Attorneys have this saying: A man who serves as his own attorney has a fool for a client. Some look at that saying as propaganda fostered by the legal establishment to scare you into hiring an attorney when you could just as easily do it yourself.

Some private investigators would say the same applies to their profession.

One must evaluate the risk-reward factor. What is the downside if your daughter catches you following her? She'll be mad, throw a tantrum, and then pout. She'll also be checking over her shoulder a lot more the next time she gets a chance to run loose. But her life isn't at stake if she catches you trying to follow her, and there aren't big bucks riding on it. If you've got the time and think you can get it accomplished, then do it. If you don't want to spend the time, and time *does* equate to money, then hire someone to get it done.

In Chapter 17, we go into great detail about how to process a crime scene if the local police won't or can't do it. In that chapter, you'll find everything you'll reasonably need to know to get the job done. Would the crime scene unit (CSU) do it better than you? Probably, yes. They would say definitely yes, but I wouldn't. I've seen some sloppy work by CSU teams. There are some techniques we didn't talk about in that chapter. Some are too technical for the scope of this book, and others you'd only use for certain types of crimes, like bomb-scene processing. If a bomb goes off, the bomb squad and CSU will be there anyway, so forget the do-it-yourself option. But if somebody broke into your shed and stole your lawnmower and chainsaw, would it be better to have a PI come out and do it? Depends upon the PI you call.

After reading that chapter, you will probably know more about the collection of evidence than a lot of PIs in the phone book, so carefully evaluate the PI you decide to hire. As with attorneys and doctors, some may specialize in surveillance, others may specialize in nursing home investigations, and others in skip tracing. Many will never have done a crime scene investigation or have a clue as to how to go about it. Interview them carefully on the phone first and find out if they're competent for the task at hand.

Admissibility—The Key to Good Investigations

There are times when it would be better to hire a professional PI. Make no mistake about this. For instance, if you reside in a state where adultery will be considered in your divorce, keep in mind what's at stake. Less alimony will be awarded to a wife who has been proven unfaithful than to one who has not been so proven.

A husband decides to save on the expense of a PI and follows his wife to her rendezvous with the lover. Later, he testifies about the tryst he observed. To his horror, his wife denies that she has a lover, and it boils down to his word against hers.

Unfortunately, people lie in court. The judges know that. Many husbands and wives have testified that they've seen, with their own eyes, their spouses being unfaithful to them. There's nothing the judge can do without corroborating evidence or testimony. In this case, the husband should have hired a PI. Then he would have had the videotapes, photographs, and the testimony from a licensed private investigator as to the spouse's action. In those states where it matters, it matters big time.

Now that you've decided to do the work of a PI yourself, make absolutely sure that it is done in such a manner as to be admissible in court if it's even remotely possible that courtroom testimony will be needed. If you are going to be a party to the case, such as in your own divorce matter, then your testimony would be considered prejudiced. In fact, it might not even be allowed, or, if it is, it would certainly be severely discounted. If the matter will never go to court and you just need the information for your own satisfaction, then read Chapter 15 on moving surveillance and Chapter 18 on clues to infidelity.

Keeping It Legal

When conducting your own investigation, be careful about violating any local, state, or federal statutes. If you're about to take an action and are not sure if it's legal, find out before you leap into it. If you don't have the time to research the applicable statute, then just don't do it.

The places where you could get into legal trouble are spelled out in the applicable chapters, but obviously, this book can't cover every potential situation. It's up to you to use good judgment and be conservative in the tactics you employ.

It's good to know the law in your particular state. Trespassing, for instance, is usually against the law. However, in most states, before you can be prosecuted for trespassing, you must be warned against it the first time. Once you've been warned, you've used up your "gimme" and the next time you're caught, you'll be arrested and charged. That's not true in all states, though, so learn your state law. Most libraries have a set of the state statutes. You can look up the applicable laws there.

I was investigating a double homicide committed by a police officer at his residence. He had been living with a woman who was married to another man at the time. The woman's husband and a co-worker of the husband came over to the officer's home. An argument ensued and the two visitors ended up dead, shot by the officer, who claimed he was in fear of his life. Both of the dead men were unarmed.

My firm was hired by the relatives of the deceased men. Many of the facts of the homicide were unclear because the only living witness to the events was the officer. A question arose as to how many shots had actually been fired by the policeman. Both dead men had been shot multiple times.

In conducting this investigation, I took a metal detector out to the officer's home to search for bullet casings. The officer's weapon, a semiautomatic pistol, ejects the shells as they are fired. We thought perhaps more shots had been fired than he'd admitted to. I had two of my other investigators with me, both also former FBI agents.

The officer in question apparently had been called by a neighbor, telling him we were on his lawn with a metal detector. He dispatched some other officers and they stopped us before we'd had much of a chance to search. They gave us written warnings of trespass on that property. If we'd gone back later and stepped onto his grass, I and my investigators who'd been with me could then have been arrested.

Sammy the Snitch

In conducting surveillances, it may be tempting to sneak onto a person's yard and peek through an open window. Such an action crosses the line from simple trespassing to "peeping Tom." Peeping through the window is probably a violation of the law. Most states have a peeping Tom law. If you get caught, you might spend the night in the pokey. Sneaking onto another person's property might also get you shot. Most courts are pretty lenient toward the homeowner who shoots someone breaking into his home. In the United States of America, a man's home is still his castle, and he's allowed to defend it, so be careful.

The police department decided we must have been on to something, though, because, after warning us off, they searched the yard for additional bullet casings and found what we were looking for. So, our initial suspicions were right. There were more shots fired than originally testified to.

Avoid the Confrontation

Your friend Sally is convinced her husband is cheating on her, and she enlists your aid to follow him one evening. Think carefully before accepting this invitation to danger. If he is unfaithful and the two of you catch him going into a motel, what are you going to do?

Sally's emotions will be redlined to the maximum. Her husband, headed into the motel room, will be very goal oriented, and if he's interrupted by his wife, he may turn his frustration at being deprived of his goal into anger toward Sally. We learned this lesson the hard way.

Carolyn asked us to follow her husband to what she believed would be a daytime rendezvous. With domestic cases, we usually maintain fairly close contact with the client. Frequently, they can advise us if the behavior we are watching is normal for the spouse or not. This case was no exception.

When we saw Carolyn's husband having lunch with another female, we advised her of that. When the husband left the restaurant and gave the female a hug and a kiss, we photographed it. The two of them drove off in separate cars, but in the same direction. The plot thickens ... shortly, both vehicles entered the same motel parking lot. We photographed Carolyn's husband and the other woman going into the same room.

Our mistake here was to call Carolyn and tell her what we were witnessing and which motel her husband was in. Twenty minutes later, Carolyn enters the parking lot of the motel with tires squealing. She races up to the door of the motel room and begins banging on the door. Seconds later, her husband appears at the door with his shirt off, his pants buttoned, but his belt hanging loose.

An argument follows. The husband whips off his belt and begins beating our client. Oh, shoot, what do we do now? As we all know, domestic disturbances may perhaps be the most volatile and dangerous situations for a responding officer. Carolyn had told us that her husband had beat her in the past.

We called the sheriff's office and then proceeded up the stairs. As is typical in domestic-violence cases, as soon as we approached the couple, they both turned their aggression on us. We backed off, and the two of them took their fight inside the room. The other woman came running out and hid behind us. In a minute, the police arrived, and they needed no directions to the room. The noise from inside was clearly heard through the walls. Both our client and her husband got a free ride in the backseat of the police car.

We made it a policy from then on never to tell a client the exact location of his cheating spouse until the following day. We'll keep him advised of what's happening, but will not tell him where the action is at the moment. Many clients aren't happy with that policy, because they want the confrontation. We don't.

If there's a history of violence in the relationship, consider all of the factors before becoming involved in a similar situation yourself. In this business, though, confrontations will happen, even when you do your best to avoid them.

Jacob was a bookie. He was a heavyset man who drove a large gray Mercedes and paid in cash. He and Martha were separated. A few months previously, Jacob had hired us to follow Martha for almost two weeks straight. I'd reported to Jacob about a man I saw entering Martha's house without knocking. I knew the man. His name was John and he was an attorney who lived across the street from Martha. Still, entering without knocking or ringing the bell seemed a little strange to me.

Jacob pooh-poohed the idea that John could be Martha's lover. He was just a friendly neighbor. Yeah—real, real friendly, as it turned out. I'm sure she was getting good legal advice from John, and at a very good rate as well.

Now Jacob wanted Martha followed some more because Martha had admitted she'd had a fling with John, but that it was over. I've heard that one more times than I can count. So had Jacob. We were back on the case. Unfortunately, Jacob had told Martha that he'd had her followed before, so now she was very paranoid and watching for us. In Chapter 21, we talk about paranoia and telephone taps. The same is true for being followed. Just because you're paranoid doesn't mean that somebody's not following you. We were certainly on Martha's tail, figuratively speaking.

One day, about 10 days into the surveillance, I and another investigator were conducting a two-man surveillance on Martha. We followed her down a busy four-lane road. A car very similar to mine was riding her bumper all the way down to an interstate on ramp. When Martha roared onto the interstate, this car still stayed right behind her. This unknown car was the same color and make as mine.

I was staying way, way back, keeping as many cars between me and her as I could while still keeping her in sight. She exited the interstate, and this other car didn't. Finally, it was off her bumper. My other investigator was further back than I was, so I speeded up to follow her off the interstate. Once off the freeway, she could have gone any of four different directions, and we didn't want to lose her.

Well, unknown to me, she'd pulled off and stopped and was just sitting there. As I drove past her, she got on my tail. I tried to pull into a nearby gas station, but she whipped around in front of me and blocked my path. She hopped out of her car and jumped right into my face.

"Why are you following me?"

"Lady," I said, thinking as fast as I could. "I'm not following you. I just pulled into here to get some gas and you're blocking my way. Are you okay?"

"I'm fine, damn it. And you are too following me. You've been following me for the last fifteen minutes. I'll tell you why you're following me. You're following me because Jacob paid you to follow me. And you're not very good at it either. How much did he pay you to follow me?"

I just shrugged my shoulders and motioned toward the gas pumps. "Lady, I'm just trying to get some gas."

"Well, I'm going to tell Jacob what a lousy PI he hired. He's wasting his money." With that she jumped back into her car and took off.

What a blow to my ego. Of course, I wanted to tell her that I'd been following her for 10 days straight and she never knew it. And that I'd followed her for over two weeks the month before and she never knew that, either. And the only reason she made me today was because it was a case of mistaken identity. Of course, she was gone, and I couldn't have said those things anyway, but boy, did I want to. I did tell Jacob. He just chuckled about it and paid me in hundred-dollar bills. Of course, what she didn't know was that my partner picked up the surveillance when she took off and we held on to her for a few more days.

Here is a short checklist of what do if you're confronted by a subject (don't use this list if you're made by the police. That's dealt with in Chapters 14 and 15, both of which deal with surveillance):

- Deny you're following the person who confronts you.

- Don't identify yourself as a private investigator.

- Never reveal the identity of your client or your subject.

- Leave the area as quickly as possible, but not so quickly as to give the impression you are fleeing.

- Stop the surveillance for the day and give it time to cool off.

- If surveillance is reinstituted on another day, utilize different vehicles and, if possible, different personnel.

Hiring the Hired Gun

There is one facet of PI work where I'd suggest using a professional, and that's body-guard work or, as it's called in the business, personal protection. In Chapter 3, we'll talk about liability insurance, but here the liability is enormous and the possibility of confrontation is almost assured.

If you're interested in pursuing this line of PI work, you'll first need to have some professional firearms training and defensive-tactics training. There is a lot more to being a professional bodyguard than standing 6 feet, 4 inches tall and carrying a big gun. Unfortunately, in our lawsuit-happy society, if a confrontation is not handled properly, then you, as bodyguard, will probably end up being sued by both your client and the person who started the confrontation.

There is a fine line between providing personal protective services and security-guard services. Most states require different licenses for each service, a PI license for straight personal protection and a guard-company license for the other. In addition, most security-guard services also provide some investigative services and frequently carry both licenses.

Another lucrative aspect of PI work that falls between personal protection and the security business is concert security and nightclub security. Each is a specialization and constitutes its own little niche in the PI market.

Pages of Last Resort

Finding a competent PI can be difficult. Going eenie, meenie, miney, moe with the listings in the yellow pages is the least attractive method of hiring a PI.

Not all PIs are full-service agencies. The first item of business in searching for a PI is to know specifically what you want the PI to do. If you simply want a background check, then detail exactly what items in a person's background you want checked out. Thumb through Chapters 7, 8, 9, and 10 in this book. You might not need a PI at all. If you'd rather pay someone else to do it, then let's look for a PI.

Here are sources for referrals of PIs:

◆ Friends who've had similar problems (personal recommendation)

◆ Attorneys

◆ Paralegals in attorneys' offices

◆ PI associations

- Insurance company claims office
- Internet referral pages
- Telephone yellow pages

Each are briefly described in the sections that follow.

Friends (Personal Recommendation)

The best way to find a PI is by personal recommendation. Find friends who have had a similar problem. Whom did they use? Were they satisfied with the services provided and was the cost commensurate with the information provided?

Attorneys

Attorneys can be a good source of referrals when looking for a PI. Many attorneys don't use PIs because their practice doesn't require it. But some do, so ask around.

Paralegals

Even if you don't know an attorney, pick a few out of the telephone book, call their office, and ask to speak to a *paralegal*. You'll get some paralegals who deal with PIs and will be glad to refer you to the one they use.

Crime Scene Clues

A **paralegal** is a person, usually working in an attorney's office, with specialized training who assists attorneys with their cases. Don't confuse them with secretaries.

PI Associations

Many states have professional associations of private investigators. Most of those associations will have web pages that post their membership directory. If a PI takes the time to belong to the state organization, then he may be a little more professional then the next guy.

You can find a list of PI associations at the homepage for ION, a private investigator referral service. Go to www.pihome.com and click on PI Information. About halfway down the list is the link that reads Investigative Associations. That's as good and comprehensive a list as you'll find anywhere.

Insurance Companies

Insurance companies use PIs all the time. Get the telephone number for the claims office for your homeowners insurance company. Call and ask to speak to a claims representative. A little telephone work and you should be able to find out which investigators your insurance company is using. If its PI does the type of work you want done, then that's a pretty good recommendation. If you're looking for someone to "sweep for bugs" (search for electronic surveillance equipment), however, the guy working for your insurance company is probably not the right one. If your needs are surveillance or interviews, then you'll hit the jackpot.

Internet Referrals

There are some websites that refer PIs. You can check www.pimall.com, for example. But relying on Internet referrals and PI websites isn't much better than looking at yellow-page ads; in both cases, the PI or agencies pays to appear in the publication.

You can improve the quality of an Internet referral by starting with ION at www.pihome.com. ION will refer an investigator to you at no charge. ION draws from a pool of investigators who have agreed to adhere to certain standards, and all of them should be suitably licensed in the 40 states that require PI licenses (see Chapter 3 for the list of states that don't require a license). ION makes its money by receiving a percentage of the fee their investigators charge.

Telephone Yellow Pages

If you have to use the pages of last resort, then here is a technique I'd suggest. Find last year's telephone book, and the one from the year before that, if possible. Sometimes libraries have old phone books. Compare the listings in the yellow pages under Private Investigators and/or Detectives. Find an agency that has been in all three books. If it can last that long, then it'll probably be around long enough to testify when your case goes to court.

When calling any investigator, don't just compare hourly rates. If your situation will go before a judge and a jury, you'll want somebody who has courtroom experience and is presentable. If you just want to see who your ex-girlfriend is dating, then you need a good street investigator with good surveillance experience. He may look really crummy, but he might be the guy for the job.

Expect to pay a retainer up front. If the PI doesn't ask for a reasonable *retainer,* then she's probably inexperienced, doesn't have a high opinion of herself or her product, or she's desperate for the work.

Crime Scene Clues

A **retainer** is money paid by the client at the beginning of an investigation. Frequently, a small portion of the retainer is nonrefundable if the case is canceled. Typically, the investigator bills his time against the retainer on hand. Once the retainer is used up, he will ask for additional funds before doing any more work on the case. This is much like a contractor who starts the job with a small advance, and is paid in installments as the job progresses.

Deciding when to be a do-it-yourselfer for any type of project, be it home plumbing or surveilling a wayward spouse, is challenging enough. And if it's in an area where you don't have much experience, the stress factor usually goes up considerably. Remember, you always have the option of hiring a professional. *The Complete Idiot's Guide to Private Investigating* gives you many of the tools you'll need to do it yourself and to help you do it right. If you're a newly licensed investigator, you'll find tricks and treats in here that would have taken you years to learn on your own. Either way, it's your decision. Just have fun doing it.

The Least You Need to Know

- Deciding whether to undertake an investigation yourself or hire a professional investigator should be balanced by what's at stake, and the financial resources and time available.

- When undertaking the investigation yourself for a matter that is expected to end up in court, it's critical that the work be done in a manner that will make the information admissible.

- Ensure that the investigation is conducted without violating any local, state, or federal laws. Know the law. If there is any doubt as to the legality of something you want to do, err on the side of caution and don't do it.

- Whether the investigation you are performing is for you or perhaps for a friend, avoid confrontations with the subject of your investigation. Never allow your client to confront her spouse at the moment of infidelity. Emotions are too high, and violence can result.

- Personal protection work is a lucrative niche in the PI business, but it also carries tremendous liability. A PI needs to have sufficient liability insurance that specifically covers this field.

◆ There are better ways to find a professional and competent PI than using the telephone yellow pages. Use referrals from friends, attorneys, insurance companies, paralegals, professional investigative associations, and qualified referral agencies.

The Path to the Professional PI

In This Chapter

◆ Learning skills to better your chances of being hired as a private investigator

◆ Getting the scoop on getting your PI license

◆ Understanding your liability and insurance needs

◆ Organizing to become a super-sleuth

◆ Finding the niche and finding the clients

◆ Marketing on the web

A career as a professional private investigator can be emotionally rewarding, entertaining, and exciting. It's much better than working for a living. Can it be financially rewarding as well? The answer is yes, under certain circumstances.

Anyone interested in becoming a PI has probably watched a lot of detective shows on TV. Remember *Magnum, PI?* (Settle down, ladies.) He drove a Ferrari and lived on a beachfront estate in Hawaii. Of course, the car was borrowed, and he lived in an apartment on the estate, not in the main house. I don't remember a single episode where Magnum collected a check from his clients.

If you've decided you want to be a professional PI, this chapter will help you get started, point out some pitfalls to avoid, and increase the collection of those checks. And in reality, collecting checks from clients is probably the only way most of us will ever get to have a Ferrari.

Getting the Experience

Good for you. You've decided to take the plunge and become a PI. The first item of business is to take this book home and read it from cover to cover. Buy it first, though, for two reasons. First, my publisher and I will both thank you, and second, getting arrested for shoplifting will probably disqualify you from ever obtaining a PI license. This book will give you a very good idea of what real PI work is all about. Your first investigative assignment is to read everything else you can on the subject of becoming a PI. Scour the shelves at the library and the bookstores. While there isn't a whole lot published on the specifics of starting and running a private investigative agency, many of the techniques used in starting other small service businesses can be applied to the PI arena.

The approach you take to starting a PI business from the ground up depends on your previous level of investigative experience. For example, if you're leaving a position with law enforcement, then your years of running criminal investigations should give you a bit of a leg up in this business, at least at the beginning. Such experience is particularly helpful when you begin marketing your services.

Is this one of those catch-22's, where you need investigative experience to get started, but can't get started if you don't have the experience? Not really. How else, then, can you get such experience? One avenue is to spend some time as an insurance claim adjuster. Their training provides good background that would serve them well in the insurance end of the PI business. Military intelligence is another pathway into private investigation. And good, on-the-job training can be received by working for another licensed private investigative agency. You can cut your PI wisdom teeth under the auspices of an established group.

This book assumes you have no previous experience in the PI field. If you do, then skip over the basics in this chapter and jump in where appropriate. But even if you're very experienced, you might pick up a few nuggets.

To obtain investigative experience, you'll need to find a job with a licensed firm. This is true in 40 of the 50 states. There are 10 states that don't require anything more than a business license. We'll talk more about that in the next section.

Having run a PI agency for nearly 20 years, I know it is nearly impossible to find a job in the this field without experience. Notice I said *nearly*, not totally. Why? There's lots of competition for very few openings. Becoming a PI seems like a glamorous occupation, and many people think they'd like to try their hand at it.

On average, my firm receives three inquires a week from folks wishing to intern. In the state of Florida, to qualify for a regular investigator's license, an applicant must have at least two years' investigative experience, or else a Bachelor's degree in criminal justice and one year of experience. Either way, you've got to get the time under your belt. How do you compete with the crowd for the few openings out there?

Step back for a minute and think about the difference between skill sets and their application to specific jobs. Someone with good skill sets that are useful in a given job can quickly be taught how to apply those skills to another job. On the other hand, those who lack applicable skill sets for the job they want carry with them a double-whammy: They'll need double the training, because they'll need to learn the necessary skills and the right way to use them. This is true in any industry.

When looking for a job with a PI firm, emphasize the skills that qualify you to do the work. Over the years, I've learned it's easier for me to teach a person how to be an investigator (applying the person's existing skills) than it is, for example, to teach him or her the photography skills and research skills that good PI work requires. Come to me already skilled, and I'll teach you how to apply those skills to this line of work. Here's your second investigative assignment: While you read this book, keep a running list of the skills an investigator needs. That ought to strip away some of the TV-induced glamour. Are you already good at each one? Can you take classes to learn, or enhance, the necessary skills? As an employer, my attitude toward a potential employee is favorably affected when I see the initiative the candidate used to improve his or her qualifications.

Phillip was a young man looking for work. He came to my office driving a 1965 Jaguar XKE and told me he wanted to be a private investigator. I think he had a James Bond complex. I gave him the courtesy of an interview, but didn't hire him.

Three months later, he came back. This time, he told me he'd been working for a photography studio and was learning photography. I still didn't hire him. An investigator has to have a decent car, one that's not too flashy, so it can be used for surveillance.

I've had two Jaguars. Both were XKE models. They were not known for their reliability. Why two? One to drive while the other is in the repair shop.

Another three months passed, and Phillip comes knocking again. Now he's had six months' experience taking photos. He can talk intelligently about *f-stops, depth of field,* and *center-weighted and averaged light metering*. I hired him.

Why did I hire Phillip this time? He demonstrated persistence and determination by acquiring a skill that is integral to the type of cases I would assign to him. Phillip worked for me for a long time and was a good surveillance man. The videotape he shot was good and always well focused.

Crime Scene Clues

F-stop refers to the setting on an adjustable, single-lens reflex camera. F-stops are numbers indicating to what degree the iris of the lens is opened or closed. The f-stop setting is one factor in determining the amount of light that passes through the lens and exposes the film. As the f-stop number increases, the iris is then "stopped down" to a smaller aperture, and less light is allowed through the lens. A larger number equals less light, all other factors remaining the same.

Depth of field refers to the apparent range of focus in a photograph. For example, in portrait photography, the background and the foreground may be intentionally blurred or out of focus while the subject, in the center of the photograph, is in focus.

Many single-lens reflex cameras have built-in light- metering capability that automatically adjusts the f-stop and the shutter speed. A good photographer will know if his **light meter averages** the measurement of the light over the entire surface of the lens, or if it **center weights** the average, giving more importance to the amount of light coming through the center of the lens, where presumably the important image is located.

The lesson here is to make yourself attractive to the firm where you're seeking employment and to be persistent. Here is a list of tips and skills you should acquire before applying with a PI firm:

- Experience in 35mm photography, digital photography, and video photography.

- Good skills in computer programs, especially Microsoft Word, Access, and Windows.

- Excellent typing skills.

- Good knowledge of the Internet search engines.

- Familiarity with the local courthouse and all public records available in your locale. The more, the better.

If a person came to my office possessing all of the above skills, I would hire him on the spot and make room for him even if I didn't need another investigator.

Sherlock's Secrets _____

Having your own surveillance equipment will be a big boost to your chances of getting hired. Don't actually purchase the cameras until you get the job, but make it clear during the interview that you've got money set aside for whatever is necessary. Most PI firms don't supply the high-tech camera equipment anymore. Each investigator has to have her own. When you get the job, buy the equipment that your firm recommends—it may still be using analog, or it may be all digital. The two aren't compatible, so you want to have what will work for your new agency.

Obtaining Licenses

There are 10 states that do not specifically license private investigators. Usually, however, at least a business license will have to be obtained. Also, in some of these states, the individual cities might require a private investigator's license in addition to a business license. Some of these 10 states, like Virginia, require proof of training. Be sure to check with the appropriate governing bodies. Those 10 states are as follows:

- Alaska
- Colorado
- Idaho
- Kentucky
- Mississippi
- Pennsylvania
- Rhode Island
- South Dakota
- Virginia
- Wyoming

ION, the PI referral agency we talked about in Chapter 2, has a list of states on its website at www.pihome.com. This site includes links to the different state regulatory bodies that oversee the private investigative industry. Click on PI Information, and then Licensing of Private Investigators.

As your business expands you may want to acquire licenses in other states than where your principal office is located. If you're working a case in your state and it leads you to a neighboring state, some states will allow you to continue working within their borders as long as the case originated where you are licensed. Others will not. Always check the licensing regulations and reciprocity agreements between states before working a case in a state where you do not hold a license. Use the preceding links and contact the state regulatory body before investigating where you're not licensed.

Twenty-two states will require the PI applicant to pass an examination before granting a license. Here are some sample questions that we found on the state of Georgia website:

Sample Question One: Someone who holds a permit from the board to carry an exposed weapon may carry a:

    A. weapon up to .45 caliber capable of holding not more than seven shots.

    B. revolver or semiautomatic handgun of no greater than .32 caliber with a 2" to 6" barrel length that can hold not more than six shots.

    C. .38 semiautomatic handgun with a clip of not more than six shots.

    D. .38 special revolver, six shots or less, with a 2" to 6" barrel length.

Sample Question Two: You are a private investigator hired to get evidence that a customer of ABC grocery store has filed a fraudulent claim against ABC's insurance carrier. The customer claims to have sustained a permanent neck injury from a fall in the store that has caused him extensive medical bills, much pain and suffering, and may permanently impair his ability to return to his employment as a house painter. In attempting to investigate this case, which of the following actions would violate the eavesdropping law?

    A. Going to the tavern and bingo parlor frequented by the suspect to attempt to catch him bragging about putting one over on the ABC store.

    B. Talking to people who know the suspect and asking them questions about him.

    C. Following the suspect to see if he does anything that a person with an injured neck probably could not do.

    D. Renting a vacant store across the street from the suspect's rooming house, setting up a camera with a telephoto lens, and attempting to take pictures of him without his knowledge.

Sample Question Three: Of the four questions below, which one is most leading?

    A. "Then what did you do?"

    B. "After the suspect ran down the hall, did you follow her?"

    C. "When did you first notice that the door had been forced?"

    D. "Where did you find the tire iron?"

The correct answers to the preceding questions are found at the end of this chapter in the section "Answers to Sample License Questions."

In order to pass the Georgia test, you'll need to be familiar with the Georgia wiretap and eavesdropping laws, as well as the laws that apply to carrying concealed and unconcealed weapons. In addition, a basic understanding of legal procedure, interview techniques, and basic investigative procedures will be necessary.

Some states like Florida, for example, will require you to possess, in addition to the local business license, three separate licenses issued by the Secretary of State, Division of Licensing: an agency license, a manager of an agency license, and a private investigator's license. Of course, there are fees associated with each license. In Florida this is true, whether you are a one-man operation or have 20 employees working out of one location. But hey, there's no state income tax, so they have to generate revenue somehow, right?

Then, in Florida, if you want to carry a weapon, you'll need two more permits: a weapon license to carry while on duty, and a concealed weapon permit to carry a firearm off duty. In the state of Florida, that makes six different licenses and permits. Do you think that's enough regulation? Maybe we could use a little bit more.

What's the Liability?

Many states will require a PI to carry a liability policy, and they won't issue or renew a license until proof of insurance is demonstrated. Some states require bonds instead of liability insurance. Check your state requirements, they vary from state to state. Florida insists on a minimum of $300,000 in insurance coverage. South Carolina requires a $10,000 bond and Georgia requires a $25,000 bond or a liability insurance policy with a $1,000,000 minimum.

The policies typically cover comprehensive general-liability coverage for death, bodily injury, property damage, and personal injury coverage, including false arrest, detention or imprisonment, malicious prosecution, libel, slander, defamation of character, and the violation of the right of privacy. Let's see, I think the kitchen sink is in there, too, but at least they had the courtesy to leave out the toilet.

The fact of the matter is, if you're trying to capture big corporate clients and convince them to use your services, it's not unusual for them to require one or even two million dollars in insurance coverage. They also will want to be named as an additional insured. If you want to go after the big fish, you've got to use big hooks.

In nearly 20 years in the PI business, we've never been sued for any action that came out

Sammy the Snitch

You will read this cautionary statement in many of the chapters in this book: If you have serious doubts about the legality of any action you're about to undertake, get a legal opinion first, or don't do it.

of our investigative effort, the only exception being a couple of automobile accidents. Despite that, in today's litigious society, only a fool would work as a PI and not carry insurance, especially if you consider the violation of privacy issue. Kind of ironic, then, that we're called *private* investigators. That's what a PI seems to do: violate the privacy of others—or at least that's what they'll claim when you catch them in some illegal or immoral act.

Privacy?

So what about this privacy thing, anyway? What's the boundary line between "acceptable" and "invasive" PI work?

Surveillance is such a large part of many private investigators' practices that, to avoid being sued, it's important to understand when a person has a reasonable expectation of privacy and when he or she doesn't. A general rule is, if the activity being observed can be seen from a public area, or an area open to the public, then the subject would not have a reasonable expectation of privacy.

A couple kissing or making love in front of an open window that can be seen from a parking lot would be fair game. How about a window with the blinds down? Many times, I've sat in one of our surveillance vans and shot video of cheating couples through second-floor blinds, because the miniblinds were shut in such a way that, from the ground-level parking area, a person could see into the apartment. If you have miniblinds, play with the slat angles and you'll see exactly what I mean.

Did that couple have a reasonable expectation of privacy? Some would say yes, because they made an attempt to close the blinds. The fact is, I could observe and photograph the activity with ordinary, off-the-shelf photographic equipment. In my opinion, they may have thought they had privacy but they didn't close the blinds properly. Their lack of proficiency in closing the blinds negated any claim they might make for an expectation of privacy.

Here's another example. Say you want to watch Jerry's backyard at night. If you have to sneak onto someone's property to peep through a window that looks onto Jerry's backyard, then you may have violated Jerry's right to privacy. Suppose, however, that you have permission from the neighbor across the back fence to stand on a chair and look over his fence into Jerry's backyard. Jerry would not have an expectation of privacy, because he'd have to assume that the neighbor can look over the fence anytime he pleases. This can be a rather fine line, so make sure your insurance payments are up-to-date. Relying on any insurance company's grace period can disgrace you out of business.

The Structure of Your Business

There are many good books written about how to start a small business. There are five basic structures that you should consider for a beginning PI business:

- Sole proprietorship

- Partnership

- Regular C corporation

- Subchapter S corporation

- Limited liability company (LLC)

A sole proprietorship means that you are the owner, the big cheese. As such, you reap all of the rewards, suffer all of the losses, and are totally on the hook if you get sued.

A partnership splits the rewards and the losses between you and your partner (if you have one). You're both still on the hook if you get sued.

A regular C corporation will require you to file corporate papers with the secretary of state's office in your state. In most states, you can easily do this yourself. Some states have downloadable, fill-in-the-blank forms on their websites. Fill them out, send them back with the appropriate fees, and you're incorporated. Or, if you're really cautious or masochistic, pay an attorney $500 to do it for you.

This corporate structure generally shields you from any lawsuits against the corporation. The disadvantage to the regular C corporation is that the corporation pays corporate income taxes on the profits, and then you, as the principal stockholder, pay taxes again on any profits that are passed onto you in the form of dividends. Bottom line, you get taxed twice on the profits. Bummer. Wish I could double-bill my customers like that.

The subchapter S corporation has the same advantages as the C corporation, including shielding you from personal liability, but any profits or losses from the corporation flow right to your personal tax return, so you only get taxed once. Yeah!

A limited liability company has the tax advantages of a partnership, not being taxed at the state or federal level, and also the liability advantages of a corporation. Some states do tax an LLC with state taxes, so be sure to check before deciding to become an LLC.

If you are just beginning a company and you are only one or two people, I'd recommend a subchapter S corporation. But check with a competent attorney and a CPA before making the decision.

Finding the Clients

Many agencies bill themselves as "full-service agencies." That's fine. Take whatever business you can get. A word of caution, though: Trying to be all things to all people leaves you spread pretty thin. The successful agencies specialize. They find a niche they are good at and then exploit the devil out of it.

When the Brown Group Inc. was marketing insurance surveillance work heavily, it was billing between $80,000 and $90,000 a month. This was in the early 1990s from a single location in northern Florida.

Sure, they did domestic work and some electronic countermeasure work, but their major market was insurance defense cases. They marketed that niche by staffing their own booths at workers' compensation and insurance liability conventions, where they gave away promotional material and freebies to prospective clients, most of whom were insurance adjusters and attorneys working insurance defense cases.

C. J. Bronstrup, a long-time private investigator, expert marketer in the PI industry, and, most recently, website designer, had some thoughts on this very matter. His website is www.InvestigatorWebs.com.

> We all have our own reasons for joining the PI profession, but making money has to be in there somewhere. When starting out, the most important part of this is defining your target audience.
>
> It is not enough to say my market is all of the attorneys in the greater Chicago area. You can't afford to reach that audience efficiently. The further you can narrow the target, the closer you can match your message to them.
>
> Beware: Lack of "technical" knowledge is not the leading cause of failure. Many fine investigators with 20-plus years of law enforcement backgrounds go belly-up every year. The major cause of failure is not having enough business. Take the time to learn how to market your business. It can propel your agency from making peanuts to a steady six-figure income almost over night.

He suggests picking an area of private investigation which you are already familiar with and marketing it. Take an area in which you possess even mediocre skills, whether it be skip tracing, property records, freight-line theft investigations, employee theft, or any other area of interest or expertise, and market that niche.

Even with mediocre skills and a good marketing plan, you'll do better than an investigator with 20 years experience and no marketing effort.

You see, the more tightly defined your area of specialization is, the more you are perceived as an expert in that field. Thus, you can command higher fees than the generalist PI. Who charges more, the general practitioner or the heart surgeon? The heart surgeon, or the heart surgeon who specializes in angio-catheterizations? You get the idea.

In my own firm, we got tired of doing insurance defense work and moved away from that to skip tracing. For five years, we skipped traced over 2,000 people a month. Recently, I was able to sell the skip-tracing portion of the business.

In the first paragraph of this chapter, we asked the question: Can this business be financially rewarding? The answer was yes, under certain circumstances. There are two ways to make the PI business financially successful:

1. Run the business yourself. Build it up until you have six to twelve investigators working for you. You will not make a six-figure income working cases by yourself. Do the math. If you work 40 hours a week, you'll be lucky to bill 24 of them. Twenty-four hours billed at, say, $50 per hour, results in weekly billings of $1,200. Fifty weeks of those billings gives you a gross income of $60,000 a year. Subtract all of your expenses, and you'll be lucky to net 50 percent, or $30,000. It is very hard to succeed as a one-man operation.

   With six men whom you pay $20 dollars an hour, billing the same 24 hours a week, all of sudden you are bringing in over $200,000 a year after meeting your investigative payroll. Sure, overhead will increase, but you should still end up with a net in the six-figure area.

2. Use the "make-it-up-in-volume" strategy. Find a high-volume niche that needs little manpower, such as skip tracing or background investigations. Each case might only gross $50 to $100 dollars, but if the volume is high and the costs are low, a nice profit can be made. If the net profit on your high-volume, low-cost product is, say, $35, and you are processing 500 of them a week, the gross profit will be over $900,000 a year. Not too shabby, huh?

There may be other ways to make high dollars in the PI business, but these are two proven ones for me. Even writing about it doesn't pay that well.

Exploiting the Full Potential of the WWW

Don't forget the Internet in your marketing strategy. Bronstrup indicates that your online marketing program and website can easily account for 60 percent or more of your business in your first year alone. "Those who ignore this advice may wake up one day to find their biggest client just got lured to another PI firm by some kid sitting at the kitchen table in his Harley boxers using a laptop computer."

In starting our new business, I've had clients already tell me that they are using a large national firm with an Internet presence. How do they know this firm is large? All they see is the website, the toll-free number, and the claims on the website. It's not a large national firm. It's that damn kid in the underwear. Excuse me while I hit the stores in search of my own Harley boxers.

I had one of the original PI websites early in 1992. At that time, there were about seven private investigators on the web, and we were the only ones taking case assignments directly over the Internet. Our bank, with whom we'd done business with for years, would not give us a MasterCard and Visa merchant account because the Internet was so new and they were afraid of it. We had to go elsewhere to set up our merchant account. Of course, that sounds silly now, but that's how early our presence was on the Net.

Even at that early stage, we were bringing in cases from all over the United States, and our bottom line began to increase because of our website. There's been a lot of shaking out in the industry since then, but a good, well-designed website can increase your business, even if you are working out of your kitchen.

Look at private investigators' sites on the web. Do they all look alike? Many of them do. They have copied their ideas from each other. Bronstrup calls this "marketing incest." This is one mistake you don't want to make. Find a good designer with original ideas. Watch out for "hotshot" kids with fancy flash pages. With those boxers, you'll never know what they'll flash at you. Make your site as professional as possible.

Choices on a web page should be kept to a minimum. Too many choices makes it easy for a prospective client to pick the wrong one, get frustrated, and leave your site entirely. It would pay to find a good designer who also knows the private investigative business. Make sure your site is simple and clean so that it loads quickly. Not everybody has a high-speed DSL line or a cable modem for fast downloads, so go easy on the graphics, or, at the very least, allow the person the option of choosing a text-only version of your page.

Answers to Sample License Questions

Answers to the sample questions provided by the State of Georgia are as follows:

1. D. .38 special revolver, six shots or less, with a 2" to 6" barrel length. Because …

   The issuance of an exposed weapons permit shall authorize the holder of such permit to carry a .38 Special revolver, holding six (6) shots or less, with a barrel length no longer than six (6) inches and no shorter than two inches or a semi-automatic handgun no larger than 40 caliber. The applicant for a weapon permit must submit proof of range and classroom training for the caliber weapon carried. All classroom training must be conducted using curriculum approved by the Board.

2. D. Renting a vacant store across the street from the suspect's rooming house, setting up a camera with a telephoto lens, and attempting to take pictures of him without his knowledge. Because …

Eavesdropping. It is also illegal to intentionally and "in a clandestine manner" overhear, transmit, or record (or attempt to overhear, transmit or record) the private conversations of others that "originate in any private place." A "private place" is defined as "a place where one is entitled reasonably to expect to be safe from casual or hostile intrusion or surveillance." Georgia courts have interpreted the statute to allow a party to the conversation to record or divulge it. For example, a pub or bingo parlor could hardly be considered a "private place."

Peeping Tom. But the Eavesdropping law also considers video surveillance matters and states: A peeping tom is defined as someone who "peeps through windows or doors, or other like places, on or about the premises of another for the purpose of spying upon or invading the privacy of the persons spied upon." Other acts that violate a person's privacy could be considered a violation of Georgia Code 16-11-62. Setting up a telephoto lens across the street from the rooming house and filming inside the premise probably would be in violation of this statute. Anything the subject did outside of his rooming house would probably be fair game.

3. C. "When did you first notice that the door had been forced?" Because …

You are leading the witness into assuming that he had seen the door was forced when he hasn't told you yet that he saw the door had been forced.

How did you do? Are you ready to take the test and get your PI license?

The Least You Need to Know

◆ Becoming a licensed private investigator is a popular dream. Making it a reality requires learning certain skills before applying to an agency, and then pursuing the dream with persistence.

◆ Forty states require PIs to be licensed. Twenty-two states also require a minimum passing score on a licensing examination. The test covers state laws on weapons, privacy issues, and general legal knowledge.

- Liability insurance and bond coverage is typically required by the states prior to issuing a PI license. Also, many clients require proof of insurance, often up to $2 million, before assigning cases to a PI.

- Business structure of PI firms generally falls within one of the following: sole proprietorship, partnership, C corporation, subchapter S corporation, or limited liability company (LLC). Each has different tax and liability consequences and advantages.

- The most successful PI businesses have found their own niche, and market that niche heavily.

- Don't forget to explore the World Wide Web as a marketplace. Internet traffic can substantially increase the bottom line for a PI firm.

Chapter 4

Tools of the PI Trade

In This Chapter

- Choosing the right vehicle
- Getting the right camera to get the shots
- Selecting the right computer
- Making a case with good binoculars
- Success is in the details—get 'em recorded

Private investigators produce a product just as surely as candy makers pull taffy and cook fudge. The product in either line of business has to, first, be pleasing to the eye of the customer, and second, be sweet and satisfying to his taste.

Every professional in every profession uses tools. Some of the tools in a private investigator's toolbox are mechanical, others may be digital or analog.

Other tools are intangible, such as skills or techniques that are learned as one matures in the trade, and whose quality directly affects the quality of the product produced. We'll learn a few of those in this chapter.

The Ferrari in the Garage

In Chapter 3, we mentioned the television show *Magnum PI*. Tom Selleck played the lead role of Thomas Magnum. In the show, he drove a red Ferrari. It wasn't unusual for Magnum to use the Ferrari while attempting to keep a person under a moving surveillance. Now, I don't know about you, but if I saw a red Ferrari in my rearview mirror, I think I would recognize it when I saw it again a few minutes later, or a few hours later. That's television for you—that's fiction.

We talk some about surveillance vans in Chapters 14 and 15, but let's examine the whole car issue here. Unless you own a whole fleet of cars, you're probably like the rest of us and have only one or two cars available to you. An investigator will have to use his car for both surveillance and marketing.

I had a very talented female investigator, Kathy, who ran one of my branch offices in another city. It was basically a one-person office and she ran it from her home. If Kathy needed help, there were other local investigators we could use as subcontractors on an as-needed basis. Sue Grafton's books had just started coming out, such as *A is for Alibi* and *B is for Burglar*, and Kathy, an avid reader, fathomed herself as Kinsey Millhone, Sue Grafton's fictional female PI. Kinsey Millhone drove a Volkswagen Bug.

The state claims offices for many insurance companies were located in the same city where Kathy resided. In fact, that was a major reason we opened a branch in that city. A large portion of Kathy's duties was marketing our company to the insurance companies' claims centers. Kathy also worked a lot of surveillance and other investigative cases in her region as well, but her marketing efforts brought cases in for us over the entire state.

I'd encourage Kathy to take these insurance claims folks to lunch as often as possible. It was a good way to let the claims people get out of the office and to mingle and joke with them and become their friend. Look through Chapter 12 and you'll see how important it is to make people your friends. It works with subjects and also with customers. Once a person is your friend, she'll feel an allegiance to you and will send you business.

When Kathy informed me she was going to buy this old, non-air-conditioned Volkswagen Bug, I discouraged her. It wouldn't make a good surveillance vehicle, nor would it be very comfortable for our clients when she took them to lunch.

If you're going to be the private investigator and run the business end, then you must have at your disposal a multipurpose vehicle, or multiple vehicles.

> ### Elementary, My Dear Watson
>
> Selection of a good vehicle for a PI is problematic. A PI should avoid anything that looks like a police car. Likewise a black van with dark tinted windows, sometimes called a "kidnapper van," makes people suspicious.
>
> Remember, people will see you. The idea is to stay far enough away so the *subject* doesn't see you. More horsepower is better in surveillance vehicles. An underpowered four cylinder car is going to make it rough when trying to catch up with the subject when he's two blocks ahead of you and moving out. Actually pickup trucks make pretty good surveillance vehicles in suburbia. Stay away from the real flashy sport cars.
>
> If the PI has only one vehicle as an option, go for the four door, eight cylinder, earth tone colored auto. It'll blend in better in most parking lots and give you room to take your clients to lunch.

Getting the Shots

Photography plays a huge role in the PI business. Whether you're working domestic cases, criminal defense, insurance defense, nursing home abuse, homicide and suspicious suicide cases, or employee theft, the quality of the photography matters. How much? Enough to make or break some cases. About the only portion of PI work where it may not be a necessary tool is skip tracing.

In nursing home cases, and almost all cases where we perform face-to-face interviews for attorneys, we ask permission to photograph the person we're interviewing. It helps us later to refresh our memories of the interview, and many of our clients want to see what this potential witness looks like. Of course, the nursing home patient is photographed to document his or her injuries. Likewise, in parental or spousal abuse cases, documenting the injuries and noting the time of the photograph and the time the injury occurred can be important. Skin bruising progresses through certain recognized patterns, and to a limited degree the approximate time of the injury can be established.

You'll use a camera to photograph crime scenes, areas where a slip and fall occurred or the intersection of a traffic accident. With domestic cases, a camera's use is obvious in catching the cheating spouse in a compromising embrace. You may wish to document two cars parked together in front of a motel or apartment.

What kind of camera equipment do you need? There are three types of cameras that each investigator should have, and also be proficient using:

- Digital still camera

- Digital video camera

- 35mm single-lens reflex camera

Digital still cameras are improving by leaps and bounds. Frankly, most investigators are cheap and will try to make their digital video camera do double duty, since digital video cameras are capable of taking still pictures as well. It's hard enough to get an interviewee to sit still while you talk him into having his photo taken with a still camera. Pull out that video camera, and he's likely to get up and turn his back on you. As far as crime scene and traffic accident photography are concerned, you'll want to take both video and stills of the scene. Sure, you could edit the video and capture stills off of it, but that's a lot more work than just shooting digital stills and uploading them to your computer. Most digital video cameras have single-shot capability as well.

The features to look for in digital still cameras are the number of *pixels*, the storage media, and the zoom capabilities.

Crime Scene Clues

Pixels are little points of light on a computer screen or a television screen that, when combined, are perceived by the naked eye as one large picture. The more pixels, the smoother the picture, yielding a better quality photograph.

Sherlock's Secrets

To access your digital photos, you have to download them to a computer. So, before buying a digital camera, it'd be smart to decide which computer you're going to use and make sure the camera's magnetic storage media is compatible. For example, many laptops have a PCMCIA card slot, which can accept a Compact Flash card with a simple and inexpensive adapter. Desktops don't usually have PCMCIA card slots. Sony Memory Sticks will require an adapter that fits in a floppy drive slot. Another techno-detail to watch for when playing matchmaker between a computer and a camera is whether the magnetic media contains a controller chip. If it doesn't, as is the case with SmartMedia cards, than you'll have to program the camera to recognize the card. This can get to be a real pain, unless you're a control-freak AA-type personality.

All the different cameras allow downloading directly from the camera to a computer via cables. The drawback to this method is speed. Cables are slower than direct digital input from a storage media. And, too, the camera's battery charge seems to rapidly dissipate during the downloading. It's a better idea to remove your storage media from the camera and insert it into your computer rather than use cable downloading. Evaluate your complete system, and this includes your digital video camera, before you buy. A good overall plan will save you heartache later.

A good digital camera will have at least 3 million pixels. Older and less expensive digitals have 1 and 2 million pixels. Like everything else in the computer world, electronics get better and less expensive pretty quickly. Four million pixel cameras are already out and will be standard issue soon.

So where do those digital still cameras keep all those photos you shoot? Rather than traditional film negatives, the digital still camera's memory is called magnetic media. Some brands have their own proprietary type of storage media. Sony, for example, uses a Memory Stick. Cannon and some others use a Compact Flash card, and others use SmartMedia. Larger digital cameras use PCMCIA cards.

With digital cameras, both still and video, check the power of the optical zoom and go for the vroom zoom. The higher the power, the better. When surveillance is covered in Chapters 14 and 15, we talk about techniques to help the investigator remain undiscovered. The farther away the investigator is from his subject, the less likely it is that the subject will become aware of the surveillance. The catch-22, of course, is that the greater the distance to your subject, the more difficult it becomes to get good photographs. This means you'll need a pretty good zoom to capture the images you need to make your case.

For your photographs to be effective in court, the subject must be identifiable. This means you have to get good, clear, well-focused shots. In addition to optical zooms, digital cameras, both still and video, will have a digital zoom feature. The digital zoom works very well, up to a point. In purchasing your equipment, all other things being equal, go first for the camera with the highest *optical zoom*, and then consider the power of the digital zoom. Most of your surveillance photography will be shot with the video camera and the 35mm camera, anyway.

Crime Scene Clues

Optical zoom on camera lenses refers to the focal length achieved by physically moving the lens further apart from each other thereby achieving a greater focal length (hence the term zooming out with a zoom lens) and increasing the relative size of the image as it appears on the film or recording media.

Digital cameras have a "digital zoom" that magnifies the image through digital technology. All other things being equal an optically zoomed image will be more clear because the image hasn't been altered or "blown up" through the digital process. The greater the number of pixels available in a digital camera makes the digital zoom more refined and the artificial enlarging process of digital zooming is now less noticeable to the human eye than in recent times. This digital zooming process will certainly improve in the future.

Except for the workers' compensation–type cases, which require the video camera, a quality 35mm camera is still the heavy-duty wrench in the private investigator's tool-box. Admittedly, this type of camera is being challenged by the versatility and light-gathering ability of video cameras, but the advantage of *single-lens reflex (SLR)* 35mm cameras is the ability to change lenses. The working lens for most PIs is a 100–300mm zoom lens. You can add a doubler between the lens and the camera body to get an effective focal length of 600mm. Anything longer than that, and you'll need to zoom in on a business loan to pay for it.

At 600mm, you'll need a tripod to steady the camera to avoid blurring the picture. A fast shutter speed will also prevent blurred pictures, but with a super-long lens on the camera, the amount of light that enters the lens is reduced, so slower shutter speeds may be required. There are SLR digital cameras available, but they're still rather pricey.

Crime Scene Clues

A **single-lens reflex (SLR)** camera is a camera where the light (the image) passes through the lens and is reflected by a mirror to the viewfinder, where it is viewed by the photographer. When the shutter button is depressed, the mirror flips out of the way, and the image passes directly to the film. The advantage of SLR cameras over other cameras, in addition to their lens-changing capability, is that the photographer sees the exact image that will appear on the film.

When after-dark photography is needed, there are two choices, neither of which requires flashbulbs or spotlights:

Sammy the Snitch

If a PI uses Tmax or any other film and pushes the film to a higher speed, then be sure to tell the processor at what speed it should be processed. If you don't, the film will come back grossly under- or overdeveloped and will be practically useless.

1. An investigator can use a 35mm camera with extra-fast film. Kodak makes Tmax film, a black-and-white product with a speed of 3200. It can be shot at 1600, 3200, or 6400, if needed. Most cameras cannot be set for film higher than 6500. However, finding a place to process black and white can be difficult. Most larger cities will have some photo shops that can do it, or that will at least send it out to a national processing center. You won't get it processed at a one-hour developer, though. Keep that in mind if you're going to need the prints right away.

2. When it comes to nighttime photography, video cameras have come to the PI's rescue. The light-receptive chips (charged, coupled devices) used in video cameras are more sensitive to light than is standard 35mm film. Therefore, after dark a video camera will probably capture a better image than a 35mm one, unless you're using a flash, which will flush you out of hiding and put your flesh at risk.

If a PI's cases regularly involve nighttime, black and white photography, she might consider having her own darkroom. The developing of black and white photos is relatively simple and not expensive. Take a class at your local community college and you'll be on your way. You'll also be able to use the school's darkroom and printing equipment at minimal cost. Color processing gets more complicated and the one-hour photo developing shops are awful convenient. With the advent of digital video and still cameras you'll be using your 35mm less and less.

Sherlock's Secrets

Sony has a feature on some of its video cameras called Nightshot, which uses infrared technology to capture images in total darkness. On most of its cameras, it's only effective to 10 feet, but you can buy an optional infrared light that will allow you to capture images up to a hundred feet away. It's worth looking at, but I wouldn't recommend buying the camera solely for this feature. It should be considered, however, when making comparisons with other video cameras. If you're targeting a niche that will require a lot of nighttime surveillance, factor that in as well.

If you're familiar with cameras in general, then go to one of the search engines we recommend in Chapters 5 and search for "digital cameras." One good site for comparing digital still cameras is www.dpreview.com. It has reviews of all the cameras, plus ratings. That site also has a pretty good learning center, where you can look up unfamiliar terms.

For digital video cameras as well as 35mm cameras, we suggest going right to the manufacturers' websites to read and compare the specifications on the cameras. Then, go to your local electronics store for a hands-on feel of the camera and personalized answers to your questions. Now, where can you find the best price for the camera equipment you want to purchase? Sounds like a question for an aspiring PI to solve. Shop around, though, because most of the brand names have a street price considerably lower than the suggested retail price.

Computer Equipment

You can't run and manage a successful PI business today without a computer and fast Internet access. If you're not computer literate, don't hang out your shield until you are. That's the bottom line. Even if you want to handle everything on paper and typewriter, you can't do justice to your clients' needs without access to the databases that are available to help you. And the databases don't accept collect calls for assistance. Chapters 5, 6, and 7 explore the wonderful world of information that is available to the PI. Come on into the twenty-first century.

Your computer should have the fastest processing chip, the largest hard drive, and the most memory (*RAM*) you can afford. Isn't that what all the guys say about the computer they want to buy? Sure it is, but in this business, we're talking tools, not toys. Why does it have to be so powerful? Thirty days after you've bought your new state-of-the-art computer, it'll be outdated and a newer, faster, larger, computer will be on the market. By starting with the best product *du jour*, you'll get about four good years in before you'll want to think about replacing it.

If you're going to skimp at all, skip the hottest new chip and get the day-old version. You can sometimes save a considerable amount of money by not buying the newest, fastest chip available, but the next to the fastest. The sometimes-slight differences in performance are not that big. Don't, however, skimp on the hard drive or the memory.

I don't recommend throwing good equipment away and having the newest just to have it. We still use one non-Windows 386 computer that we've had for well over 10 years. We use it for one very specific purpose. There is one program on it that is not compatible with Windows, and when we need that program, running it on that old computer is the only option available.

Crime Scene Clues _____

RAM is an acronym for **Random Access Memory.** It is the memory that the computer accesses when it processes information and runs programs. If there is not enough RAM in a computer, then the information being processed is swapped back and forth to the hard drive, which slows down the processing speed, causes programs to lock up and the computer to crash, and can actually hasten a hard-drive failure.

Computer programs get larger and require more RAM every time a new version is issued. If you're having stability problems, programs crashing, or the computer is locking up, try adding more RAM to your computer. Increasing RAM can solve a whole host of problems. In your new computer, include the most RAM you can afford.

What Are the Bells and Whistles?

There are lots of bells and whistles you can add to your computer, but don't tell your wife *The Complete Idiot's Guide to Private Investigating* suggested the high-quality sound-card with the subwoofers. Not true. Do, however, add a CD burner.

We sometimes ship reports with embedded photographs to our clients on CD. Likewise, you can put short video clips onto a CD instead of duplicating tapes. Your clients can look at the video clip and get a good idea of the degree of fraud in an insurance defense case. The client can do this from his desktop computer and not have to fool with finding the remote to the television and the other remote for his VCR.

Using Microsoft Access, we developed a database for one client where we had hundreds of potential witnesses. Each witness record included a complete copy of the interview and an embedded photograph of the witness. We put the database on a CD, and with each change, we'd send the client a new, updated CD that contained everything.

A fast color printer is a necessity. You've taken the digital picture and now you want to give a copy to your client. You can run down to your local photography store and wait an hour, and they'll print it for you. Or you can run back to your office and print it yourself, if you have the right equipment. A high-quality color printer, using premium photo paper specifically designed for color printers, will give you a print nearly indistinguishable from a print made at a photography shop.

> **CAUTION**
>
> **Sammy the Snitch** _____
>
> The only problem we've found with sending CDs containing our reports, photos, and video to clients is that sometimes the client's computer hardware is not up-to-date enough to play the CDs! We've had to encourage clients to upgrade their version of Access before they could run the databases we've developed for them. Nevertheless, even if the client can't use the CD you send him, he'll recognize you as a top investigator, who is above his peers in professionalism and on the crest of new technology. That's a good impression to leave with a client.

Applying the Bells and Whistles to a Case

It was 11:30 at night on Friday, May 10. The lights in the apartment I'd been watching had gone out about a half hour before. My client's husband, Jonathan, from whom she was separated, had taken their three-year-old son with him for the weekend. Part of the separation agreement was that Jonathan would not cohabit or otherwise spend the night with single females while he had custody of the child.

I'd followed Jonathan to the girlfriend's apartment complex and watched him and the little boy enter. His SUV was parked in front of the apartment, and the girlfriend's car was parked next to his. I walked up to the vehicles and, using a large, black, permanent felt-tip marker, I drew an inverted V on the sidewall at the very top of the right rear tire on both cars. If the vehicles departed and then later returned, I would know it by checking the position of the V. It would be nearly impossible for the V to be in the exact same position relative to the fender as when I drew it.

Next, I backed off a ways behind the cars and took out my trusty Cannon digital camera. At that hour, I had to use the flash, but since the subjects were inside, the risk of being discovered was next to nothing. I took three shots of the two cars and the front of the apartment. My objective was to record both vehicles and the address in the same photo. An advantage of digital cameras is you can see immediately if you got the picture you wanted. With the first picture, I was too far away, so the flash didn't illuminate the license plates. That's why I took two more, checked them, and discovered they were fine. Then I scooted out of there.

Back at the office, I inserted the date and time onto the face of the photographs, using Adobe Photo Deluxe, a program that came with the camera. I ran off two high-quality prints of the photographs, one for my client and one for her attorney.

At 7 the next morning, I was back at the same apartment complex. Both cars were still there. The inverted V was in the same relative position as I'd left it. There was dew on both car roofs and front windshields. I felt the grill area on both cars, and they were cold. My conclusion? Neither car had moved since 11:30 the previous night, indicating that Jonathan had spent the night with his girlfriend, son in tow.

I shot two more photographs of both cars and hustled back to my office. This time, I inserted "May 11th 7 A.M." onto the prints. Three or four weekends of this, and we had what the client wanted. The case went to court and Jonathan's attorney stipulated to the facts in my report without me having to testify. The client told me that out of all the money she'd spent going through the divorce, she thought the most productive use of her money was what she spent with my firm. Gotta love those satisfied clients—and gotta love those digital cameras.

Binoculars: The Better to See You With, My Dear

There are two other pieces of gear that are essential to a private investigator. One of those is a good pair of binoculars. Some investigators try to use opera glasses. These are small binoculars that fold, and will fit in a small purse or pocket. The size has its advantage, for sure, but it's outweighed by the lack of quality. A good pair of binoculars will make you a more productive investigator.

The binoculars should be 7×50's. At that power and that size, the image does not "bounce" around too much. A good set of binoculars will be filled with nitrogen or some other inert gas. This gas is injected into the binoculars between the lens and the eyepieces. This prevents moisture and dirt from getting into the binoculars.

Don't spare the expense on the binoculars. There is a big difference between an inexpensive pair and an expensive one. It might not be noticeable when you're inspecting them in the store, but the light-gathering aspects of binoculars vary significantly, usually in proportion to the price tag. On a nighttime surveillance, quality binoculars will gather more light and actually make it easier to see your subject's activities.

Some binoculars have a compass built into the viewfinder. Knowing where north, south, east, and west lay is very handy. If you're in radio contact with another investigator and your subject is on the move, you can tell the other investigator exactly which direction the subject is moving or toward which direction the activity is shifting. It's a lot clearer to say "The subject is moving east around the end of the shopping center," than to say "The subject is moving toward my right, around the end of the shopping center." The other investigator probably doesn't know which way you're facing and will be unsure as to which direction he should be looking.

My friend and long-time investigative associate Robert Plance was working a case with me on the island of St. Croix, in the U.S. Virgin Islands. Our subject, the plaintiff, was a claimant in an insurance case. The subject had a set of corrals and several horses stabled there toward the east end of the island.

There were two viewpoints we could use to get good video of the subject working around the barn. One was in a clump of brush, just off a dirt road that passed the corrals. From there, Bob could see one side of the corral and the barn. I climbed a hill, quite a distance across the main road, and concealed myself in the brush there. I could see the other side of the barn and corral that Bob couldn't see.

The subject had six sons ranging in sizes from small to extra large. Without good binoculars, we would have shot hours and hours of videotape of the two older sons, who looked very much like their father. Wouldn't we have been embarrassed going into court with video of the wrong person?

As it turned out, we obtained lots of good video of the father and not the sons. The case was settled for a nominal amount. In the process of following the father, we inadvertently stumbled upon a love nest he had with a female other than his wife. We always wondered what his wife would have thought if we'd gone to court and she'd heard the testimony about that.

Recording the Facts

One aspect of PI work is the report writing. You've heard this in a previous chapter and you'll hear it again before the book ends: PIs produce a product. A private investigator's clients only see the written or photographic results of our work. They don't see the gallons of sweat on the floor of your car after a hot afternoon surveillance. They don't feel the fear of a near collision on the freeway when your subject exits suddenly and you have to jump three lanes of traffic to stay behind him. To them, your product is your report. That's all they'll see—that, and any evidence you collect.

The written report needs to appear professional. We talk in greater length in Chapter 23 about formatting your reports. Here, we'll discuss the process of getting the facts down so they're not lost or forgotten.

Some surveillance investigators handwrite their surveillance logs. That works, but it is tedious. A better way is to have a microcassette recorder and dictate the surveillance as you go along. With that method, all of the details—license plate numbers, right and left turns, and the rest—are captured as they happen. Nothing important is left out or forgotten. You'll have a more detailed surveillance log. Down the road, that may become important. People really are creatures of habit, and as you work a subject, his patterns will develop. If this is all laid out in your surveillance logs, then the next guy working him will have the benefit of your experience.

Even with a recorder, though, I'd recommend you keep a pen and paper ready for quick notes. You should always jot down any important license plate number as you see it, because sometimes, in dictating, we transpose numbers. Write it down immediately. You may need to call the tag in to your office and have the registration run. You don't want to have to listen back through your entire surveillance log to find a tag.

As long as we're on the topic of surveillance logs, here is one piece of advice you won't find in any other book. Back at the office, take the surveillance videotape you've just made and watch it on a monitor. Dictate while the tape is running. In your dictation, note the times of significant activity. When the claimant picks up that 50-pound bag of fertilizer, note that in your log. You don't have to mention every bend and each motion of his body, but do enter into the log the time of any activity you think is important.

When you show these tapes in court, the judge will not want to watch the entire thing. After a few moments, he'll ask you to fast-forward the tape to the "good parts." With the time and date on the tape, and the same time and date in your typed log, you can go right to the good parts and skip over the long, boring, and unimportant parts. We'll discuss this some more in Chapter 24.

If you're just beginning a business, you might not have a secretary. I'd suggest not hiring one until you find that the volume of report typing you're doing is actually keeping you from working on cases. At that point, hire a part-time secretary, and you'll become more profitable.

The importance of producing a high-quality product cannot be stressed enough. The candy maker's fudge must first look good enough to eat. To keep clients coming back, the fudge has to taste even better than it looks. Likewise, your product should look professional, and as the client reads through the report and views the photographs, the contents should be even more pleasing to him.

In one of the examples in this chapter, we talked about Jonathan spending the night with his girlfriend while having his three year old for the weekend. Who do you think his wife, or her attorney, is going to recommend the next time somebody asks them for the name of a good private investigator? In fact, his attorney, recognizing my good work, now refers clients to us. The product looked good and tasted even better. Success, in this case, is sweet.

The Least You Need to Know

- An investigator needs a car that is practical for both surveillance and carting clients to lunch.

- Three important tools of the trade are a digital still camera, a digital video camera, and a 35mm single-lens reflex camera. Important factors for digital cameras are the optical zoom and the number of viewable pixels.

- It's impossible to run a PI business without a computer. In buying a new computer, it's recommended to purchase the computer with a recent processor, a very large hard drive, and as much RAM as you can afford. Also, a fast color printer and a CD burner should be at the top of the list.

- An investigator should have a good pair of 7×50 binoculars.

- Use a good quality microcassette recorder to dictate during a surveillance rather than handwriting a surveillance log. Do keep a pen and paper ready to jot down license plates, as well as dictating them.

- A high-quality finished product will please your clients and fatten your bottom line.

Part 2

Getting the Scoop

Now that you've decided exactly what you're looking for, it's time to learn where to find it.

In this section, we'll examine the sources of information that PIs use around the country to get the scoop on the subjects of their cases. You'll learn how to skip trace on the web, and prowl the courthouses and get access to federal, state, and local records. We'll also show you how to log on to those secret private databases that professional PIs use.

Skip Tracing on the Web: Part One, the Internet

In This Chapter

- ◆ How to find and use the best search engine
- ◆ Problems with using free Internet white pages
- ◆ Begin a search with these important steps
- ◆ Where to find good white-page sites … at a price

There is not a soul in the United States or Canada who has not at least heard of the World Wide Web (WWW). Unfortunately, there are many misconceptions about the kind of information that is available on the web. In this and the next chapter, we'll clear up some of those misunderstandings. We'll show you step-by-step how to use the web to locate a person and find his or her current address and telephone number. If you still can't find him or her, you'll understand why, and where to search next. We'll also explain why sometimes there is information on the person you are searching for that's partially incorrect, out-of-date, or just plain wrong. Later, in Chapter 16, you'll learn how to turn out-of-date information into a current address.

In the Internet Beginning

The WWW was originally developed to exchange information between government-granted universities, laboratories, and other hallowed halls of learning. The lines of communication for the web were structured in such a way that in the event of a nuclear attack or other major catastrophic event, even though one section of the Internet or a host provider might be disabled, communications between the remaining parties would still be possible.

Remember, we're talking about communication at the speed of light, 186,000 miles per second. Your modem may be bottlenecked by downloading or uploading at 56K bytes of information per second, but once that data is out of your computer and headed toward its destination, it is traveling at close to the speed of light. You'd think the quickest way to route an e-mail from Miami to New York City would be a direct line up the East Coast of the United States. But if there is a slowdown or outage somewhere along that line, the Internet might route the e-mail from Florida to California and back to Washington, D.C.; at the speed of light, what's a few thousand miles one way or the other?

Imagine a huge spider web 3,000 miles in diameter. You might break one little strand in the web, but the rest of it remains intact. That is the way the World Wide Web was originally organized.

I'm going to assume you have some familiarity with the Internet and your *web browser*. If you don't have any familiarity with the Internet, then you may want to pick up *The Complete Idiot's Guide to Online Search Secrets* or *The Complete Idiot's Guide to the Internet*. You'll find both books helpful to you in developing your *skip tracing* skills on the web.

Crime Scene Clues

A **web browser** is the software program you use to "surf" on the Internet. Most likely it is Microsoft Internet Explorer, Netscape, or even the browser within AOL. **Skip tracing** originally referred to collection agencies' attempts to locate a debtor who'd "skipped out" on his obligation. It generally now refers to any attempt by a private investigator to find an individual. Perhaps this person is intentionally eluding creditors, or is merely a witness whose address is not currently known, but is sought by attorneys for an interview or a deposition. Universally, however, a person who is eluding his creditors is referred to in the business as "a skip."

Navigating the White Pages

On the Internet, you'll find hundreds of websites that have a name-search capability. You input a name and it'll give you back a list of possible matches. You refine your search, narrow the list of possibilities, and increase your chances of finding the right person if you have his or her address, city, state, province, or postal code.

Following is a list of websites that have "white-page telephone" listings. The list may be outdated to some extent because Internet sites come and go more often than you change your socks.

- ◆ www.lycos.com
- ◆ www.yahoo.com
- ◆ www.msn.com
- ◆ www.superpages.com
- ◆ www.anywho.com
- ◆ www.whitepages.com
- ◆ www.questdex.com
- ◆ www.teldir.com
- ◆ www.canada411.com

Several of these websites have white-page "phone books" where you can search many countries from around the world. Canada, in particular, is very well represented.

For our purposes right now, it is more important to learn how to find these databases yourself than to choose which one to use exclusively. Some are better than others, but they change frequently. Once you learn how to find them on your own, you're in the money. So let's go.

Elementary, My Dear Watson

The Internet contains listings similar to the white-page listings in your local telephone book. These are residential listings and will have names, addresses, and phone numbers. Sometimes the address won't be available if it is not published in the local phone book. The web listings will not contain nonpublished numbers, cell phone numbers, or pager numbers. There are also listings called yellow pages, which have mostly business listings (very similar to the yellow pages of your phone book). White pages and yellow pages are usually maintained in separate databases and you search them separately, just as you would in your printed telephone book.

Utilizing Search Engines

On the Internet we use *search engines* to find specific websites that are of interest to us. All web addresses are actually numbers. We as humans relate better to letters than numbers; names are easier to remember than a string of numbers. When you type in a website by name, the computer then converts that name (a string of letters to the computer) to a string of numbers and sends you to the appropriate site. That's what your browser does. It acts as an interface or interpreter between you and all of those numbered sites out there. If you know the number that corresponds to the website, you may use that rather than the name (for example, the Yahoo! website is 66.218.71.89).

Most actual site addresses are usually *http://* followed by *www.*(the name of the engine).*com*. The *.com* end of the address could be *net, gov, edu, org,* or a number of other dots, including country names. Don't worry about what the dot endings, or extensions, mean. You do need to use them, though. You need to type in everything after the *www*. Most browsers (Netscape, Explorer, and AOL) let you type in just the name without the *http://* or the *www*. The browser will insert the rest for you.

Crime Scene Clues

Search engines are Internet sites that allow a user to input search criteria. The engine then searches its own database of researched Internet sites and provides you with a list of sites that most closely meets your search criteria.

Some search engines on the Internet are as follows:

- Google (www.google.com)
- Mamma (www.mamma.com)
- Northern Light (www.northernlight.com)
- Ask Jeeves (www.ask.com)
- WebCrawler (www.webcrawler.com)
- Datavor (www.datavor.com)
- Excite (www.excite.com)
- Go.com (www.infoseek.go.com)
- Lycos (www.lycos.com)
- MSN (www.msn.com)
- AllTheWeb (www.alltheweb.com)
- AltaVista (www.altavista.com)
- Teoma, formerly Direct Hit (www.teoma.com)
- LookSmart (www.looksmart.com)
- Yahoo! (www.yahoo.com)

One of my favorites is Datavor (www.datavor.com), which searches its own database along with 30 other search engines (and their databases). You can easily click on any of the other 30 search engines and see those results in a separate window without losing your spot at Datavor. Pretty nifty.

If the preceding list is not long enough for you, you can go to any of the sites listed and type in "search engine" to come up with an even larger list.

Internet search engines, in simplified terms, come basically in three varieties:

- ◆ The first is a crawler-type computer software program, also referred to as spider, robot, or worm. This software "crawls" around the Internet, logging all of the pages into its own database, indexing or copying what it finds there. It then follows links from one Internet site to another, enabling the search engine to literally crawl throughout cyberspace, logging web pages as it goes. Google claims to have over a billion pages logged into its database.

- ◆ The second type is a metasearch engine, or metanavigator, that searches multiple crawler databases looking for items that match the requested search criteria. With these types, one search request might search 30 other databases and return a list of possible matches. A good example of this is Metacrawler.com.

- ◆ The third is a virtual library, which is basically a huge library of material that also contains links to additional Internet resources. Sometimes these virtual libraries also function as a metanavigator, performing searches. Yahoo! is an example.

Each has its advantages; within each category there are many variations, including how the material is scored, evaluated, and matched with what was requested.

Each search engine will have a search-request area, usually a white box where you can type in the word or words you want to look up. Click on the Go or Search button and a list of Internet sites that provide information about your subject will appear on your screen.

When the engine completes your requested search, it will provide a list of possible sites that match your search criteria. These sites are usually listed in descending order, beginning with those considered to have the highest match percentage to your subject. As you examine this list, you will notice areas or names in blue type. These are the site addresses or locations; the blue type indicates a *hyperlink*. If you

Crime Scene Clues

A hyperlink is an area, picture, word, or phrase on a web page that you can click on in order for your browser to take you to another page or website whose content is linked in some manner.

move your cursor over these blue words, the cursor will change to a small hand. When the hand appears, click the link to be taken directly to the site. If you right-click this link, it will open or give you the option to open a completely new browser window for the site. This is convenient for keeping the main search-site match list available without having to click back numerous times to return to it (in case you want to link to another search result).

Find That High School Sweetheart

We all have friends, relatives, or old high school or college buddies with whom we've lost contact. The web is a great tool for tracking these people down, though it may not necessarily be the best.

Likewise, if you're searching for somebody who owes you money, there is a good chance he or she may be in debt to others as well. In that case, the free white-page part of the web may not be of great help. If folks are hiding or moving frequently, the free search areas of the web probably haven't caught up with them yet. In Chapter 9, you'll see where you can find more current information.

Elementary, My Dear Watson

There appears to have been a significant increase over the past five years in the percentage of nonpublished and nonlisted phone numbers. This is probably due in part to subscribers attempting to avoid telephone marketing companies.

Most telephone companies allow subscribers to request a "nonpublished" telephone number, which means that their name, address, and phone number will not be published in the printed directory for the phone company, and the number is not available through directory information. However, the name and address do appear on the computer screen in front of the directory information operator. See Chapter 11, on how to get the phone company to reveal this information.

A "nonlisted" telephone number means that the number is not published in the directory but it is in the information operator's database. Operators will provide it when asked.

Also, the name and telephone number can appear in the directory without an address.

If the person you are looking for hasn't moved in the last couple of years, works a steady job, and pays his or her bills, then you have a good chance of finding him or her on the web.

The First Principles of Skip Tracing

When locating old high school or college friends, there are a couple of basic principles you need to be mindful of:

- Person-to-person contact is a good place to start.
- Search the right last name (keep in mind that married women often change their names).
- State and city of last known whereabouts is a plus.
- Occupation may be a good identifier.
- Take advantage of multiple search engines.

It is easier, quicker, and usually more reliable to pick up the telephone and call a mutual acquaintance than it is to search blindly for someone on the Internet. Even if your friend doesn't know exactly where your old girlfriend is, he may have heard something about her. He might be able to tell you who does know, or may know what city and state she is living in, what her current last name is, or her occupation. The more investigation you do and information you gather about her current status before you begin your Internet search, the greater your odds of success.

If you are searching for a particular female, remember that her name may have changed if she's gotten married. If you happen to know her date of birth (even just the month and year, if not the exact day), that tidbit of information might help narrow the search down a great deal, as you'll see in Chapter 9 when we get to searches using pay-per-search data providers.

The good and the bad of searching for someone on the Net is that it is in reality a World Wide Web. That being the case, you might literally be able to find someone halfway around the world. The negative side of that coin is that the world is so large, it can make locating a person even more difficult. For that reason it is best if you can narrow the scope of your search. For example, if you know the state or province, or better yet, the city where the person is most likely residing, your chances of finding him or her increases a thousandfold.

Another good way to narrow the search even more is by occupation. If you know your old college buddy serves in the military, or even specifically what branch he is in, you might use a military-locator database. A white-collar civilian may belong to professional organizations: lawyers, the bar associations; doctors, the AMA; security consultants, the ASIS; truck drivers, electrical workers, or garment workers, the unions. Don't forget to check the alumni association of your college.

Did your ex-girlfriend get married and you know what state the ceremony took place in? In Chapter 6, we'll deal with state records, but keep marriage records and voter-registration records in mind. A marriage record will have her maiden name (or most recent name) and her new name as well.

Searching on the web may require many different approaches. You have to be a good detective and utilize the tools available. Some searches return better results than others, and some are more specific toward certain subjects than are others.

Ready, Set, Go

In this section we're going to go step-by-step, searching for a common name. First, let's start with the basics of a search. Suppose we are looking for me! Steve Brown. That's a pretty common name and we can use it as an example in this book without worry of being sued.

So let's start with Lycos. Go to www.lycos.com. There under Tools near the top is White Pgs. Click on it and the window at the top of the screen says "WhoWhere?" You can fill in the name of Steven Brown and search for a phone. A whole bunch of Steve Browns all across the country will appear. It doesn't tell you how many matches it found and I haven't counted them, but there are a bunch.

That's not going to get us anywhere. Go back to that search page. In small letters under the last name field are the words Advanced Phone Search. Click that.

Now you can refine your search by putting in the city and the state. See why you called your old buddy to find out as much as you could about the person you're looking for?

If you don't know the city, just put in the first and last name and state (in this case, Florida). If you put in Steve Brown, you'll get 64 listings—but none of them are me. How come? I do live in Florida.

The reason I'm not included in those 64 names is because my name is not Steve, but Steven Brown. So try it with Steven. You'll get 87 returns. Actually, I am in that group of 87, but how are you going to know which one I am? If you know me as Steve Brown—which everyone does—you now have 151 possibilities.

You can do a people search at Yahoo! and you'll get 153 choices. That's pretty close to Lycos (makes you wonder if they're using the same search engine). But if you just use

S. Brown, the number goes up to 200. (Lots of single women list their phone only using their first initial.) Which one are you going to choose?

Another source for a people search is the Microsoft Network, at www.msn.com. Its white pages give 158 listings for Steve Brown in Florida, an additional 90 for Steven Brown, and a total of 250 if you search for S. Brown.

CAUTION

Sammy the Snitch

While searching these sites, you'll see lots of ads and highlighted text for other search services, including US Search.com, Classmates.com, KnowX.com, and other companies that conduct searches of public records. Remember, there is no free lunch. The free website searches make money by selling advertising to these pay sites. Don't be fooled into paying $5, $20, or even more for searches when you can get them for free. Read a little further in this chapter and you'll see where.

The problem with all of these sites, except for one, is that the information is very old ... and you don't know how old. The MSN white pages have a reverse number lookup, where you can put in the phone number and get the subscriber information for that number. I put in my phone, which I've had for eight months, and the previous subscriber name is shown. I'm not.

Let's look at two more sites.

Superpages (www.superpages.com) has multiple searches available for free. You can search by name or reverse search by phone number. If you put in the name Steven Brown or my phone number, you will still get information that is over eight months old. However, Superpages tells you when the record was first entered into their database and when it was last updated.

In my case, enter Steven Brown of Jacksonville Beach, Fl., and you'll find me at the old address. If you click on the blue-highlighted More Info after my name, a map showing that address pops up. Also, the fact that I was first listed at that address and telephone number on June 1, 1997, and updated on June 1, 2000, is

Sherlock's Secrets

When using your telephone to call directory information, the phone company charge usually runs between 75¢ and $1.00. However, information operators will run two searches for the one price if you ask. When the computer answers your call, say that you need to speak to an operator and don't say anything else until a live person answers. Give the operator both names you want searched. That way, you can get two for the price of one.

revealed. At Superpages, at least you have a time frame of when I may have lived there. That is important, because even though the information is no longer current, you have someplace to start. In Chapter 16, we'll take that outdated information and use it to get the current address from the post office.

One last white-page site, at www.anywho.com, is run by AT&T. It is one of the better free sites for names, addresses, and phone numbers, and has business listings as well. When I searched my name, I found my current address and two of the phone numbers I have here. Anywho did not show the third number, which I've had for 60 days. Likewise, they did not have my secretary's boyfriend's phone number, which he's had for about four months. So the information is dated, and unfortunately we don't know how dated it is. But it is clearly more current than any of the other free sites I've checked, so let's give them a gold star.

Where are you going to go to get more current telephone information? You can call the directory information operator, but that will cost you nearly a dollar a try. There's got to be a better way … and there is.

The Pay Sites

There are at least two reputable sites where you can buy current telephone information at rates less than your phone company will charge you. Currently these sites charge between 20¢ and 30¢ a search. Both of these sites are reselling to you the Regional Bell Operating Company (RBOC) telephone-information data. There are others that resell this information, but they are geared toward high-end commercial users, or as of this writing they charge more.

The first of these is Reach Directory, a product of Masterfiles (www.masterfiles.com). You'll need a credit card to use Reach. You'll be charged $60, which includes a $10 processing fee and $50 worth of searches. On this site you get daily updated telephone information (as current as the phone company info, because it *is* the phone company info). You can search by name or do a reverse search by number. The nifty part of Reach is that you can also search by address. If you have an address and want to know the telephone number at that address, plug in the street address and presto, there is the number. The address search runs about 33¢ per search. Individual, business, or reverse searches are 20¢ each.

You won't get nonpublished numbers or cell phone numbers. If you search by name and the individual has a nonpublished number, you will see "NP" next to the name.

Suppose you find a phone number written in lipstick on a cocktail napkin in your husbands coat pocket. If you want to know the subscriber's name and do a reverse search, searching the number, and it turns out to be a nonpublished number you will get a "no record." The same goes for cell phones and pager numbers.

As of the publication date for this book, Reach will also provide a search based on an individual's social security number, and another search which should show relatives of the person you are looking for. The company puts out a good product, but it's not free.

The other pay site is 555-1212.com. At this site (located at www.555-1212.com), you have two choices after registering. With a credit card and $9.95 you can buy 100 basic phone searches. The basic searches are not current, and according to the people who run the site, are updated every 90 days. For $19.99 you can buy 100 overnight searches, which means you are buying information that is updated nightly just like Reach Directory. The RBOC data is updated every day, and this site updates its directory information from the RBOC every night.

At 555-1212.com, you can also run searches by address and do reverse-number lookups. Again, since you are dealing with RBOC information, you won't get cell-phone numbers and nonpublished numbers.

There is talk of cellular companies or third party companies publishing telephone directories of cell number subscribers. We'll just have to wait and see if that develops. There is so much competition between cell companies and customers jumping from one company to another, any directory, to be up-to-date, would have to be web based.

As for nonpublished numbers, obviously they'll not be a directory for them, otherwise they'd no longer be "nonpublished." There are methods of getting those numbers and we talk about that in Chapter 11.

The two sites do have a couple of other useful features. Once you have registered, you can use their area code lookup feature for free. You can search by area code number, or by city and find the corresponding area code. They also have country code lookups.

One extremely helpful bonus that 555-1212.com has is the neighbor feature. After performing a search and retrieving a number, you have the option of asking about the neighbors. Do this and you get a list of everybody in the neighborhood, with their phone numbers and addresses. This works really, really well. I can't tell you how many times I've used that feature from another database I subscribe to. Even if I can't get a number for the person I'm looking for, perhaps because they have a nonpublished or unlisted number, I find a number for the person next door or across the street and get the information I need.

There are other pay sites such as QuickInfo.net and SearchAmerica. Both of these sites provide a good product, but are geared toward the professional private investigator and collection agency and may not allow individuals not holding a license to access their databases. We'll discuss these two databases and others like them in greater detail in Chapter 9.

One other site worth mentioning is the BellSouth Yellow Pages, at www.yp.bellsouth. com. Its white-page search is like the other outdated free sites, but the yellow-page site is pretty good.

I am sure there are more out there. Now, after reading this chapter, you know how to go and find them. The Internet white pages can be a valuable and productive avenue for skip tracing. The best part is that most of it is free.

The Least You Need to Know

- ◆ Query old friends and associates to gather information on your subject before you begin your web search.

- ◆ The Internet uses search engines to direct you to content-specific websites; some are better than others.

- ◆ Use multiple web search engines for better results.

- ◆ Free white-page directory information is usually very out-of-date.

- ◆ There are pay sites that resell the Regional Bell Operating Company data.

6

Skip Tracing on the Web: Part Two, Public Records

In This Chapter

- ◆ Determining if your subject is dead or alive
- ◆ Locating prison inmates
- ◆ You're in the Army now: military locators
- ◆ Finding an e-mail address for your first love

Skip tracing is as much of an art as a science. When you're trying to locate somebody, you assemble as much data as you have on the person and then search the logical places. There is a big difference between looking for somebody that you've only lost contact with and somebody that is actually a skip, meaning someone who is intentionally hiding perhaps from creditors or has some reason to keep their whereabouts a secret.

Old high school friends would probably as much like to find you as vice versa. They're not hiding their identity. They haven't put their phone in somebody else's name, and their mail goes to their home address, not some *private mailbox*.

If a person is really on the run, it's highly unlikely you'll find his or her current whereabouts on the free Internet sites. Professional pay sites are a different matter, and we'll go through them in Chapter 9. If someone owes you money or if you run a collection agency, and you're sure that person is still alive and is not in the military, go right to Chapter 9. Read those two chapters and do it yourself for next to nothing, or you can pay someone like me big bucks to find them for you.

Crime Scene Clues

Private mailboxes are commercial establishments, such as Mail Boxes Etc. Mail is delivered to their business and then put into a box setup much like post office boxes at the U.S. Post Office. In addition to the regular street address and box number for a private mailbox the address is suppose to contain the initials PMB (private mail box).

As I mentioned in Chapter 1, if you're going to be a do-it-yourselfer PI or become a professional PI, then you have to "think outside the box," or "sideways." Most folks, when attempting to locate someone, think only of telephone directory information, whether it's on the Internet or on their telephone dial. Due to so many telemarketing campaigns and a growing desire for more privacy, it's becoming more and more popular to have a phone number that is either nonpublished or nonlisted. If you only utilize telephone databases, you're out of luck. But there are lots of other databases where people show up. Use them.

Wanted Dead or Alive—Searching the Death Master File

Is the person you are seeking a birth parent, someone who's age you're unsure of, and who may be elderly? It's possible he or she is already deceased and you don't know it. It would be a good idea to check that out first before spending a lot of time and money searching for him or her elsewhere.

There are lots of sites on the Internet where you can search something known as the Social Security Death Master File. Some sites will let you search it for free. Others, of course, want you to pay. As in any database search, you need to know exactly what records are being searched and when they were last updated. The Social Security Administration sells that part of its data, and it's not cheap.

I had a new client from another state call me just this week. He asked me to locate a cousin of his that he hadn't heard from for several years. He had her last known address and telephone number, but couldn't locate her through directory information or find anything current about her by using the free white-page searches on the Internet.

I quoted him a minimum price of $250, which he agreed to, and I set about searching for her. First, I called the number he'd given me, and sure enough, it was disconnected.

There were lots of directions I could have gone in trying to find her, but since he'd told me she was elderly and lived alone, I checked the Death Master File.

She was listed there. The Death Master File gave me her social security number; day, month, and year of death; and county of last known residence. I waited a few days to get back to the client because I didn't want him to think it was too easy. I called him and related the sad news. He could have saved himself $250 if he had bought this book and read it instead of calling me.

Keep in mind that this search is not all-inclusive, and the number of deaths listed before 1980 are not many compared to those after that date. For instance, my father, who died in 1975 and had a surviving spouse, is not listed. My mother, who died in 1988 and did not have a surviving spouse, is listed. Like any database, it is a resource that is not necessarily definitive in all directions. If the person you are looking for is there, then they are probably deceased. But, if their name is not listed, it doesn't mean they're not deceased.

You can take any of the search engines set out in the preceding chapter and insert "Death Master File" in the search box. You'll get a list of websites that will run the search for you. Some are free, others want to charge as much as $49; several run in the $5 to $15 range. Even one of the best professional pay databases (see Chapter 9) that I subscribe to charges $5 for this search. Many of the free ones are updated very infrequently. Likewise, the pay sites may only update their data every three months, and some only every year.

The good news is that you can get the best search of the Social Security Death Master File for free at a site that is updated monthly. Interestingly, it's offered at two different sites, both owned by the same company, but the RootsWeb.com search is better than that of its counterpart, Ancestry.com.

Go to www.rootsweb.com. On the left side of the web page is a link to the Death Master File. This search is free and by far the best and most current available that I've found anywhere. Don't ask me why, but we have done identical searches at both websites and the RootsWeb.com site performs better. It finds individuals that Ancestry.com doesn't. Go figure.

Searching the database is fairly straightforward. The more exact information you have, the better. With that said, it's also true that too much information is not good. For example, try searching for my mother, Brookie Bellamy Brown. If you search her full name, no hits are returned. However, if you search Brookie B. Brown, just using the initial for the middle name, you get a hit.

Her last residence is shown as Tempe, Ariz. That's not exactly right. While she did maintain a residence there, that is not where she was residing at the time of her death.

Any information that you receive from databases, whether they are free or you paid big bucks for them, must be looked at with a broad view. Sometimes the information is exactly right, but just as often, the "facts" returned may have part of the truth, but not necessarily all of it. Just as a good mariner doesn't rely on only one source for his navigational data, a good investigator will check the facts through multiple sources before testifying that they are accurate and complete.

Go Directly to Jail, Do Not Pass Go, Do Not Collect $200

One of the unpleasant things you have to consider when searching for someone is the possibility that he or she has been incarcerated, whether in a federal facility, a state prison, or a county or city jail.

To find a federal prisoner, go to www.bop.gov. This is the Federal Bureau of Prisons website. On the left side of the screen, there's a hyperlink to Inmate Info. Click on that link and then click on BOP Inmate Locator. There, you'll find a search screen where you can input your search criteria by first and last name, FBI number, inmate register number, INS number, or DCDC number. If you are at your computer, just for fun, search John Gotti and see what comes up.

Elementary, My Dear Watson

In the spring of 2002, there were a little over 150,000 inmates housed in about 100 different federal detention facilities. The federal prison system only houses individuals convicted of federal crimes. According to the U.S. Department of Justice, Bureau of Justice Statistics, over 6.3 million people were on probation, parole, or housed in federal, state, or local jails at the end of 1999.

These records not only show you everyone who is currently incarcerated, but also gives their anticipated release date and the institution where they're housed, the institution's address, and its telephone number. The database records begin in 1982 and should show anybody who has spent time in a federal prison since 1982, even if he or she is now released.

I searched my own name and found 10 Steve Browns and 45 Steven Browns (and no, I've never spent the night in a federal prison), so be sure and search all possible name variations for the person you are skip tracing.

This database won't show what the crime was that got them into the federal penitentiary. I'll show you how to find that in Chapter 8.

If you're pretty sure the person is in jail but he or she doesn't show up in the federal prison database, then you'd need to start searching the state prisons and county jails.

You can go to www.corrections.com. At that website, click on the More Links option and you'll see an alphabetized list of links. One of the choices, Inmate Locator, gives links to various states and Los Angeles County that allow Internet access to information on the inmate population of those respective correctional institutions.

Many states will also allow you to search for individuals on *probation* and *parole* as well, not just those folks who are still locked behind bars. If you add parolees and probationers to your search, then you're considerably expanding the number of people in these databases. So, when searching the prison databases, don't overlook these options. The databases usually have a separate search or a button you have to click on to include the probation and parole population.

Crime Scene Clues

Probation indicates that a person was convicted of a crime, but rather than sentencing him or her to a jail term, probation is given to see if that person can not violate the law, stay employed or any other terms of their probation given to them to follow over a specified time period. **Parole** means an individual was sentenced to and actually spent time in jail, but was released earlier than the original sentence called for. He or she also must not violate any conditions of their parole or they face having the parole revoked and being sent back to prison.

The information in the preceding list will certainly change. Most of the state, web-based inmate locators work very well. Some states, such as Utah, only allow access to sex offenders, while the other states listed will let you search their entire prison population.

You're in the Army Now—Military Locators

Currently, no websites run by the military will allow the public access to the military locator databases. However, there is another method of obtaining a military person's location.

If you are a family member and have an emergency, you can call the numbers that follow and a representative of the specific branch will find your family member for you.

If you are a private investigator or nonfamily member, or a family member without an emergency, you can write to the following addresses, include a check for $3.50 (a fee set by Congress), and give the individual's name, social security number, and as much information as you have. Family members do not need to pay the $3.50.

The current exceptions to this method are the Coast Guard and the Navy. The Coast Guard may respond over the telephone and there is no fee. The Navy, due to current security considerations, will not respond, but will forward mail to the individual.

- Air Force
  AFPC-M.S.I.M.D.L.
  550 C St. W, Suite 50
  Randolph AFB, TX 78150-4752
  210-565-2660

- Army
  Army Worldwide Locator
  U.S. Army Enlisted Records &
  Evaluation Center
  8899 E. 56th St.
  Indianapolis, IN 46249-5301
  703-325-3732

- Coast Guard
  Commandant
  U.S. Coast Guard Personnel
  Command (C.G.P.C.)
  2100 2nd St. SW
  Washington, DC 20593-0001
  202-267-1340

- Marine Corps
  USMC – CMC
  HQMC – MMSB – 10
  2008 Elliott Rd., Suite 201
  Quantico, VA 22134-5030
  703-784-3942

- Navy
  Navy Personnel Command
  PERS – 312
  5720 Integrity Dr.
  Millington, TN 38055-3120
  901-874-3388

E-Mail Addresses, and How to Get 'Em

If we're using the Internet to locate somebody, then we might as well use the entire Internet. There are databases of e-mail addresses, which typically get their information from scanning the *Usenet* postings. If you post to a Usenet group or the person you are looking for posts, then there is reasonable likelihood that the e-mail address may be found in these databases. Most of these databases are free.

Also, many people will voluntarily add their names and e-mail addresses to these databases. It is certainly worth a try. Remember, if the name is common like mine, you will end up with numerous possibilities. If you're not sure of the name, most of these databases allow the use of *wild card* searches.

You can usually do a reverse search in these databases as well. If you have an e-mail address and want to know who it belongs to, then use the reverse search feature.

Crime Scene Clues _____

Usenet groups are like bulletin boards on the Internet. You can post messages to these groups and include photographs (called binaries). They are organized according to subjects. Your typical Internet Service Provider will subscribe to about 3,700 of these groups and make them available to you. Subjects range from anything to everything, including alt.private.investigation. A good way to get started using Usenet groups is to download a free software program called Free Agent. It can be found at www.forteinc.com.

A **wild card** allows the use of only partial names in searches. This is accomplished by inserting an asterisk after the beginning of a name. For instance, if you're not sure if a person's name is Rick or really Richard, you can input "Ric*" (without the quotation marks) and the search will return the following names: Rick, Richard, Ricky, and Ricardo.

The list that follows will give you a place to start, but all of the search engines listed in the Chapter 5, can be used to find e-mail directories. Just input as a search parameter "e-mail directory," without the quotation marks, and you'll be off and running.

- www.iaf.net
- www.theultimates.com/e-mail
- www.bigfoot.com
- www.411locate.com
- www.e-mailfinder.com
- www.worldemail.com

Sherlock's Secrets _____

Could the individual you're looking for be a Jr., Sr., a II, or a III? Try adding the wild card asterisk at the end of the last name. That will get any suffixes that are appended to the last name.

There is a lot of borrowing and linking between websites, so don't be surprised when you get the same search results from several different Internet sites.

High School Reunion Time

My agency receives one or more requests every week to track down some person's old high school sweetheart. Perhaps a client, now divorced, has fond memories of warm summer nights from his high school years and wants to know if his high school girlfriend is by chance available. There is a website that registers classmates, and you can search it for free. That site is Classmates.com, at www.classmates.com. If you find your school friend there and you want to e-mail her, you have to pay a $36 fee for a year's membership. But, hey, isn't that a lot cheaper than hiring me to find her for you? If she's not listed, it hasn't cost you anything. She won't be there unless she's listed herself. Maybe you should list yourself and she'll find you.

The Internet has some great tools for skip tracing. In my business, we skip trace more than 2,000 people a month. Do we use the Internet? You bet. Do we use the free sites? You bet. Why pay for a search of the Death Master File when I can get a better search for free? I use prison inmate locators every day; some of the people I'm looking for are in jail. The military locators? It's hard to beat the price at $3.50.

The telephone searches? I use the two pay sites we discussed in Chapter 5, www.masterfiles.com and www.555-1212.com. Remember the neighbor search? Even if your subject has moved, you'll likely find a neighbor who can tell you where they've gone. And then you get to start all over again. Oh, the joys of skip-tracing.

Putting It All Together

Here is your final exam for the last two chapters. Like all of the examples in this book, it is true and from our case files. Now is your chance to test your knowledge of skip-tracing. I'll give you a clue. Skip ahead and read Chapter 8, then come back and solve this skip-tracing case.

Mariah Sue, in 1999, needed a new place to live. She had two small sons, was working, and making a pretty good living. Mariah, saw a one-bedroom condominium that she found attractive. It was clean, had a community swimming pool and was close to work. The owner, let's name her, Peggy Ferrar, owned several of these condos and rented them all.

Mariah Sue gave Peggy a check for $2,100 as a deposit to hold the condo for a few days until she could make up her mind if she wanted it for sure. Peggy, said, fine, no problem, if Mariah Sue didn't want the condo she should call her and let her know within seven days.

Three days later Mariah decided that a one-bedroom condo was too small for her and two boys and called Peggy. Peggy wasn't home and Mariah left her a message on the recorder informing Peggy of her change of mind and requested that she tear up the deposit check.

Fast forward to 2002. Two Sheriff's deputies show up at an old address of Mariah's to arrest her on a worthless check charge of $2,100. The people at the old address know Mariah and call her, but don't tell the deputies where she is.

Mariah checks with the District Attorney's office by telephone and verifies that there is a warrant for her arrest and she needs to bring either the $2,100 plus costs down to their office or a receipt from Peggy Ferrar showing that it's been paid.

Mariah is beside herself trying to reach Peggy, but the number she had for her has been disconnected. She tries telephone directory information but can't find a listing for her. Peggy was an older lady and Mariah is thinking perhaps she is dead. She calls the State Bureau of Vital Records and pays them $30 dollars to search the death records for the last three years plus a $25 rush fee. They promise to mail her the search results within two weeks.

Okay, now you have the facts. Using what you've learned, how would you find Peggy Ferrar?

As we learned at the beginning of this chapter there is a quicker and free way to determine if Peggy has passed on, unless it happened within the last few months. So you are correct. First you'd search the Social Security Death Master File.

You search the Death Master File and it's negative. Okay, what next? In the county that Mariah Sue lived, she could have gone on line to the county property appraiser's website and searched by address the ownership of the property she was going to rent. That's what I did.

The property records showed the address was owned by Frank Ferrar and June M. Ferrar. I presumed the middle initial "M" in June's name probably stood for Margaret and Peggy is a nickname for Margaret.

I went to www.555-1212.com but you could have also gone to www.masterfiles.com and searched Frank Ferrar. There was a listing for him at an address close to the condo that Mariah was going to rent. Just for fun, I went back to the property appraiser's records and checked the ownership of that address as well. It showed Frank and June M. owned that property, too.

In less than 30 minutes I'd found Peggy for Mariah Sue. Total cost was one search at www.555-1212.com or www.masterfiles.com. Again for giggles, I searched the free white page listings on the Internet and found the Ferrar family was also listed in the free sections we talked about in the previous chapter. So it could have been a totally free search.

As it turned it out, just in case you're interested, Mrs. Ferrar was not about to forgive the debt and insisted that Mariah Sue bring the money over to her right away. That was an expensive lesson for Mariah, but it could have been a little less expensive if she'd read this book first.

The Least You Need to Know

◆ The Social Security Administration has maintained a database of deceased individuals, known as the Death Master File, since 1980.

◆ The Federal Bureau of Prisons has a prisoner locator database, and some states have websites that allow searching the inmate, parole, and probation population.

◆ Members of the armed forces can be located by mail, except for the Navy, which will only forward mail to its sailors. The Coast Guard will frequently respond to telephone calls.

◆ There are some websites that maintain databases of e-mail users.

◆ For finding high school chums, Classmates.com is cheaper than hiring a PI.

◆ Using a little common sense and knowing what databases are available can save you time and money and maybe even keep you out of jail.

Chapter 7

Taking Advantage of Big Brother

In This Chapter

- Using the Secretary of State records to find that missing person
- Getting access to state occupational licenses and the information they provide
- The nitty-gritty of the Drivers Privacy Protection Act
- Utilizing the utility companies
- Private books and the public library

In an industrialized culture, society lives and dies by its records. Governments control their people by tracking them. They use a census for planning purposes, watching changes in living habits, and making sure that every person is taxed appropriately.

The various governments—federal, state, and local—have a mountain of records on each of us. Some of these records are open to the public and some are not. We're all familiar with birth certificates, marriage licenses, driver's licenses, and death certificates. But you may not be acquainted with the multitude of other public records that are accessible to you.

Why Should You Care About Public Records?

Are you asking yourself right now, "Why should I care about public records?"

When a 25-year-old plumber came to me and wanted help in finding his girlfriend, I was a little wary. He explained that his girlfriend lived with her parents and they had moved to another part of the city and wouldn't tell him where. When I asked how old the girlfriend was, he told me that she was 16.

In taking cases, I don't usually make moral judgments. I guess it's sort of like being a prostitute; I pimp my services to the highest bidder. There are exceptions, though, and I do have my standards.

I told the plumber to take his money someplace else. Having teenager daughters myself at the time, I could understand the forces of love for a daughter that would make the parents move the family across town in order to keep her away from this older guy. Me? I would have had him charged with statutory rape, but .... The reality was, if this guy had read this chapter, he could have found them without my help, but I didn't tell him that.

Are you seriously dating somebody? You'd better read this and the next chapter to understand how the records system works so when you get to Chapter 18, you'll know how to run a background check on your bride- or husband-to-be.

And what kind of information, you may wonder, is actually out there?

State Records

States maintain a variety of records that are valuable for background investigations. There will be variations between states as to how the records are organized and where you can locate them, but for the most part they will follow what we'll set out here.

Corporate Records

Most states maintain records of companies incorporated there at the Secretary of State's office, Division of Corporations. In these records you can find the names of the officers and directors of a corporation. Typically the *registered agent* is identified and the physical address of the corporation is given.

Why would we care about the officers of some corporation? Suppose you are looking for Steve Brown in Florida. You might just go online from the computer in your bedroom, during a commercial break on the television, and pull up the Florida Secretary of State's website and find your man in a matter of a few keystrokes before the game starts again.

Most of these Secretary of State corporate-record websites can be searched by the name of the corporation or by individuals associated with the corporation.

Go to www.sunbiz.org, which is the Florida Secretary of State website. In the very center of the screen is a white block that says Site Index. Scroll through the index until you get to Corporations, Trademarks, and Limited Partnerships. Clicking that will take you to the Corporations on Line search page. Click on Officer, Registered Agent Name List, and the search window comes up. Type in Brown, Steven K., and 9 of the first 10 listings that come up are corporations that I've had some affiliation with. That's a lot easier than searching all of the 250 Steven Brown listings on white-page directories, as we saw in Chapter 5.

Crime Scene Clues

A **registered agent** is an individual who agrees to be available to accept service, subpoenas, or other legal documents for a corporation. In the event you need to sue a corporation, your attorney will have to physically serve the lawsuit to the registered agent, the person who will accept notice of the suit on behalf of the corporation.

Of course, if you don't know my middle initial, than you'll have to wade through about 175 listings in the corporate records. Maybe there's a better search if you're trying to find me.

Professional and Occupational Licenses

Many people work in professions that require some sort of state license, from PIs to hairdressers, to nurses, to massage therapists. It's good to know how to check the various state Internet sites and find those licensees. The person you're looking for may be there.

Let's see. You talked to an old high school chum, as I suggested in Chapter 5, and he told you, sure, he remembered Steve Brown. Brown was in the FBI for a while, and last he heard, he'd left the bureau and was running a PI firm somewhere down in Florida. But for the life of him, he couldn't remember where in Florida.

So you go back to www.sunbiz.org. At the top of that page you'll see the following hyperlinks: Help, 411, Feedback, and Directory. Click on Directory. Up pops a list called State of Florida Agencies, Cabinet Agencies, and Other Organizations. In that list you'll see the word "State," which is the link to the Florida Department of State site. If you want to know about oranges instead, click on Citrus, or maybe you'd like Fish and Wildlife. If you clicked on State (the link to the Florida Department of State) and then next clicked on Licensing, you can see who in the State of Florida has a current private investigator's license.

Search Steve Brown and there are only two choices. You found me. But what's that? Oh, darn, you click on my name and a notice appears that says "RESTRICTED. The home address and telephone number for this individual is restricted from public record in accordance with the Public Records Act, Section 119.07(3)(i) F.S." The State of Florida is kind enough not to publish a private investigator's home address and telephone number, thank you very much. This keeps the irate husbands from knocking on my front door. Of course, if they really wanted to find me I'm dead meat, because all they have to do is read the rest of this chapter and any dummy could figure out how.

But perhaps the person you're looking for is a massage therapist, or a nurse, or a doctor. The information is all there for you to see. From the main Florida screen you can go to the Department of Health and search all of the preceding professions by name. It's a great way to find somebody and a very good way to determine if the professional person you're going to see is actually licensed.

Remember these state sites like all Internet sites are prone to changing their menus. So if you don't see immediately what you're searching for, look around the site a little, explore it until you do find it.

Elementary, My Dear Watson

There is much talk lately about identity theft and how to safeguard your social security number. The truth is, your social security number is pretty much a public number. It can be found on your voter's registration information, which is public. You give it out to banks, telephone companies, utility companies, and credit card companies. In fact, eight states use the social security number as their driver's license number.

Identity theft is a problem for merchants because of the charge backs from the credit card companies. The merchants may lose big bucks. Your liability for illicit charges on your credit card is only $50. Getting the credit bureaus to straighten out your credit history is another story. (Good luck. I've never seen them receptive at all.) The bottom line is, a theft of your identity doesn't create a huge liability for you the individual, just a huge nuisance.

Driver's Licenses

Every state issues driver's licenses. The information on a driver's license usually includes name, address, date of birth, some descriptive information such as height and color of eyes and hair, and frequently the person's social security number.

Driver license information is still one of the single best sources for identification purposes. Many database searches require basic data on the person you are searching for besides just a name. You'll need, at the very least, a date of birth and or social security number. So how do you do that? Easy. Remember the lesson on wild card searches in Chapter 6. With some of the pay databases that we'll discuss in Chapter 9, you can use a wild card search with the driver's license information database and almost always get the social security number and date of birth you'll need to search other databases.

CAUTION

Sammy the Snitch

Most of us have neighbors or friends who work for a police agency. Don't be tempted to ask your police friend to pull someone's driver license information for you. You'd be asking him to violate several laws, including theft of information, and he'd be guilty of a direct violation of the Drivers Protection Act, which has criminal penalties for this kind of behavior. You and your police friend could be convicted criminally and fined, and your friend would certainly be fired.

Driver's license information is good information. It is almost universally helpful in locating someone or in helping to verify that you have found the right Steve Brown. Most states have laws that require drivers who are licensed in the state to report a change of address to their DMV within 10 to 30 days of a change. Not everybody reports their new address to the DMV, but when they don't they are in violation of their state's statutes. At least every few years when the license is renewed, the newest address is probably used.

Also note that states discourage the use of a post office box or postal mailbox (the kind in those postal packaging stores) as an address on a driver's license. Therefore, if you can legally get this information, at least you will have a physical address from where you can begin your search.

Getting driver's license information is becoming more difficult. You will probably have to go to a professional PI to get it for you. But if you're planning on becoming a PI, you should subscribe to one of the providers we'll talk about in Chapter 9. A PI shouldn't charge you any more than $25 for driver's license information. If he's a professional, he should make sure the use is in compliance with the Drivers Protection Act, or else he leaves himself open to a civil damage suit including actual damages (set by the statute as a minimum of $2,500), punitive damages, and attorney fees.

Elementary, My Dear Watson

In 1989, Robert John Bardo hired a private investigator to get the home address of actress Rebecca Schaffer, who at that time played on the television sitcom *My Sister Sam*. The PI got the information from the California Department of Motor Vehicles (DMV) and sold it to Bardo. Schaffer was expecting Francis Ford Coppola to come to her door to discuss an audition for his film, *Godfather III*. When the bell rang, Schaffer opened the door and found Bardo there instead. She asked him to leave and closed the door. Bardo went away but returned very upset. He rang again but hid so that Schaffer had to step out of the apartment to see who was there. Bardo shot her once in the chest and fled.

As a result of this incident, the U.S. Congress passed the Drivers Privacy Protection Act, effective June 1, 2000. This act prohibits the release of information pertaining to driver's licenses, but included 14 specific exceptions. Licensed private investigators are listed as exception number eight, as long as the information is used for one of the other 13 reasons.

The bottom line is you can no longer walk up to your local DMV and request this information that used to be publicly available.

Driving History

Most states will allow you to have a copy of your own driving record. This will require a trip to your local DMV office, showing some identification, and paying a small fee. If you want the driving history of somebody other than yourself or somebody in another state, again you will need to hire a professional PI who has legitimate access to this information. States do sell driving history information, but usually only in bulk to resellers. Resellers buy this information from the state and sell it primarily to insurance companies and large trucking firms. They download the information from the state daily, which means thousands and thousands of records. The entire department of motor vehicle record database is downloaded or purchased on tape every day. Because of some irregularities they've encountered in reselling the information to private investigators, the resellers almost entirely refuse to provide it to PIs anymore, even though there is a specific exemption in the law for private investigators.

Consequently, these records are now even harder to get than the driver license information, and not all PIs subscribe to the services that provide this. I wish I had better news about obtaining DMV information, but the Driver's Privacy Protection Act has put the squeeze on it.

Sammy the Snitch _____

Beware, if you're a PI and you're selling this information, you could get busted. Some states like Pennsylvania run tests, sort of undercover operations, to see if their information is being sold without the proper safeguards. The State of Pennsylvania canceled its contract with one reseller, who had sold this information to a PI firm, who in turn sold it unknowingly to an undercover state operative that was testing various websites. Many of the resellers are no longer providing this information to private investigators because these PIs were selling this information through their websites without verifying to whom the information was going or verifying that the information was being properly used. Nevertheless, a good PI will have his sources and be able to get it for you. The cost will probably be in the $25 range.

State Records on the Web

As you read in a preceding section, many states have some of their records available for free on the Internet. Your local counties are getting online big time, more so than even your state governments. Get your wallet out, though, because some counties are charging for access to their records via the Internet and generating revenue. The process of searching county records online is in the midst of a big change as this book is written. In a few years the counties will probably find what works best for them and you, their client, and most will likely be pretty standardized. They'll probably polarize at one extreme or the other, pay or free.

A fellow named Marty called me and wanted to check a potential tenant's criminal record. The rental unit was in a garage apartment attached to his house and he wanted to make sure the applicant wasn't an ax murderer or worse. The prospective tenant had recently arrived in Florida from Colorado.

Sherlock's Secrets _____

Before paying a PI to run a search for you, use the search engine skills you developed in Chapter 5 to see if what you are looking for is now available on the Internet. More states and counties are coming online everyday.

Until just recently, Colorado would provide a statewide criminal search as long as we mailed a letter requesting the information with a prepayment. We waited three to five days for the request to be processed and then mailed back to us, which was a pretty decent system compared to many states. But Marty was in a hurry. You can still use the mail system if you want, but what many states are doing now is quicker and cheaper.

We hadn't checked any criminal records in Colorado for a while, so before going through the laborious process of dictating the letter, waiting for my secretary to type it, writing out the check, and waiting until the next day for it go out, I did a little searching on the web.

Guess what? Now all you need to do for Colorado criminal records is go to www. cocourts.com. For a $5 fee, you can access up-to-the-minute information on the complete Colorado court system—every criminal court including both *misdemeanor* and *felony* charges are searched in every county with one click of the mouse. It may not show arrests if the charges were dropped, but if the case made it to court, it should be there. Marty paid $45 for that search. He could have paid $5 and done it himself just as quickly as I did.

A particularly useful site that you might want to bookmark is www.brbpub.com/pubrecsites.asp, run by BRB Publications Inc., which lists most of the Secretary of State sites for each state, the sex offender sites, and county sites, such as the property appraiser's office, within the states.

Crime Scene Clues

Criminal offenses are categorized according to the severity of the offense. Less serious crimes, those typically involving a potential penalty of less than one year, are called **misdemeanors**. Crimes that are punishable by a one-year jail term or longer are called **felonies**.

The list is not all-inclusive and some of the links have obviously changed because they don't work, but it's not a bad beginning. For example, you won't find the Colorado court site as I described in the preceding section, so that simply highlights the need to conduct your own search.

BRB also sells books in the genre of searching public records. You can browse its catalog at the same website.

The Big Red Book

Things are changing so fast in the public-record-search area that before the books can even get printed they are out-of-date. That being said, many of the sites they list will still be functional. The brand-new ones just won't be listed.

There are two books that are essential to have if you are in the business of doing records checks. There are many other similar books available out there—but in nearly 20 years of performing record searches for clients, I rely on these two together more than any others. In my office we call the first the Big Red Book. The other book is the *Sourcebook to Public Record Information* published by the folks with BRB. We'll talk about the Sourcebook in greater detail in Chapter 10, "Performing Background Investigations," when we go step-by-step through the process of checking a person's background.

The Big Red Book is officially known as the *Guide to Background Investigations*, published by T.I.S.I. (1-800-247-8713, www.usetheguide.com). The book is revised every two years. It's NOT cheap. The current price is $199.95, or $169.95 for the CD version. The ninth edition of the book is over 2,000 pages long and covers more than 15,000 sources or records. It weighs about 6 pounds, so make sure you've been working out and gotten buff before picking it up.

It tells you where to look for the records you need in each county, state, or federal jurisdiction, as well as how much the record will cost and the hoops you have to jump through to get what you're looking for. It also lists the websites for the various state agencies and county clerks.

The academic section lists more than 4,000 U.S. colleges and universities. This section is sorted first by state, then alphabetically by university name. Each entry gives instructions on which records are available and the procedures to follow to get them, including whether they can be obtained by phone or mail.

Federal courts fall into districts, as explained in Chapter 8. The federal records section of the book sorts by state and county. You'll be able to find your county and tell under which federal district and bankruptcy court it falls.

The Canadian section tells you how to get a Canadian driving and criminal history. It also lists more than 200 Canadian universities.

Utilizing the Utilities

I walked up to Jean Macmillan's house and knocked on the door. Jean used to work at a nursing home that was being sued by my client, an attorney, for negligent care. My client was considering taking her deposition but couldn't locate her and asked me to find her, interview her, and take a recorded statement if I could.

Jean had a nonpublished number and had moved from the address listed on her driver's license. The state records for certified nursing assistants, which I searched through the state website, reflected the same address as her driver's license.

I could have gone to my telephone source and paid him the usual $50 for her phone number and address (for which I would have billed my client $125), but my client, the cheapskate, didn't want to invest a lot in Jean unless she had something to say that was going to help his case.

So how did I find Jean's house? I went down to the local electric company's office and looked her up. There I found her address and her current telephone number, which the phone company wouldn't give to me because it was nonpublished. I also learned that her average utility bill was $157 a month (like I really cared).

The records of utilities that are owned by a municipality (city, county, or village, for example) are frequently considered public information, and therefore accessible for you to search.

Sherlock's Secrets

It has never done me any good to try and bully a private utility into giving me information concerning a person's account. They usually clam right up. There's still a way to get that information. First, you have to know all you can about the person you are searching for: name, previous address, social security number, date of birth, and previous phone number. If possible, go to the old address and get the meter number off the electric meter. Watch out, though. If someone else has moved in, they may not take kindly to you snooping around their backyard.

Next, you call the customer service number for that electric company and pretend that you are the person you are looking for. Just make sure you read Chapter 11, about how to best block your Caller ID information. When the representative asks you for a social security number, give her your subject's number. Say that you seem to be having trouble getting your mail at your new address and you're not sure you got your last electric bill from the previous address. Also, you think the meter at the old address was faulty. When was the last time that old meter was calibrated? Give her the meter number. Giving the old meter number usually convinces the customer service person that you are the person you say you are.

While the customer service person is looking up the calibration date, mention that you're having some of your mail switched to a P.O. box, and oh, by the way, what was the closing date of the last bill they sent to you? And what address did they send it to? She'll give you your subject's new address if she has it. Remember, it's possible that the person you are searching for skipped and didn't pay his last utility bill. The customer service person will ask if you want your bill to go to your new P.O. box; tell her no, what they have is fine. If you feel like pushing your luck, ask what telephone number she has for you. Nine times out of ten you'll end up with both the new address and the new telephone number.

If you're looking for Steve Brown and he skipped on his bill, she'll try to pin you down as to when you're going to pay up. Promise her anything you want. Just be sure you followed the instructions about blocking Caller ID before you begin.

It's not unusual to live in an area where the electric company is private, and therefore their records are considered to be private. If that happens to you, try the water company. Usually water is a public utility, and so are the records—but not always. If either one or both are owned by the city, county, or state, then you are home free.

Call the utility company and ask them if subscriber or customer information is a public record. They'll tell you if it is or not. If it is, they'll probably have a computer set up somewhere in the front of their main office for public access. They may require you to sign a log in sheet and provide some identification.

Remember the 25-year-old plumber at the beginning of this chapter, the one looking for the 16-year-old girlfriend? All he had to do was go down to the electric company, which is owned by our county government, and search the current subscriber list for the parents' names. Or, he could have gotten the change of service details from the parents' old address to the new address. It's all public information and available to anyone who wants it.

Public Libraries and Private Books

You don't have Internet access, you don't want Internet access, and you don't own or even want a computer. But you do live within the boundaries of the United States or Canada. Chances are, then, you have Internet access and don't even know it.

Your public library probably has computers already online and logged onto the Internet. Using the public library's computers, you can take advantage of all the information in this chapter, the preceding ones, and those that follow. But your library also has other reference books that are invaluable resources.

The two main resources a private investigator uses at the library for skip tracing are, first, the *criss-cross directory* (also known as the *reverse directory*, or the *city directory*). Second, you'd be surprised how useful old telephone directories are.

The main branch of larger library systems have telephone books for not only their own city but for major cites around the country, and also for many other towns within your own state.

If you have a telephone number or street address located in a town other than your own, call the library in that town and ask for the reference desk. If you're polite, the reference desk librarian will look up the address, name, or telephone number you give them in the local criss-cross directory and give you the information. I've never had one refuse a request yet. But then, I'm a nice guy.

The library probably has the telephone directory for your town going back 10 years, or sometimes longer. When skip tracing someone whose address you have is no longer valid, you can look in the library's old telephone books and find out when, within the parameter of a year or so, your subject moved. Next, go to the criss-cross directory and identify the neighbors who lived there when your subject did. Use the current criss-cross to see if any of those neighbors are still living there, and go out and talk to them. They may well remember your subject and might be able to tell you where he or she moved to, and possibly even an employer's name. See Chapter 13, which deals with this in greater depth.

Crime Scene Clues

Criss-cross directories, sometimes called **reverse** or **city directories,** are privately published by Cole, Polk, Donnelly, and others. These directories sort their listings by name, address, and telephone number. You can take a telephone number, check it in the "reverse" listing, and find the subscriber information. Likewise, you can search the directory for an address within the city, and it will give you the person living there and the phone number.

Frequently, these directories give additional information about the person living at a residence, such as how long he or she has lived there, how many people live in the residence, their occupations, and income level. Not all city directories give all of that information; it depends upon the publisher and their research efforts. So if you only have one phone number to check, and don't want to subscribe to either 555-1212.com or the Reach Directory, then try the criss-cross at your library.

The Least You Need to Know

- Secretary of State records are usually public and include officers and directors of corporations.

- State records frequently include license information for professions in medicine, nursing, private investigating, and almost every other occupation licensed by the state.

- Driver's license information is increasingly difficult to get. Your best bet is probably through a licensed PI.

- Utility companies are frequently owned by a municipality, and their records, which show changes in address, may be public.

- The library has useful reference books such as criss-cross or reverse directories and old telephone books. You can call a library reference desk in another city and someone will probably look up the information you need.

Chapter 8

Prowling the Courthouse

In This Chapter

- ◆ Locating property-transaction records
- ◆ Understanding the lower and higher court system
- ◆ Learning how to search for local criminal records
- ◆ Examining the federal system
- ◆ Obtaining computer access to federal case indexes
- ◆ The ins and outs of the bankruptcy court

Christine called me last week. She and her boyfriend are getting married soon. The problem is, he's not divorced yet from his first wife. They've been separated for four years but no divorce, hence they've never agreed to any formal alimony or child-support settlements. The soon-to-be ex-wife is asking for more money than Christine thinks she's entitled to. Christine, being no dummy, knows money out of the fiancé's pocket means less money for her.

She wanted to know how much the ex-wife was paying each month in mortgage payments. Christine thought the ex-wife had grossly inflated the figure to bump up the child-support payments. Proof of a lower mortgage payment would result in lower support payments.

I actually was kind of rooting for the kids in this case, but I don't make up the facts, I just report them. So in Christine's case I shrugged my shoulders and took her American Express credit card number over the telephone. She could have saved herself $225 if she'd read this chapter.

Need other reasons to read this chapter? Have you ever bought a house? Or might you buy a house in the future? If so, if you're smart, you will want to know how much the seller paid for it, and how much he still owes on his house, before you make your offer. You don't *have* to know those facts, but knowledge is power. Your realtor probably won't know or won't think to tell you if she does. If you've done your research and know the seller has a gazillon dollars worth of equity in the house, then you can submit a low-ball offer and he may just accept it. If you know the house is free and clear, you may ask the seller to finance the house for you instead of using conventional financing.

But if the house has a first, second, and third mortgage recorded on it, the seller probably needs every penny out of the house he can get. On the other hand, though, you also know he is probably desperate to sell since he's making three mortgage payments. Desperation equals lower prices, and if he can't lower the price because there is no equity in the house, he might throw in that riding lawnmower or the pressure washer you saw in the shed out back because he has to get the house sold now.

Have you ever thought about going into business with a partner, a buddy from work maybe? You'd better find out if he has any judgments against him before you sign those partnership agreements. Merrill-Lynch had a slogan that said, "Investigate, then invest." That's still good advice.

The Local County Courthouse

There are four main areas of interest for investigators in the county courthouse, not including the courtrooms where you'll be called upon to testify. We'll cover your testimony in court in Chapter 24. The areas we want to look at are sometimes called different names in different counties, but every county has them.

Making the Official Records Speak

For some reason, searching the official records seems to confuse a lot of my investigator interns. I think they feel it is a waste of time and they should be out on the street following somebody. A good private investigator knows the courthouse and all of its nooks and crannies, inside and out.

Official records are those records that are recorded at the courthouse for all the public to see. By "recorded," we mean the document is entered into the official records in a particular book and on a certain page. In the pre-computer era, a notation was handwritten into a large ledger-type book saying, for example, a certain mortgage from such-and-such a lender was recorded against a particular piece of *real property*.

Crime Scene Clues

Real property is described as anything that is not personal property. Real property is anything that is a part of the earth or attached thereto which can not be easily moved. Think dirt.

The existence of this mortgage was physically entered into a book on a particular page number. An index was made somewhat alphabetically and you could hand search those indexes by year to see if there was a mortgage recorded or not. As the pages of one book were filled up, the county recorder's office would begin a new book. The books were numbered and hence you would find a legal description of a mortgage, noting it was recorded on such-and-such book and on that particular page number.

These book and page numbers are noted, and anybody who may have a claim or want to establish a claim or lien on or to any particular piece of property is free to search through these official records. You'll find notations regarding other mortgages, liens, judgments (or satisfaction of mortgages, liens, or judgments) that might pertain to a particular person or piece of property.

When you purchase a piece of real property, a deed is recorded in the official records of the county. If you borrowed money to buy the property, most likely the mortgage company or bank also recorded the mortgage. The lender does this as a sort of notice to all the public that it has the first mortgage on that property. If it wasn't recorded, and you borrowed some more money on the property, the next bank would record its mortgage and it would have the first mortgage recorded. If you failed to pay the mortgage on the second loan, the second bank could foreclose and the first bank would just be out of luck. This is why when you buy a piece of real property, there should always be a title search to make sure all the mortgages, liens, etc., recorded on that property are paid or satisfied before you take title to the property.

Now, why do we as investigators care about all of this? I'll show you why. Remember Christine at the beginning of this chapter? The house the ex-wife lived in belonged to her father. All I had to do was go into the official records and search his name to find the mortgage on her house. In fact, I found the house was purchased in 1979 and a mortgage placed on it. I found a satisfaction of the mortgage recorded in 1989 and another mortgage was placed on it. That mortgage was satisfied in 1999 and another higher mortgage was placed on it at that time. On this last refinancing it looked like she pulled some cash out of it and refinanced it for 15 years. The mortgage was for $72,000. Unfortunately for my client, since this mortgage was for only 15 years, her payments would have been higher than for a 30-year mortgage.

> **Sherlock's Secrets**
>
> I hear people complain all the time about our public servants. Let me tell you, I've searched for information in courthouses all across the United States. I've never found a more helpful bunch of people in my life than at the local county courthouse. They've always been more than willing to show me how to do the search I need, or if I act pathetic enough, they'll even do it for me most of the time.

I took a financial calculator and figured out what her payments were for principal and interest based on a $72,000 loan for 15 years. I had to guess at the interest rate because the promissory note wasn't recorded with the mortgage. But it wasn't too hard to go back three years and see what the average 15-year loan was going for in April of 1999. Principal and interest came to about $607.58.

Christine needed to know the amount of the mortgage payment. Now I had the first piece of the puzzle, the principal and interest payment.

The Property Appraiser

I went across the hall to the property appraiser's office. (I could have, but actually that's a fib. In our county, as in most counties now, the property appraiser's records are online, and before I went to the courthouse I looked up the latest appraisal on the website.)

The appraiser's office showed the value of the property, the type of construction (which was brick), and this year's current tax amount. In this case the property taxes were about $1,200 annually. This meant the ex-wife's mortgage company would have added about $100 per month to the principal and interest payment for the property taxes.

I called my insurance agent to see what a typical homeowners insurance policy would cost for a brick home. He gave me a figure of about $485, which is about $40 per month. Add the three figures together (principal and interest, $607.58; taxes, $100; and insurance, $40) for a total of $747.58.

Bingo. In 30 minutes I had the information Christine wanted. Let's see, $225 for a half-hour's work is what Christine paid me—that's $550 per hour. Better than minimum wage, for sure.

The State Civil Court Systems

State court systems in most states are divided into higher courts and lower courts. Some states have other courts, like water courts and traffic courts, but we won't deal with those here. Criminal courts and federal courts we'll touch on later in this chapter. Don't let the names of the courts confuse you. Some of my investigative interns just don't seem to get it, but it's real easy. Just think of higher courts and lower courts and everything will fall into place. We'll talk about civil cases first.

Higher Civil Courts

The higher courts and the lower courts have different names in different states. In Florida they are called circuit courts and county courts; Arizonans call them superior courts and justice courts; New Yorkers call them supreme courts and county courts. Let's forget the names and just call them higher and lower courts.

The higher courts deal with more important cases. More important usually equals more money. Everybody has heard of small claims court. Small claims in most jurisdictions means sums of money *where the damages sought are less than $5,000. In some states it is even less.* In lower court cases, frequently people do not use the services of an attorney and represent themselves. I'm sure you've heard the old saying that a person who acts as his own attorney has a fool for a client. I've always found this to be true. So if you find yourself in small claims court, you might want to reconsider representing yourself.

Civil actions such as divorces, malpractice, libel, and other suits are likely to involve money amounts over $5,000 and are held in the higher courts. Petty actions like residential rent disputes will be found in the lower courts.

My client, Mary Beth, whom I'd known on a personal basis for a long time, called me. She said her husband was in jail on charges of spousal abuse (toward her) and she had a restraining order against him. He'd blackened her eyes, dragged her around the house by her hair, and beat her with a clothes hanger.

You probably can't imagine how many times I've had clients tell me their husbands beat them with a clothes hanger. It seems to me if we're going to mandate trigger locks on handguns, we should require trigger locks on coat hangers, too. There are a lot more women out there struck by hangers than shot by handguns.

Mary Beth had been married to Lionel for just under a year. She wanted to know if he'd had physical altercations with any of his previous three wives. Where do we go to look?

Right, to the office of the clerk of the higher court. I reviewed all three of the previous divorce files. There was one restraining order in one of them alleging physical brutality. I found the personal data on the ex-wives and tracked them down. Each of his ex-wives told me Lionel had been physically abusive to her. In fact, he had been arrested multiple times for abusing each one.

Lionel's relationship with his second wife was a little different. She told me they used to beat each other up. Now that was a new one for me.

If Mary Beth had come to me before she married Lionel, she would have known about his propensity for violence and perhaps been prepared to diffuse it or even not marry him at all. At least now she knows it was probably not her fault. It amazes me, though, how few people do any sort of prenuptial background investigation, especially when we're talking second, third, and fourth marriages. In this case this was Lionel's fourth marriage and Mary Beth's fifth. I also checked the criminal records for Lionel and we'll talk about them in the following section on criminal courts.

Mary Beth is still married to and living with Lionel. He goes to anger management classes every Tuesday night. I'm not holding my breath on this one.

Lower Civil Courts

We conduct background investigations for a local landlord. This fellow rents high-dollar furnished homes located in a golfing community on short-term leases. One of the checks he insists on before renting a house to a prospective tenant is to search the lower court records from whatever county the renter previously resided in. He's been involved before with tenants who will pay the first month's rent and then begin some kind of action in small claims court, and end up living rent-free month after month until he can finally get them evicted. If we find any previous litigation where they were the *plaintiff*, he refuses to rent to them. If they were a *defendant*, he wants the details of the suit and then makes a decision.

> **Crime Scene Clues**
>
> Legal actions require a minimum of two parties. The **plaintiff** is the party who initiates the action or lawsuit. The **defendant** is the person on the receiving end of the action.

This commercial client figures even though it costs him a little bit more to have us run a civil-records search, he saves big bucks in the long run in attorney fees and loss of rent.

In most court actions the plaintiff's name is listed or shown first on the complaint. The defendant is being sued or arrested by the plaintiff. In criminal cases the plaintiff is the government and the person being charged with the crime is the defendant. Usually you'll see a criminal case listed as, for example, *the State of Florida V. Brown.*

Cases are indexed in the state court system by the plaintiff's name and cross-referenced by defendant's name. In *Kramer V. Brown*, Kramer is the plaintiff and Brown, the defendant. In a court index you might find the notation, Brown adv. Kramer. "Adv." stands for adverse, the reverse of versus. In that case, Brown is still the defendant and Kramer is still the plaintiff. In some states, instead of adv., the abbreviation "ats" is used. Ats is an acronym for "at the suit of."

Lower court records are also at the county courthouse. Large counties may have annexes or "sub-courthouses" in different locations around the county for the convenience of the taxpayer. Usually the annex will have computer links to the entire courthouse system so a check can be run from any annex. When in doubt, ask if a search at an annex will search all of the records in the entire county. If not, then go to the main courthouse. In smaller less computerized counties you'll probably have to go downtown to the county courthouse. There the clerks working in the Clerk of the Courts office can direct you to the records you're looking for and will gladly show you how the system is organized.

Miscellaneous Civil Courts

In addition to the higher and lower courts, as described in the preceding, there are also in many jurisdictions other courts such as traffic court and municipal court, depending upon the state, county, and city. You'll need to do a little research in your city of interest to see what the courts are called there. The easiest way to remember is to think in dollars. The higher dollar value at risk, the higher the court. The more serious the offense, the higher the court. Fewer dollars at stake means the item will be heard in a lower court. Traffic violations, less serious still, move on down to the traffic or municipal court.

State Criminal Courts

State criminal courts, not including the appellate courts, are divided into higher and lower courts just like the civil courts. We will deal some with these courts in Chapter 10.

The criminal courts usually carry the same name as the civil courts. In Florida they are the circuit court (higher court) and county court (lower court); Arizonans call them superior court (higher court) and justice court (lower court).

Remember Mary Beth from the preceding section on higher civil courts? Well, when she was downtown shopping, prior to marrying Lionel, had she only paid a visit to the courthouse and checked the criminal records on her husband-to-be, she would have found that charges against Lionel were still pending even as she walked down the aisle at her wedding. She didn't make the stop, so she never knew it.

Elementary, My Dear Watson

Cases in the state criminal courts are usually prosecuted by attorneys working for the local or county government. They are sometimes called state's attorneys, district attorneys, or county attorneys. They are, in fact, attorneys for the state, district, or county, which is the plaintiff in criminal actions. These are often elected positions. Most states have a state attorney general's office that may get involved in prosecuting cases. Those cases usually originate from state law enforcement bureaus as opposed to the local police or sheriff's office.

I can't stress enough the value of checking criminal records on your husband- or wife-to-be prior to getting married. You have all the tools right here in this book to do it yourself. If you grew up with your intended spouse, high school sweethearts and all, then maybe you know all there is know about the person. But if you're from different towns and states, spend the few dollars or whatever it takes and find out for sure. If you don't want to do it yourself, then hire me or another PI to do it for you.

There is no magic bullet that can guarantee a long, peaceful, and happy marriage. We all know that. But you can sure improve the odds a lot on the peaceful part of the equation by doing your homework before you wed. Mary Beth wouldn't be wearing sunglasses today to cover her black eyes had she taken the trouble to check into Lionel's background. It's not hard.

Federal Courts

The federal judicial system breaks down a little differently than the state systems. Excluding the federal appeals court and the United States Supreme Court, the three basic federal courts are the federal civil, federal criminal, and bankruptcy courts.

The United States government also has its attorney, similar to the district attorney within the state system. This federal government attorney is a political appointee and he will be out of a job if a rival political party wins the next election. He has the title, appropriately, of the United States attorney (USA). The cases are usually prosecuted by an assistant United States attorney (AUSA) who is usually a career employee. In one U.S. Attorney's office there will be dozens of AUSAs, separately frequently into attorneys who prosecute criminal cases and attorneys who handle federal civil cases. The office of AUSA can be a lifetime career or sometimes is used as a stepping stone from public service to private practice.

There are several different methods available for checking federal records. You can walk into the local federal courthouse and search at the clerk of the court's office for records belonging to that division of that specific federal district. But that's a little difficult if you live in Los Angeles, which is in the Central District of California, Los Angeles Division, and want to search San Francisco, which is in the Northern District of California, San Francisco Division. The answer to your problem is the PACER (Public Access to Court Electronic Records) system.

Elementary, My Dear Watson

Each part of the United States, Puerto Rico, Guam, and the Mariana Islands is broken down into federal districts. There are 94 federal districts in the United States. Districts do not cross state boundaries. The districts are also broken down into divisions along geographic and population lines. Florida, for example, has three: the Southern District, which naturally covers the southern part of the state; the Middle District, which covers the central part of the state and, not so naturally, the northeast corner of the state; and the Northern District, which covers the panhandle portion of Florida.

The federal courts have been developing this electronic search system, which is available through a dial-up service or via the Internet. Dial up simply means you have to dial a specific number via your modem to gain access to the information; you cannot simply open your web browser and enter the URL to view the information on a web page. Think of dial-up as a direct connection from your computer to another computer via a telephone line. If you plan on accessing a lot of federal court searches, subscribing to PACER is the way to go. You must first register, which you can do online for free. It takes about two weeks to receive your system password by mail. They will not e-mail or fax it to you.

Thereafter, there is a charge of 7¢ per downloaded page. Not all district courts are on the Internet system. Some of the PACER systems are dial up. Access on the dial-up system runs 60¢ per minute. You will not be charged both the page cost and the per-minute expense. The government will invoice you once every three months for usage of the system. If your bill for using the system is less than $10 per year, it will forgive the debt and not expect payment. (It would most likely cost more than that to physically bill you.) Each court maintains its own database, so they are all a little different. You can access the PACER system by going to http://pacer.psc.uscourts.gov.

After registering for PACER, be sure and register for the U.S. Party/Case Index. This is a national index of almost all of the district court cases. It is updated each night. By utilizing this index, you can conduct a nationwide search (except for the few courts which don't participate) for federal court cases involving whatever individual or entity you are interested in. If you find a case that peaks your interest, you can go to that file through the PACER system and view the contents. Fees are the same as for the PACER system.

The U.S. Party/Case Index is a great tool if you don't know for sure where a particular case may have been filed. In addition to the civil cases and bankruptcy cases, you can also search for federal criminal cases. Federal criminal cases are those cases brought by the FBI (Federal Bureau of Investigations), DEA (Drug Enforcement Agency), ATF (Bureau of Alcohol, Tobacco, and Firearms), the Secret Service, and other federal agencies when they allege a violation of federal law.

By searching the U.S. Party/Case Index (USPCI), you can basically perform a national federal criminal conviction search. Don't confuse this with an NCIC (National Crime Information Center) rap sheet. We'll talk about rap sheets and NCIC in Chapter 10.

> **CAUTION**
>
> **Sammy the Snitch** _____
>
> Don't forget, as of this writing there are seven U.S. district courts not on the USPCI. So if you are looking for any cases that may have originated in these seven courts, you'll have to go to that court via the PACER system and do a search. Those seven districts are: Alaska, Arkansas Western, Guam, Idaho, Indiana Southern, Nevada, and the Northern Mariana Islands District Courts.
>
> Don't tell your client you've done a complete federal criminal court search without a disclaimer excluding the above courts.

The Bankruptcy Courts

Filing for bankruptcy is a federal matter. Personal and business bankruptcies all fall under federal statutes and therefore are handled in a federal court. The bankruptcy law was designed to give individuals and businesses a "fresh start."

Bankruptcy courts are organized differently than the other federal courts, have their own set of rules, and actually trace their origin back to a different part of the Constitution.

Searching the records at the bankruptcy court is similar to the district courts. Most of the bankruptcy courts are on the PACER and USPCI systems.

To understand the records you review, it would be helpful to know that bankruptcies are filed under four different chapters:

- Chapter 7, liquidation: for individuals and businesses

- Chapter 11, reorganization: for larger corporations

- Chapter 12, reorganization: for family farmers

- Chapter 13, reorganization: for individuals and smaller businesses

Liquidation means all of the assets (with some allowable exceptions) are disposed of and all debt (with some exceptions like debt to the government) are discharged.

Reorganization stops collection activity on the part of creditors and gives a business or individual a chance to breathe while working out a plan of action in coordination with a trustee appointed by the bankruptcy court.

Elementary, My Dear Watson

The U.S. Bankruptcy law is derived from the statutes of the United States. The U.S. statutes are divided into sections called "Titles." Most (not all) of our federal criminal statutes are contained in Title 18. The laws regarding bankruptcy are found in Title 11. Title 11, United States Code is called simply Bankruptcy. Title 11 is divided into 13 chapters. Chapter 7 deals with liquidations, usually a business. Chapter 11 gives the rules for reorganizations and Chapter 13 lays out the law for adjustments of debts of an individual with regular income.

You can find the full text of those chapters at the Cornell University Website, www4. law.cornell.edu/uscode/11.

I get requests to perform due diligence searches all of the time. This can be a check of an individual, but more often of a company's reputation, ability to perform under contract, and verification that there are no liens or judgments filed against the company. A good due diligence search will also encompass any lawsuits, pending or potential, or other current or potential areas of liability, such as a pending bankruptcy. There are some private investigative agencies that not only specialize in due diligence searches—it's all they do.

Most clients request a bankruptcy check as part of a due diligence to determine if the person with whom they are going to be doing business with has filed for bankruptcy in the past or may be in the middle of a bankruptcy now.

If you're thinking about doing serious business with a company or individual, you should check the appropriate bankruptcy court before signing any contracts.

The Least You Need to Know

- Real property transactions such as sales and mortgages are recorded in the official records of the county and are public records that can be reviewed.

- State court systems have higher courts that deal with more important cases (think higher dollars) and lower courts which handle less important cases (think lower dollars).

- The criminal divisions of the state court system are nearly identical to the civil divisions. Higher courts handle felonies and lower courts deal with misdemeanors.

- The federal court is divided into districts. Some states have only one federal district and others have several, depending upon population and geography.

- Federal court records are available by computer through the Internet or by dial up using the PACER system.

- A national search can be conducted in the federal court system by using the U.S. Party/Case Index, also available through PACER.

- There are four main chapters used in filing bankruptcy petitions. A due diligence search should always include a search of the bankruptcy court records.

Chapter 9

Accessing Private Databases

In This Chapter

- ◆ Getting acquainted with the credit bureaus
- ◆ Credit headers, God's gift to the PI
- ◆ The impact of the IRSG and GLB
- ◆ Cooking the data for the data providers
- ◆ Examining the differences between data suppliers

Are you serious about PI work? Do you want to know how PIs find people? Where do they find those professional resources seemingly available at their fingertips? Then this chapter is for you.

If you have no intention of ever becoming a private investigator, and no curiosity as to how it all works, or where PIs get their information, you may still want to read this chapter. Why? Because if you ever hire a PI, you'll be able to better negotiate a price for his or her services. You'll also be able to determine if the PI you're thinking of hiring has the resources to do the job. If he or she doesn't, you might want to look elsewhere.

Mark Davis, an accountant, came to my office. He'd recently received a notice from the IRS and wanted to find a former client whose taxes he'd done several years ago. The address and phone he had for her were no longer any good. He did have her social security number from her tax return. Using the database resources we're going to examine in this chapter, we located her in about 30 seconds. We waited until the next day to tell him that, though, because he wouldn't have wanted to pay our fee.

Was the fee justified? The location fee we charged him wasn't a time-based fee. We weren't billing him by the hour. The fee was based upon us having the expertise and resources available to first, know which database to search; second, evaluate the information we found; and third, verify that the information was accurate. Now I'm going to show you how to do that, too.

The Credit Bureaus

A good professional PI will subscribe to a variety of data providers. Each data provider has its strong points and its weaknesses. In this chapter we'll examine several providers that are oriented toward the private investigation professional.

We look at these databases as tools. Just as there are different types of hammers for different jobs, likewise there are different databases a PI will utilize, depending upon the job requirements. You wouldn't use a ball peen hammer to frame a house, you'd use a claw hammer. You use a tack hammer for tapping in tacks and a sledgehammer for pounding posts. If you used a sledgehammer for putting a tack up, you'd lose all your profit repairing the hole in the plaster. Likewise, if an investigator uses his most expensive data provider for a $25 case, he won't last a year in the business.

A lot of information that goes into private databases is derived in one way or another from credit bureau files. The three main credit bureaus are …

- TransUnion (www.transunion.com).

- Equifax (www.equifax.com).

- Experian (www.experian.com).

Credit bureau files contain, of course, information about payments on credit accounts that you currently

> **Crime Scene Clues**
>
> A **judgment** is a final determination by a court of competent jurisdiction setting forth the rights and liabilities of the parties in a lawsuit. Usually the term judgment refers to a money judgment where the court may decide that a plaintiff is owed money by a defendant in a case. These judgments are recorded in the official records at the clerk of the courts office and are public records. Credit bureaus review these records on a regular basis and include them in your credit file if the judgment is against you.

have or used to have. Information, with a couple of exceptions, stays in your credit file for seven years. After seven years, it disappears, or at least that's the theory. One of the exceptions to the seven-year rule is a bankruptcy filing. That stays in your file for 10 years.

In addition to credit information, your credit file might also contain data from public records, such as we discussed in Chapter 8. This could include ...

- Bankruptcy filings.
- Tax liens.
- *Judgments.*

Public data information is not considered credit information and not subject to the Fair Credit Reporting Act (FCRA), which we'll discuss in a few minutes.

Credit Headers, God's Gift to the PI

But surprise, guess what? Also in your credit file is identifying personal information which we can use to locate you, and because it is not subject to the FCRA, it is not considered credit information:

- Your name (and previous names, or "also known as" a.k.a.s)
- Your date of birth
- Your social security number
- Your telephone number
- Current and previous addresses
- Current and previous employers

The credit bureaus, therefore, sell (they're in the business, after all, to make money) what is called "credit header" information to various databases or resellers.

Subscribers to these databases can access them without having to comply with the FCRA, which is a big deal.

Generally, private investigators wouldn't have a good reason to pull a credit report except for pre-employment backgrounds. Permissible purposes for pulling a credit report on an individual under the Fair Credit Reporting Act are ...

(1) In response to the order of a court having jurisdiction to issue such an order, or a subpoena issued in connection with proceedings before a federal grand jury.

(2) In accordance with the written instructions of the consumer to whom it relates.

(3) To a person whom the credit bureau has reason to believe ...

(A) intends to use the information in connection with a credit transaction involving the consumer on whom the information is to be furnished, and involving the extension of credit to, or review or collection of an account of, the consumer; or

(B) intends to use the information for employment purposes; or

(C) intends to use the information in connection with the underwriting of insurance involving the consumer; or

(D) intends to use the information in connection with a determination of the consumer's eligibility for a license or other benefit granted by a governmental instrumentality required by law to consider an applicant's financial responsibility or status; or

(E) otherwise has a legitimate business need for the information in connection with a business transaction involving the consumer.

The Fair Credit Reporting act does contain provisions for criminal and civil prosecutions for abuse of the credit reporting system. It provides as follows: Any person who knowingly and willfully obtains information on a consumer from a consumer reporting agency under false pretenses shall be fined under title 18, United States Code, imprisoned for not more than 2 years, or both.

Sammy the Snitch

If you're thinking about becoming a professional PI and subscribe to these data providers, be warned. They do audit their clients' accounts from time to time to ensure that you are adhering to the IRSG principles. Don't pull information from these data suppliers for reasons that don't comply with the IRSG guidelines.

The IRSG and the GLB

The responsible database suppliers that sell to PIs, attorneys, and law enforcement have for years subscribed to a set of self-regulatory rules known as the Individual Reference Services Group (IRSG) Privacy Principles. The clients of these databases, people like you and me, have to promise to adhere to these IRSG principles or lose our access. So we do.

Congress recently passed what is known as the Gramm-Leach-Bliley Act (GLB). This is a broad-based act that deregulated a lot of banking activities and also included a privacy provision. The privacy provision pretty much turns the IRSG principles into law, which is why the IRSG is disbanding. If you want to see the entire set of IRSG principles, you can find them at www.irsg.org. Though the IRSG is disbanding, the data suppliers still adhere to them and require that PIs follow them.

The Data Stew in the Data Providers

We've talked about credit headers, which are a very valuable source of information because most people have some sort of credit activity every few months. It might be getting a new telephone service, applying for a new job, renting an apartment or, of course, applying for credit somewhere.

One nice aspect of credit header data is that normally the information is time stamped. The credit bureaus indicate the date the record was most recently updated. This does not mean the date somebody last used his credit card. That would be nice, but that information is not reported to the credit bureau; only the credit card company retains that information. Normally, when people apply for credit, they are required to include on the application the name of their employer, residence address, and home telephone number (a great source for those nonpublished numbers).

Here are just some of the database records that are in the pot and frequently incorporated into these databases:

- Credit header data

- Magazine-subscription lists

- Telephone directory information

- Postal change of address

- Licensed drivers

- Marriages and divorces

- Book-club lists

- Registered vehicles

When you combine all of these records into one huge database, searchable by name, or social security number, or name and date of birth, you can imagine the possibilities. Remember in Chapter 6, where we talked about wild card searches? The wild card searches in these databases are practically unlimited.

Data Providers

Data providers have amassed literally billons of records. They sell the ability to search through those billions of records to private investigators and others. Generally speaking, the larger the database and the more comprehensive the search, the more expensive the search becomes. A good private investigator will play the data searches like an instrument, knowing from which data provider he can pluck the piece of information he needs to make his case or find his witness.

If you wish to subscribe to the data providers we've listed here, most of them will require you to be a licensed professional (not necessarily a PI) with a valid business need. They sell access to their data to law enforcement, PIs, attorneys, collection agencies, insurance and related service companies, and other businesses.

> **Sherlock's Secrets** _____
>
> A factor to keep in mind with these data providers is that some are more regional than others. When they started business, they likely began acquiring data within their own state first and then expanded to a broader coverage area. If you've just set up shop as a PI and the paint's still wet on the sign over your door, keep the geographic coverage areas of a potential data provider in mind. It can make a significant difference to the effectiveness of your work, and your bottom line.

Because of the Gramm-Leach-Bliley Act, some data providers no longer provide credit header information. Some only provide data that was in their database prior to July 1, 2001, the effective date of the GLB. However, the GLB doesn't prohibit the selling of credit header information, it just restricts it. Therefore, most of these data providers that list here do resell the credit headers, but only after you confirm that the reason you want it is in compliance with the GLB. Here is a list of eight permissible reasons to access credit headers. The wording is not set in stone, and different data providers word their purposes differently, but most of them are encompassed in the following:

- Necessary to effect, administer, or enforce a transaction
- Law enforcement investigations
- Law firm and attorneys
- Insurance or claims investigation
- Fraud detection and risk management

- Due diligence or institutional risk control/dispute resolution
- Collection actions
- Government agency or court related

Finding lost lovers, relatives, birth parents, or other people for personal reasons or developing a news story do not fall within the permissible guidelines.

ChoicePoint AutoTrackXP

AutoTrackXP was originally developed by Hank Asher of Database Technologies (DBT) in the early 1990s. Since it was located in southern Florida, he began with Florida public record information. He marketed it heavily to private investigators and attorneys. These two groups are regularly discriminated against by the credit bureaus and usually denied permission to become members of the various credit bureaus. AutoTrackXP was well received and grew and grew and grew, expanding its database until it had a nationwide scope.

DBT went public and was quickly bought out by ChoicePoint. Shortly after the buy-out, DBT nearly doubled its rates, forcing budget-minded PIs to search for more affordable alternatives. AutoTrackXP is still one of the granddaddies of databases. Its website is www.autotrackxp.com. If you're in the PI business, you need to at least look at what it offers. Then you can compare AutoTrackXP to any other data providers you're considering.

In AutoTrackXP, one of the more popular searches is called Faces of the Nation. AutoTrackXP describes its Faces of the Nation search as this:

> "The Faces of the Nation database provides easy access to over 13 billion records that can be used to locate and identify individuals. The information within Faces of the Nation is compiled from hundreds of sources. Searching for an individual is as easy as using a name, date of birth, address, social security number, phone number, or a combination thereof to locate a subject. Upon locating an individual, reports can be used to cross-reference other related databases to acquire additional information, as well as accessing all available credit bureaus real-time to bring back additional credit header information."

Thirteen billion records is a lot. The claimed coverage area is the United States, Puerto Rico, and the Virgin Islands. You can search through all of those records, at the speed of light, using any of the following criteria:

- City, state, first name
- City, state, last name
- County, state, last name
- Date of birth, first name
- Date of birth, last name
- Last name
- Phone number (with area code)
- Phone number (without area code)
- Social security number
- State, first name
- Street address, ZIP code
- Street name, ZIP code
- ZIP code, last name

I'm not going to enumerate similar lists for the rest of the data providers, but I wanted you to have some idea of what's out there and how flexible these databases are.

Elementary, My Dear Watson

Database coverage in Puerto Rico is available, but it is problematic because the architecture of the Spanish name is different than Anglo-Saxon names. Most Anglo-Saxon names have a first name or given name, a middle name (but not always), and a last name, which is taken from the child's father (although now we're getting a lot of hyphenated last names with females keeping their maiden name). First, middle, and last. Simple, right?

Hispanic names include a first name (given name), a middle name, a last name taken from the child's father, and a second last name, or fourth name, which is taken from the child's mother's maiden name.

When I was assigned with the FBI to the San Juan, Puerto Rico, office, my name was Steven Kerry Brown Bellamy, Bellamy being my mother's maiden name. I still have credit cards from down there that read "Steven B. Bellamy." Try explaining that to a clerk in the department store when he wants to compare my driver's license, last name Brown (hence the B in the credit card) with the credit card showing Bellamy as the last name.

Most databases only have three fields for names: first, middle, and last. By the year 2010, it is projected that 15 percent of the United States will be Spanish-speaking, and by 2020, it could exceed 20 percent. These databases are going to have to accommodate the Spanish name structure or they'll have very poor search results, like they do now in Puerto Rico, south Florida, and the southwestern states.

An attorney client of mine was looking for a witness in an automobile accident case. He knew her first name, which was very unusual; let's call her Shantoya. He also knew she was from Jacksonville, Fla. He had no other identifying information. Since there are several suburbs around Jacksonville, we searched Faces of the Nation by state, first name. There are a couple dozen Shantoyas in the state of Florida, but not that many around the Jacksonville area. That was a $5 search, and we had his witness located in less than five minutes. If the witness's first name had been Steve, though, forget it.

In Chapter 7 we talked about the difficulty of getting driver's license information. If you are going into the PI business, such information can be extremely useful. Here's how to find it. AutoTrackXP's Drivers of the Nation search includes driver's license information from the following states:

- Alabama
- Colorado
- Connecticut
- Delaware
- District of Columbia
- Florida
- Hawaii
- Idaho
- Illinois
- Indiana
- Iowa
- Kansas
- Kentucky
- Louisiana
- Maine
- Maryland
- Michigan
- Minnesota
- Mississippi
- Missouri
- Nebraska
- New Jersey
- New Mexico
- New York
- North Carolina
- North Dakota
- Oklahoma
- Oregon
- Rhode Island
- South Carolina
- South Dakota
- Tennessee
- Texas
- Utah
- Vermont
- Wisconsin

While you may not be able to get the driver's license information from all states, you can get vehicle license tag details from many of them that are not in the preceding list. Do you have an Alaskan license plate number and you want to know who the registered owner is? AutoTrackXP has a license plate search feature available for 42 of the 50 states. The price runs from about $24 to $44.

AutoTrackXP also has a series of reports that collates all the data that a search can produce and sets the data out in standard format. AutoTrackXP, in my opinion, is superior to other data providers in its reporting format, with the exception of the IRB reports (see "Accurint—IRB" later in this chapter). Here are some available options:

- The **Basic Report** will include, when available, current address information from two consumer reporting agencies, historical address information, date of birth, information related to social security numbers, drivers' licenses, phone numbers, and more. The information in the Basic Report is derived from a broad array of databases so it provides a solid overview of the subject of your search. This report currently costs ten dollars.

- The **Associates Feature** can be incorporated into the Basic Report. In addition to the information provided by the Basic Report, the Associates Feature provides, when available, the names of an individual's relatives, other people who have used the individual's address(es), neighbors with listed phone numbers, as well as spouses in Florida and Texas. This is a terrific feature because even if you can't find your subject, you will probably find a relative or associate who can tell you where your subject is currently residing. You get all of that for an additional two dollars.

- The **National Comprehensive Report** contains the information from the Basic Report as well as linkages to AutoTrackXP's other extensive national and state databases for a summary of assets, drivers' licenses, professional licenses, real properties, vehicles, and more. Using advanced search techniques, AutoTrackXP precisely identifies and integrates the information that specifically matches the individual being sought. The result is a National Comprehensive Report providing an extremely focused and thorough composite. This report costs $15 and you can add the associate feature for another two dollars.

Note that these descriptions are taken from their individual website. If you want more information,

QuickInfo Online Searches

E-InfoData has three products of interest to private investigators:

- Colorado Court search (www.cocourts.com), which we talked about in Chapter 7.

- FlateRateInfo, which we'll talk about in the next section.

- QuickInfo, located on the Internet at www.quickinfo.net.

Because E-InfoData is based in Colorado, you will find that the QuickInfo product has stronger coverage in the western United States. However, it also has good coverage in Florida, Georgia, Iowa, Ohio, and a host of other eastern and Midwestern states. The competent private investigator will have access to many different pay databases. They each have their strengths and weaknesses. QuickInfo is big into voter registration records, which are not found on many other databases.

All of QuickInfo's databases are basically public record searches. It's a very user-friendly database and the prices are reasonable. The nice part about QuickInfo is it's very good about telling you when the records were last updated. The employees are great folks to work with.

A lot of QuickInfo data is archival and the inclusive dates of the records are clearly shown. For instance, if you're searching for a witness that you know lived in a particular locale a few years ago, you won't find him or her in a search of current voter's registration data. Since QuickInfo has data archived from previous years, you might locate the person in the older data. It's a good way to get identifying information, date of birth, social security number, and so forth, which you'll need in order to perform credit header searching.

The QuickInfo website also has a real-time phone finder, based on the Regional Bell Operating Companies (RBOC) information. The current charge is 50¢. It also has a feature called Fetch, the Wonder Dog. Click on Fetch and he will search through over 100 regional databases around the country. If he finds nothing, there is no charge. When he does find a record, Fetch charges you $7.50. It's a good search tool if the record you are looking for is in a state where QuickInfo has coverage.

QuickInfo tells you specifically which states they cover and what information from those different states is available in their archives. Fetch will search those public records and combine all of the information he finds into one report for you.

FlatRateInfo

FlatRateInfo is located on the web at www.flatrateinfo.com. If you anticipate performing a lot of searches throughout the year, it's the best bargain on the Internet. FlatRateInfo—you can probably guess by its name—only charges one rate for unlimited use by a single user for the entire year. The current rate is $1,400 annually. This may seem like a lot, but if you're skip tracing 2,000 people a month like my firm does, then those $5, $10, and $15 searches will add up really fast, and FlatRateInfo becomes very economical.

FlateRateInfo describes their service as follows:

> "At the heart of the FlatRateInfo.com system is the QI National People Locator, a powerful searching tool containing over 600 million records from most U.S residents, including social security number, current and previous addresses, date of birth and aliases."

The National People Locator includes credit header information. However, the credit header database is only updated on average once a month, so a search on FlatRateInfo could easily produce different results from the same search on another site with up-to-the-minute credit header data. But you can run a whole busload of searches at FlatRateInfo and it doesn't cost a dime more.

In my PI business, FlatRateInfo is the first primary source we check when doing *locates*. Once we have the person identified, we can verify that the address and other pertinent information is current through other means, which you'll have to do anyway.

Crime Scene Clues

A **locate,** in PI terms, means finding an individual whose whereabouts is not known by your client. It differs from skip-tracing in that the person is not hiding his whereabouts, although the terms locate and skip-tracing are frequently used interchangeably.

The National People Locator can be searched by any number of criteria, similar to what we listed for AutoTrackXP. It's very versatile. Also, FlatRateInfo has the Social Security Death Master File, which we covered in detail in Chapter 6, so if the person is deceased, you can find it there.

FlatRateInfo provides access to a number of public databases such as U.S. pilots, bankruptcies and liens, national property, U.S. aircraft, ZIP codes, and more.

FlatRateInfo has a nifty little social security number verifier that notifies you if a SSN is valid or not, and what state it was issued in.

Sammy the Snitch

Just a word of caution about searching the Death Master File. Be sure and check the date that FlatRateInfo last updated its Death Master File. If you're not certain the data includes the dates you need, then go to RootsWeb.com and search for it there.

Another search I like a lot is the InteleTracer. It is like a reverse telephone number search, only better. You can input a telephone number without the area code and it will search all of the RBOC, then list how many matching phone numbers and in which states that number was found. Click on the state you think it might be and InteleTracer will give you the subscriber information for all of those listings in that state. For instance, I searched my home number and

InteleTracer found 17 matches in 12 states, including Florida. A click on Florida brought up the subscribers who were located in Miami, Hialeah, and Orlando, as well as my home phone number. All of this was done without an area code. Pretty cool, huh?

Accurint—IRB

In the preceding section, I mentioned Hank Asher had started AutoTrackXP. After ChoicePoint bought out what was then DBT, Hank went on to other things. One of his latest successes is Accurint, at www.accurint.com. Accurint is another pay-per-search data provider with a twist. Accurint's per-search initial cost is only a quarter, and what a quarter's worth you get. In many of our searches we never have to go beyond that.

Accurint describes its data processing in these terms:

> "Accurint uses a name, past address, phone number or Social Security Number to obtain the current name, address and phone number of targeted subjects. Using proprietary compilation of data sources and association algorithms, Accurint's ability to deliver high-quality matches and find rates is unparalleled. Accurint can also provide previous addresses and location information for relatives, associates, and neighbors."

> "By leveraging unmatched capability for processing billions of records per second, Accurint has compiled the world's largest set of accessible location data. Accurint searches more than 20 billion records that cover recent relocation to historical addresses dating back 30 years and more."

Accurint is available to law enforcement, collection agencies, and companies with internal collection departments. It is not available directly to private investigators. However, the information is available to PIs through the International Research Bureau (IRB), which resells access to the Accurint data.

IRB is located at www.irbsearch.com. You can't beat the price. At 25¢, it's a bargain. If you perform a comprehensive search similar to what we saw at AutoTrackXP, the price goes up to between $1 and $5, depending on the depth of the report you choose.

IRB also offers a directory assistance search for 10¢, but it's difficult to tell how up-to-date the data is. It does not appear to be real-time RBOC data like 555-1212.com and Reach Directory. The phone search does have a reverse feature, which actually seems to work better than the regular forward search. A nice feature about the phone search is that if there is no record found, then there is no charge.

SearchAmerica

SearchAmerica, located at www.searchamerica.com, has more basic features than the data providers already discussed. It doesn't provide a comprehensive report that correlates data, nor does it include possible relatives and associates. At a little over $2 each, the credit header searches are one of the more affordable searches of this kind. It's not geared to public-record data like QuickInfo, for instance, but SearchAmerica is a good data provider and we use it regularly, especially in view of the rates.

There are other data suppliers out there. Use the search engines to find them. ChoicePoint, in addition to buying AutoTrackXP, also bought IRSC and CDB Infotech. IRSC was strong in California and the western states. Presumably all of this data is being merged into AutoTrackXP, giving it greater depth. That makes AutoTrackXP really convenient, but be aware that there are cheaper alternatives.

The Least You Need to Know

- ◆ Data from credit bureaus is used by private investigators as a primary source for skip tracing.

- ◆ The three credit bureaus providing credit header information are TransUnion, Equifax, and Experian.

- ◆ Credit bureau files contain not only your credit history, but also what is known as "header information" which includes your name, date of birth, social security number, current and previous addresses, and current employers.

- ◆ The Fair Credit Reporting Act limits access to your credit data but not to the header information.

- ◆ A set of principles known as the IRSG and a new law, the Gramm-Leach-Bliley Act, have restricted the use of credit and credit header data.

- ◆ There are multiple sources available to licensed private investigators for credit header data. Each of these data providers has distinct strengths and weaknesses.

Performing Background Investigations

In This Chapter

- Tricks to uncovering personal identifiers
- Finding criminal records
- There is nothing civil about civil lawsuits
- Dancing with the previous employer
- Verifying the degree of education
- Having a meaningful discussion with the personal reference

Every third inquiry for services a private investigator receives is a request for some type of a background investigation. Generally the new caller has no idea what she's looking for, only that she needs somebody checked out, doesn't have a clue on how to do it herself, and has no idea really of what is encompassed in a background investigation. The professional investigator first has to determine the actual need of the client and then educate her as to what is possible and what is not. Many of us have a vague notion of what a "background check" may include, but are not really clear as to the specifics.

Let's look at some typical problems everyday people have:

- A father and former husband is concerned about the ex-wife's new boyfriend. The ex-wife has custody of the children, and the boyfriend appears to be a slimeball. If the father can prove his ex-wife is letting some degenerate hang around his kids, perhaps the father can get custody.

- A woman has her wedding planned and the date is soon, but some doubts linger in her mind about the soon-to-be husband. Some of the things he says just don't add up.

- A small business owner has a new employee and wants to make sure the person he just hired is honest, hardworking, and dependable.

- A mother and father are thinking about hiring a nanny full-time. They want to ensure the new nanny is not a child abuser, or worse, a molester.

- You have a new cleaning lady. You're going to be out of town on cleaning day. Do you give her a key to the house?

- Your new boyfriend claims to be a secret agent, or an ex-Navy SEAL, but his beer belly has you wondering. What else is he lying about?

The preceding six points are real problems from real people. Their lives are tied in knots until they can get answers to their questions and resolve the doubt in their minds.

To find the answers to your questions, there are five ingredients that make up a good basic background or pre-employment check:

- A criminal-arrest and/or conviction search

- A civil-records search

- Verifying and checking with previous employers

- Interviewing personal references

- A driving history, if applicable to your needs

This type of knowledge is power. In this chapter I'm going to show you how to get that knowledge.

Obtaining the Basic Goods

Before beginning any background check, you must assess the level of detail and the depth of the check you desire. Regardless of what type of background investigation you intend to perform, you must have the first three items here, and the fourth is highly desirable: name, date of birth, Social Security number, and current address.

Finding the Name

If your purpose for the background is pre-employment, you'll have all this information on the candidate's application. Other than pre-employment, most of us don't start out with much information about the person. That's why we want a background check done.

You'd think that knowing the name of the person that you want to check out would be a simple, commonsense item, but you'd be surprised at how often that little detail is difficult to come by. I can't tell you how many times husbands have come to my office because their ex-wife is seeing some new boyfriend and they are concerned about who this guy is, what he does for a living, and whether he's had any run-ins with the law before. The trouble is, they don't know the new boyfriend's name.

A good father who does not have custody of his children *should* be concerned about another male who is living with his children or may have influence over them. The last thing you want is somebody who is abusive or with a history of child molestation living with your kids. If the client doesn't know the individual's name, how do you, the PI, find it? Here are four good methods that work:

> **Sammy the Snitch**
>
> You need to be sure that the name the child gives you is, in fact, the first name. We have spent many useless hours and incurred countless database charges because our client told us the person's name was Scott, for instance, only to find out later that Scott, which is the name he goes by, is actually his middle name.

- If you're on good terms with the ex, just ask her. Most of the time, however, our clients aren't on very good terms with the former spouses.

- If the kids are old enough, ask them. If they are young, they may only know a first name or the name by which the ex refers to him. If you can get a first name, that's a start.

- If you are allowed regular access to the ex's house, perhaps when you're picking up the kids, check the Caller ID on the telephone if she has the service. Chances are the new friend has called the house and his telephone number and name might be right there. Even if his name isn't shown, his number might be recorded. Chapter 5, tells you how to do a reverse phone search. Even if you have a list of 30 numbers, spend 20 bucks at 555-1212.com to buy a hundred searches (the smallest package available), and run all 30 numbers.

♦ Jot down the license tag on the guy's car. This means you'll have to be there when he shows up. That might be easy, and it might not, depending on your situation. If you can't be there, perhaps there is a friendly neighbor who will do it for you. By running the license, you'll get name, date of birth, social security number, and an address (a bases-loaded home run). As a professional, I always go right for the tag.

Finding the Date of Birth

In order to run a criminal record check, you need two things: name and date of birth. A social security number is nice, but not necessary. Race and sex are also helpful as identifiers, and in running criminal records you usually have to include both items in the request. Race and sex should be easy for you, although these days, with spiked hair and baggy clothes, a person's sex might not be clear.

Crime Scene Clues

A **pretext** is a subterfuge or a ploy used by private investigators to encourage an individual to reveal information about himself or another party without being aware of the true reason for the conversation. In the course of responding to what appears to be a normal everyday query, the individual unsuspectingly releases the information the investigator actually is seeking.

Once you have the person's name, you'll need the date of birth. Go down to your local voter's registration office and check the voter's records, which are usually considered public information and will include name and date of birth. Interestingly, you can look at the voter's registration records, but often they won't let you write anything down. That's to keep people from coming in and making marketing lists. You'll just have to remember the date of birth until you can step around the corner and write it down.

If the new boyfriend is not a registered voter, head for the clerk of the court's office and check for previous marriages and divorces. There you will find all the identifiers you need.

Excuse me, you say, but I've spent half a day running around the courthouse only to discover the new boyfriend is not a registered voter and was divorced in another state. Now what do you do? If you're absolutely determined to do it yourself and not pay a PI (who can tap into one of the subscription databases we discussed in Chapter 9, and have it for you in a in a matter of minutes), then you have to make a *pretext* call.

Before attempting this, see Chapter 16, for detailed instructions on how to perform pretext calls. The following pretext we've used quite successfully in the past to uncover date of birth. It cannot be used on the subject himself. It is best used on a close relative like a parent or sister, or on a roommate. In either case the subject cannot be present when you make the call.

Call the phone number you got off the caller ID when you're sure the subject is not home. If you know anything about the subject's parents, call them instead. Be sure and use one of the tricks we will discuss in Chapter 11, to block your phone number before calling.

When Mom answers, tell her you found her son's wallet in the parking lot of a nearby shopping center, referring to the store by name. (If the mom lives out of state, better still.) Explain you're not sure that you have the right family, but you'd like to get the wallet back to its owner. If Mom asks how you got her number, tell her it was in the wallet. If Mom will just confirm the date of birth you found in the wallet, you'll make arrangements to return the billfold. Tell her you'll need the person's current address to take the billfold to him. Now you've turned your base hit into a double (date of birth and address), and you're going for a triple.

That pretext always works if handled as I've outlined it. If you want to push it, ask her to confirm the social security number also. Mom may not know the social security number off hand, but she'll go and look it up for you. (Now it's a triple.) The most important thing, though, is to get the date of birth. If you get the address and SSN, consider them bonuses.

Locating the Address

If you can't make the pretext call to get the address, there are other methods of obtaining it. Keep in mind that the address is not usually required as an identifier except in searching civil court cases. Usually, in civil cases, a person's date of birth and SSN are not listed. A party in a civil case is identified by his name and address. Not a problem unless the name of the person you are searching is Steve Brown and there are twenty of them in the city. Then you have to have the address to differentiate between all of those Steve Browns.

If you've gotten the name and date of birth, the address is a cinch and there are two quick ways to find it. The vehicle tag, of course, is by far the easiest and most direct approach. Sometimes, though, people change addresses and don't notify the DMV so the vehicle registration may not always be current. The good news is eight times out of ten, it is. The other easy method is by using the telephone records. Reverse search the number you got off the Caller ID and, unless it's a cell phone or a nonpublished number, you'll have the address.

Sometimes, clients really want the address for other reasons. Maybe the client needs to see for himself what's really going on at the new boyfriend's house, or maybe the client needs to prove that his ex-spouse has moved in with a man. This can figure into alimony adjustments in a big way.

Here are two more surefire ways to locate the address:

◆ If the person dating the ex is a reasonably mature person, of medium or higher means, and lives in a single-family residence, then check the local property records (real property tax rolls) at your property appraisers office. If he's a younger person living in an apartment, that won't work.

◆ Follow the subject home. That always works. Be sure and read Chapter 15, before you attempt this. There are a lot of tricks of the trade that go into a successful surveillance, so study up. The last thing you want is for your ex to find out that you've tailed her new boyfriend to his apartment. And you don't want a confrontation. This is very important.

The Criminal in Our Background

In Chapter 8, we talked about getting records from both the clerk of the court and the state criminal record system. Now's your chance to put that knowledge to work. Yeah, it means you've got to spend a couple of hours driving to the courthouse and getting someone to help you. Actually, at most courthouses you'll spend more time looking for a parking space than you will inside looking for records. Twenty minutes, in and out, is all you should need if you're only checking criminal cases. Be sure and check both the upper and lower courts. In the lower courts you'll find the misdemeanors.

Remember, a lot of misdemeanors began as felonies and were *pled down* to misdemeanors. So you want to review the file and examine the original charges.

Suppose your subject has only been in town a few months, but you know exactly where she lived for the previous eight years and that it was in another county or even another state.

Or, maybe you're running your own business and want to check the criminal background of a potential new hire. You don't want to be running down to the courthouse every time you interview a new applicant. The next two sections have some options for you.

> **Crime Scene Clues**
>
> To **plead down** means that the prosecuting attorney's office, in order to expedite the flow of cases, as well as lessen his load and the burden on the court, reduces charges from higher offenses to lesser offenses. He or she does this if the defendant agrees to plead guilty to the lesser offenses.

The Sourcebook

In Chapter 7, we talked about the "Big Red Book." Let's take a look at the second-most informative book we use, affectionately referred to as the "Sourcebook." This is the *Sourcebook to Public Record Information* (published by BRB Publications, Inc. Tempe, AZ www.brbpub.com). This book lists every state, all of its courts (local, state, and federal), and how to get the records you need. It also tells you whether to mail your request, fax it, or telephone it in. In addition, it lists all of the different licensing agencies in a state along with each agency's telephone number and website address, if it has one.

Let's take Missouri as an example. A statewide search is available. The Sourcebook indicates records are available from 1970 on. Convictions are reported, but no arrest data unless the arrest is less than 31 days old. The search fee is $5. Personal checks are accepted, but no credit cards. Turnaround times vary, depending upon how you make your request; requests by mail take three to four weeks, while in-person requests are processed while you wait. The address and telephone number for the criminal-record division is there also.

Oh, you say, but you can't wait three to four weeks to see if your subject has a criminal conviction record in Missouri. Go to the Sourcebook publisher's website at www.brbpub.com. You'll find a database named Public Record Retriever Network (PRRN). The PRRN is a group of folks who make their living pulling public records. If you enter Cole County (Jefferson City), where the Criminal Record Division for the state is located, you'll find two members of the PRRN listed. One is out of state and the other is right there in Jefferson City. Guess which one I'd pick? Give the local company a call and you'll get a price quote on going over and getting the record for you, same day or next day. Pretty slick, huh? If you don't have computer access, BRB Publications also publishes a book with the same information named the *Local Court and County Record Retrievers*.

If you're in a hurry, get one of the record retrieval sources to pull the record for you, but it'll cost you more than the $5 the county charges.

Oh, how did I know that Jefferson City was in Cole County? Because in the Sourcebook, there is a county locator for each state that lists cities within the state and indicates which county they're in.

If you're running your own business and want to do your own pre-employment backgrounds, then you need either the Sourcebook (currently retailing for $74.95) or the Big Red Book, the *Guide to Background Investigations* (currently retailing for $199.95).

The Local Sheriff's Office

This is very important. While you're at the courthouse, chances are your local sheriff's office or city police department is not far away.

Walk across the street to the police department and check their records. Why? Because they may have records of incidents that never went to court because nobody was ever charged. In some states you can get the arrest records, for a small search fee, typically about $5, right there while you wait.

Suppose the new boyfriend was beating up his live-in girlfriend. The next-door neighbor calls the police when she hears the girlfriend pleading for help. The police arrive, but there is no blood spread around, so they calm the couple down and leave. Before they leave the scene, they write up a domestic disturbance incident report. Nobody was arrested, no charges were filed. There will be nothing in any court file. But still, you'd like to know about that incident, wouldn't you?

Frequently patrol officers will stop somebody who is acting suspiciously or loitering. When they do, they always ask for identification and usually run a computer check on the subject to see if there are any wants or warrants on him or her. In most jurisdictions the officers will fill out what is known as a *Field Identification* (FI) card, or they may write an incident report if they were responding to a call. Those FI cards and incident reports contain a lot of information and should be reviewed.

Crime Scene Clues

A Field Identification card is a card used by patrol officers when questioning persons who may have been acting suspiciously. It will contain the subject's identifying data, the date and location of the incident, and a short synopsis of why the subject was questioned.

That's why, if possible, always check the local police jurisdiction's files in addition to the court records when performing a criminal background check. When you check the local police department they'll do the searching for you. Usually you write the name and other identifying information on a form and hand it to a record clerk who searches for the information while you wait. There is almost always a nominal, $3 to $15 charge for this search.

The Big Lie About National Criminal Checks

There is a big misconception about national criminal checks and we need to expose it here. There is one, and only one, possible way to do a national criminal-history search. That is by searching the FBI's Identification Division records. The records at the division can be searched by fingerprints, or you can initiate a search of the Computerized Criminal History section of the Bureau's *NCIC* computer, which can be searched by name and date of birth. Anybody in the pre-employment screening or background investigation business, who is honest, will admit that there is no other national criminal-history check. Period. A search through the FBI's records and the NCIC computer is only available to law enforcement and a few other federally mandated organizations.

Some "search firms" sell what they call a "national criminal check." Usually what they're selling is a search of a popular national database. This database compiles publicly printed arrests and court cases by getting its information principally from the major newspapers and magazines. If you're conducting a background and your subject was arrested but the arrest wasn't printed in the papers (and most aren't), then it's unlikely that it will show in what these folks bill as a "national criminal check." Don't buy it. Save your money.

Crime Scene Clues

NCIC stands for the National Crime Information Center. Among other things, NCIC maintains a huge database run by the FBI where subjects with outstanding arrest warrants are listed. Also listed are stolen properties and missing persons.

The Sometimes Not-So-Civil Cases

In Chapter 8, we talked at some length about how to find different records. Many times, clients aren't so interested in the property records, the official records where deeds and mortgages are recorded, but rather they have a very legitimate need to search the civil records.

I have a client who is suing a business for discrimination. He wants to know if any other former or current employees have sued this business for the same reason. A pattern of behavior by a corporate entity is important in winning large judgments in these types of suits. It also gives your attorney a ready pool of witnesses who can testify, "Yeah, they did the same thing to me."

Checking civil-court files in prenuptial investigations is important because divorce files contain some of the most bizarre allegations you'll ever see. Husbands and wives in the midst of a bitter divorce spill all the dirty secrets about each other, including drugs, sex, adultery, violence, anger, and perverted behavior. It's all right there in the divorce file, a public record, for anybody who cares to read about it. Certainly, were I to remarry, presuming my new wife-to-be had been previously divorced, I would want to review her divorce file before popping the question.

A while back, a female stockbroker called me, indicating she was going to be married in 10 days. She had some lingering doubts about her fiancé, who was from another state, and thought that before the big day came she should check a little into his background. "A little late," I thought, but we took the case.

I had my man in the western state that the gentleman was from start with the civil records and the local police department. Guess what? In the clerk of the courts office he found a marriage record but no divorce on file. True, he could have gotten divorced someplace else, so we kept on digging.

Across the street at the police department, guess what we found? Nope, not an arrest record, but a missing person report filed by his still-legal wife, nearly a year before. Apparently the man just upped and left his family of 20 years and headed east, leaving behind his wife and three sons. They had no idea where he was, or if he was dead or alive, but they did know for sure that he hadn't been divorced. Well, what's a little bigamy between friends?

The kicker is, my female client decided she was still in love with the guy, postponed the wedding, and waited until the divorce was final from his first wife, and then married him anyway. At least she knew what she was getting into. After all that, do you still think doing a prenuptial background is silly?

The Previous Employer—Outfoxing HR

In your small business, a position has opened up and you need to fill it. You've interviewed new candidates and think you have it narrowed down to the person that meets all of your requirements. Now is the time to do your pre-employment background check. Checking the person's civil records might be excessive, but at the minimum, you'll want to check to see if he has a criminal background. You should also talk to his former employers.

The application will list his most recent employers. Anyway, it should, or he may have just left some off because he departed on unfriendly terms. You won't know until you check.

If the firm he came from is large, it will have a Human Resource (HR) department. By all means, call it. Most likely all an HR rep will tell you is that yes, he was employed there. If you're lucky, the rep will give you the dates he was there as well. Not a big help, huh? So here's what you do. When you're interviewing the candidate, be sure and get the name, telephone number, and telephone extension of his immediate supervisor. After you've tangoed around the dance floor with the HR department, call the supervisor. Read Chapter 12 first. You have to get "buddy-buddy" with this person on the phone. Tell her a joke, make her "like" you. Get her to relax and let her know that this is not an official call ... more of a social call. Then ask, "You know, just between you and me, what kind of worker was so and so?" You'll be amazed what people will tell you if you ask. Once you become their friend, they'll frequently give you the real scoop.

Giving the Third Degree to Education Verifications

My firm performs a lot of pre-employment background investigations. In fact, we run a separate company that has pre-employment checks as its sole function. The education verification is the simplest part. Pick up the telephone and call the registrar's office at the school. Ninety-five percent of the time, a person in the office will tell you if the candidate went to school there, what years, how many semesters, and if he or she obtained a degree. Five percent of the time, the office will ask for a release. There's no trick here, except to make sure that your employment application includes a release that will let you search criminal, credit, previous employer, and educational institution records.

This is the one pre-employment search we do where the applicants lie the most. It's incredible. They'll claim to have degrees from universities when they don't. They'll indicate three years attendance when they only attended one semester. It goes on and on.

Think about this. If applicants misrepresent facts or lie on their employment application, what does that make them? If you hire them anyway, don't be surprised when you catch them in a lie later on.

Getting Really Well Acquainted with the Personal References

We always check the personal references when our clients ask us to. Some clients do and others don't. There are a lot of honest folks out there and occasionally we get a personal reference that tells us what a rotten scoundrel our applicant really is. If you're going to check the references, then you need to probe and not just ask hokey dead-end questions. We like to ask questions that solicit and expose both the positive and negative attributes of the candidate. Ask a question where you expect a positive information and then ask for the negative information. Here are some suggestions:

- ◆ In what ways has the applicant demonstrated to you he is dependable?
- ◆ Can you give examples of when the applicant was not dependable?
- ◆ Can you give me an example of the applicant's honesty?
- ◆ Can you give us an example of a time or occasion when the applicant was dishonest?
- ◆ What would you say are the applicant's most special talents or areas of expertise and strength?

◆ What areas would you suggest are his weaknesses? Where does he most need to improve?

◆ We're considering the applicant for such and such position. Is he proficient in that area, and how are you aware of that?

Take those seven questions and tailor them to your particular needs. You'll find out quickly if the personal reference really knows your applicant or not. If you have three references and none of them have known your candidate for very long, you may want to probe a little further into his or her background.

The Least You Need to Know

◆ A basic background check usually includes criminal history, civil record search, previous employers, and personal reference contacts.

◆ You must have at least the name and date of birth to conduct a background search, and preferably a social security number as well. There are some tricks to obtaining this information.

◆ There is no "national criminal" search other than NCIC, which is run by the FBI. Don't be fooled.

◆ Civil suits, particularly divorce files, contain many allegations between suing parties and provide good leads for additional witnesses.

◆ Information can be obtained by bypassing the HR department of previous employers and going directly to a former supervisor.

◆ Applicants routinely lie about their educational credits.

◆ Personal references can be good sources of information, if you ask thoughtful, probing questions.

Part 3

Learning the Basics

Once you've learned how to search the public records and the private databases, it's time to learn actual investigative techniques.

In this section, you'll learn how to get more information from the phone company than you thought possible. You'll uncover the tricks PIs use to get nonpublished numbers, cell phone numbers, and subscriber information. Methods of conducting investigations that provide proven results are taught to you, step-by-step, to help you with your own case. You'll see how to conduct an interrogation and how to carry out an effective surveillance.

Chapter 11

Winning the Telephone Game

In This Chapter

- Outflank the telephone company's defensive line
- Slash directory information costs in half
- Nonpublished numbers and how to verify subscriber information
- Phone breaks, pager breaks, and cell breaks
- Finding the elusive nonpublished number
- Determining a pay telephone's location
- Phreaking the phones

The telephone is a tool. I know, all this time you thought it was a voice instrument used primarily for ordering pizza. Surprise, surprise, it's really the most basic tool in the private investigator's toolbox. A competent PI can find out more information using the telephone than any database can possibly provide. A PI may not always have access to his computer, but he should be able to lay his hands on a pay phone or a cell phone—unless he's in the Virgin Islands, where the pay phones don't usually work anyway.

We're going to examine the ins and outs of using the telephone to enhance your PI career. In order to make the best use of the phone, sometimes you have to outwit the person you're calling, and frequently you have to outsmart the telephone company itself.

Sword Fighting the Operator

The phone companies are in business to make money, so naturally they sell some of their data to generate an additional revenue stream that adds profit to the bottom line. Thirty years ago, the phone company gave away its data. There was no charge back then for directory information. Now, you'll pay anywhere from 25¢ to $1.25 for a single call to directory assistance.

Just as the Germans outflanked the Maginot Line in France during World War II, you also have to outflank the telephone company's defensive lines that are built between its data and us, the customers. There used to be only one set of bunkers between you and the data. Now there are two: the computer-operated voice information service and the directory assistance operator.

I'm sure everyone has experienced the frustration of dealing with the computer-answered directory information system: "What city, please?" "What state, please?" "What listing, please?" You answer the questions, give the requested listing, and then receive a telephone number that turns out to be the wrong one. Or, maybe you've just spent a buck for a phone number, but you needed the address, too, and you didn't get it because there was nobody live on the other end of the phone to ask for it.

Perhaps that digital goddess gave you Steve Brown's telephone number (one out of sixteen in the metropolitan area), and actually the one you wanted is listed as S. Brown. There goes another buck, or two or three, depending upon how many times you call back to get the wrong information.

As we talked about in Chapter 5 the best solution is to go online and use one of the pay directory information sites, like 555-1212.com or Reach Directory, which will cost you less than 20¢ for a printout of all 16 Steve Browns and all the S. Browns, with addresses, so you can peruse them while you're drinking your lemonade and figure out which one you need.

All that's fine if your computer is always handy, booted up, and already online. The reality of life is that you're not usually home, your hard drive has crashed, and the cable or DSL is down. It's a lot easier to pick up the phone, dial 411, and get the number that way. But in order to get the address with the number, you have to outflank the first line of defense, the computer-operated directory information service, and get to a living, breathing operator. You also have to outsmart the computer if the number is nonpublished and you want to verify the address, which we'll deal with a little later in this chapter.

Here's how you do it. You dial 411. The computer answers and asks, "What city, please?" You say, "I need to speak to someone please." The computer will continue to run through its programming, asking the remaining questions. Don't answer them. Mumble something unintelligible, but not obscene, if it makes you feel better. Eventually, the phone company will put forward its second defensive line, and a live directory information operator will come on.

Congratulations, you've just won your first skirmish with the guardians of the telephone databank, but you haven't won the battle yet. If, at this stage, you restate your question, you just lost the skirmish and the battle. You ask for Steve Brown, the operator says, "Just one moment, please," and boom, you hear the computerized voice giving you the wrong number again. Bad move.

> **Elementary, My Dear Watson**
>
> Directory assistance operators are partially rated by how many calls an hour they can handle. The faster the operator can get you off of her screen and back to the computer, the more calls she can handle and the better her rating. The better her rating, of course, the more money she'll eventually earn.

Now, after you've mumbled your way to a live operator and she asks, "What listing, please?", the winning strategy is to immediately, forcefully, and politely say, "Please don't put the computer on. This is going to be a little complicated." If you've begged just right, you may find an operator willing to step up to the challenge and help you get the information you need. Then give her the listing information you're seeking. If you know the street, give her that at the same time. If you want the street address, be sure and ask for that upfront. Say, "I'd like the street address *and* the number for John Q. Public." About 20 percent of the time, she'll forget to give you the address and you'll end up with the computer giving you the number. I'll take an 80 percent win rate against the telephone company anytime.

Getting a Twofer

In the preceding section, you learned how to outfox the telephone company computer. Now, let's cut the cost of that call to 411 in half. If you do it right, you can get two listings for the price of one. When you're dealing with the computer you get one shot, one number, for about a dollar. If you need two or more listings at the same time, fight through the computer system like before until you get the live operator to finally answer. In addition to telling her not to put on the computer, also tell her you have two listings.

Sherlock's Secrets

When dealing with directory information operators, the old adage "It's easier to catch flies with honey than vinegar" has never been more true. Show an interest and a concern for the operator, her problems of dealing with rude callers, and the fact that she needs to get you off the line. Tell her you're sorry to be taking up so much of her time. You'll win her over and she will take all the time you need her to. Frequently, being nice results in getting her to search other cities, like suburbs, or giving you other options that you didn't think to ask about. She may say, "I don't have a Steve Brown on Beach Boulevard, but I do have an S. Brown on Beach. Would you like that listing, too?" You won't get that level of cooperation unless you use the honey technique.

Directory information operators will give you up to two listings on one phone call. Frequently, they will give you the first listing and then the operator says, "Here's your other listing." The operator disappears and the computer gives you the second number. Remember, she's trying to get to the next call as quickly as she can. But you received your two numbers and got them for the cost of only one.

The Secret to Verifying Nonpublished Numbers

In the private investigation business, sometimes knowing where your subject lives is just as good as knowing his or her telephone number. If the PI wants to conduct surveillance on an individual, he doesn't necessarily need the telephone number, but he does need the address so he can get out of bed in the dark, well before dawn, and venture out into the cold, while every sane person is still sleeping (isn't PI work fun?), and set up the surveillance on the residence prior to the subject leaving for work.

The PI has run the subject's name in the databases and they show an address for him, but he's not sure if the address is current or not. The databases are not infallible, and as we discussed in Chapter 9, the databases pull a lot of the information from credit bureau files. Not everybody applies for credit every month, so the address might not have been updated for six months or more.

Next, you, the PI, check directory information, where you can get a phone number as well as an address. If you call 411, the recording and the live operator might both report the listing you want is nonpublished. What do you do? You certainly don't want to get out of bed and go to the wrong address. You can run all of the other checks we talked about in the skip tracing chapters (Chapters 5 and 6), but here is the easiest way to verify the address when your subject has a nonpublished number.

With a possible address in mind, and knowing the subject's telephone number is non-published, mumble your way through the 411 computer until you get the live operator, as we talked about in the preceding section. Next, tell the operator you'd like her to check a listing for you. You think the number is nonpublished but you'd like to verify the address.

The operators don't get this request very often because most people don't know you can verify an address on nonpublished numbers. Be prepared to have her say she can't give you the address. When she says that, you tell her that's okay; you already have the address, you just want to verify it. Give her the address where you think the subject is living. Either she'll confirm it or she'll tell you no, it's a different address. She might not be willing to give the address to you, but she does have it in front of her on the screen, and she can and will verify it for you if you give it to her first. If you've got the right address, then set the alarm for about 4 A.M. and go to bed early.

Elementary, My Dear Watson

Some long distance companies use third-party subcontractors to handle directory assistance inquiries. Sometimes these subcontractors will not verify addresses on nonpublished numbers. If you're using any of the Regional Bell Operating Companies (RBOC), you shouldn't have a problem. If you run into one of these subcontractors who refuses to verify the address for you, then simply hang up and dial 1 plus your subject's area code and 555-1212. That should put you into the RBOC directory information network and you should get an RBOC operator who will verify the address. Also, there are other private telephone companies out there besides the Bell System companies, and they may have different rules. Altogether, the technique in this section works 99 percent of the time.

Area codes seem to change within some states every week. Here are two good area code locators; www.555-1212.com and www.mmiworld.com/telephone.htm. There is no simple solution to keeping up with the area code changes but these two websites help.

Breaking the Number

Obtaining a *telephone break* can be one of the most challenging and exasperating problems facing a private investigator. A wife will come to you with a telephone number she found in her husband's billfold or coat pocket. The wife suspects the number may belong to a female, and she wants to know for sure.

In obtaining a telephone break, you have to first satisfy yourself that the client means no harm to the subscriber. The very last thing a PI wants is to find that, by breaking the phone number, he has enabled his client to go to the subject's address and attempt to physically harm that person.

Next, arrange the price with your client. On a listed number, the price should be about $25. It's hardly worth the paperwork if you charge any less. A nonpublished number, cellular number, or pager number break should cost the client about $125.

Start with the easy checks. Go to www.reachdirectory.com or to www.555-1212.com and run a reverse search on the number. There's a good chance the number will be a regular listed number and you've just turned a 25¢ search into an extra $25 in your pocket.

> **Crime Scene Clues**
>
> A **telephone break** is the process of taking a telephone number, with no other identifying information; and obtaining the subscriber information, including name, the service address if it's a landline, or the mailing address if the number rings to a cellular telephone or a pager.

If those two searches come back as "no record," then you'll know that, in all probability, you've got a nonpublished, cellular, or pager number. But there are some other possibilities. For example, if the client had picked the number off of her Caller ID instead of finding it in her husband's billfold, it could be a trunk-line number, such as a T-1 line, from a commercial establishment.

Your next step is to call the phone number and see who answers. In this day of voice mail and answering machines, there's a 50-50 chance you'll get a recorded greeting, and more often than not it will include the subscriber's first name, or even last name. And if the number is assigned to a pager, you'll know that right away, too.

> **Crime Scene Clues**
>
> **Data brokers,** also known as **information brokers,** are individuals or companies that have access to specialized sources of information or use advanced techniques to gather information and then resell the information to the private investigator. An example of this would be asking an information broker to obtain a nonpublished telephone number, or a list of credit card charges that the PI couldn't get himself.

If you find out your number is a pager, nonpublished, or a cell phone, *data brokers* and *information brokers* are useful tools, too. The next few sections will explain more options.

Breaking the Pager

If the number goes to a pager, as a PI you have two possibilities:

- ◆ You, the PI, can go to an information broker who specializes in telephone numbers, pay him $50 to get the subscriber information, and turn around and charge the client $125.

◆ You can page the number and wait for the return call. If you decide to page, here are four rules:

1. Use a phone that has Caller ID.

2. Use a *safe phone* that you can answer with a "hello" (not a business phone).

3. Use a phone that is neither your home phone nor a number that anybody associated with you would recognize.

4. Consider paging the number later in the evening so that the page is returned from the subject's home.

Now, when the page is returned, answer the phone with a business name. Make one up, but not a PI firm name. Pretend you are the switchboard operator of a very small company. The person returning the call will tell you that she was just paged from your number. She will probably ask you what kind of business you're in. Your response to her question is very important and can make the difference between her hanging up and your getting the information you want. Tell her, "Oh, it's complicated, give me your name and I'll see who paged you."

Eight times out of 10, you'll get the name. The other two times, the person will hang up. If she does hang up, wait 15 minutes, and page again. If she calls back, this time she'll give you her name. If she won't return the page again, then hopefully the Caller ID will give you a lead. I would immediately run a reverse on the number from the Caller ID. If you waited until evening to page the number, there's good chance your subject may have called from her home. You should get what you're looking for right there. If you didn't take my advice because you couldn't wait until evening, then she may have been calling from a business telephone. Give it 30 minutes and then call the number from the Caller ID and see who answers. If it's a business and she answers, you've got her. If she doesn't answer, ask the person who does whether any salespeople just left, because somebody returned a page from there about 30 minutes ago but didn't leave her name. Does anyone, by chance, know who that might have been?

Crime Scene Clues

A **safe phone** is a telephone that has the following characteristics: It is not traceable back to the user; it does not reveal its number to the Caller ID services on outgoing calls, and it does have Caller ID service for incoming calls; and it is set up in such a way that it can be answered in any manner necessary and is used for only one case at a time. As a good PI you should have one of these phone lines available in your office at all times.

Breaking the Nonpublished Number

Getting subscriber information for nonpublished numbers is difficult. A PI can always resort to a telephone information broker, pay the $50 and get on with his life. But if you're not a licensed PI, most of these data brokers won't deal with you.

So here is a technique, a pretext call, that works most of the time. Actually, in my 20 years in the business, I don't recall it ever having failed. In Chapter 16, we talk at length about the do's and don'ts of pretext telephone calls. You need to read that section before attempting this particular pretext call.

The pretext goes like this: You call the number from a safe telephone. When it is answered, identify yourself as a representative of a major pizza home-delivery company (be specific—use the name of a pizzeria in your local area that the person you're calling will recognize). Tell him if he'll answer three quick questions, you'll send him a coupon for a free large pizza.

The questions are ...

1. Have you ordered home-delivery pizza from (insert the name of the company) within the last three months?

2. If so, how many times per month do you call for home delivery? If never, do you know where the closest home-delivery outlet is?

3. Are you familiar with Sicilian-style pizza and have you ever ordered that?

Now, you don't give a hoot about the answers to the preceding questions, so just get through them as quickly as you can. Next, thank him very much for his time. Tell him you'll send him a coupon for a free large pizza and thank him again for his participation in this survey. To what address should you send the coupon? If he's gone with you this far, he'll always give you his address. And what name should you address it to? Bingo, you've got his name and address. If he wants it to go to a post office box, take the box information (it might come in handy later), but tell him that these coupons can't be mailed and the delivery folks will drop one off, so you need the street address and apartment number, if any.

Breaking the Cell Number

Again, the easiest way for a PI to get a break on a cellular telephone number is to pay the information broker. It is quicker for me to fax the number to my phone guy and get a fax back from him the next day with the information I need. The client is footing the bill, anyway.

Elementary, My Dear Watson

I've been told by people in the telephone directory assistance business that cellular phone directory information will soon be available. Why the change? The industry's announced reason was that cellular time was so expensive, the cellular providers didn't want their customers to be bothered with spurious calls. The real reason was they didn't want to give up their customer database because of the fierce competition between cell phone companies. But now, with the explosion in cell phone use, the thinking is changing and in the very near future you'll find cellular directory information available at different sites on the web. I'm sure you'll be able to do a reverse search as well.

Why the turnaround by the cellular companies? The regular carriers are making big bucks selling their directory information to resellers. With the intense competition in the cell phone market, the cell companies want in on that same kind of profitable action. It'll generate another revenue stream for the almighty bottom line.

If you're not a PI and don't have a "phone guy," then you'll have to go to a PI to get it done, or call the number and pretext it. You can use the same pizza pretext that we used for the nonpublished number, with a few changes in the questions. Start like this: "We know we've called you on your cell phone, but this will take less than 60 seconds and we'll send you a coupon for a free large pizza from (name the pizza company) if you'll answer two questions for us:

1. Have you ever used your cell phone to order a pizza from us?

2. Have you ever used your cell phone to order any other type of carryout food, so that it would be ready when you got there? If so, what type and how often?

Thank you very much for your time. At what address should we send you the coupon for the free pizza? And what name should we address it to?"

We've had pretty good success with this pretext for cell phones. It is not unusual for the person answering to say they don't have time to talk right then. If they say that, ask if it's okay if you call them later. There's no gimmick and you're not trying to sell them anything, so most people are willing to cooperate.

Sources for Nonpublished Numbers

Just because your telephone number is nonpublished doesn't mean I can't get it. "Nonpublished" simply means the telephone company won't give it to me willingly. The subscriber has requested the phone company not release his phone number for publication. Fair enough.

What we find, however, is while the subscribers have made that request to the telephone company, they violate their own instructions by giving it to the cable company, the electric company, the water company, the pizza delivery company, the newspaper for home delivery, service and repair companies of all kinds, the credit bureaus, their employer, the schools their children attend; the list of folks who have the "nonpublished" number goes on and on and on.

As we discussed in Chapter 7, in many locales the utilities are publicly owned and so their records are public. All you have to do is go to the source, examine the records, and you can get the infamous nonpublished number.

If the utility records where you live aren't public, then look at your list of friends and see if any of them or their spouses work at the cable company, the newspaper, or any other place where your subject has probably left his number. If you think of someone, ask him or her to get the number for you. But there are a couple of reasons why you don't want to ask this favor of anybody you know who works for the telephone company.

First, it is a violation of the telephone company rules for employees to divulge proprietary information, and second, it could be considered theft of information. The likelihood of either you or your friend being prosecuted for it are nil, but still, your friend could lose his or her job.

If you can't think of anyone, then you'll have to get a little more creative. You will need to know the social security number and the address of the person whose telephone number you're seeking.

Call the local cable company from a safe telephone and pretend you're the subject. You're thinking about making changes to your service and would like to review your service with them.

CAUTION

Sammy the Snitch

Occasionally, in some jurisdictions, a private investigator's techniques may be considered borderline legal. I would never advocate breaking the law, but to get the information you need, you may have to go right up to the line. Clients ask me all the time to break the law, tap a phone for them, pick a locked file cabinet that doesn't belong to them, fabricate evidence, and lie for them in court.

If you have any questions as to the legality of a PI technique in your city, don't do it. There is always more than one way to get the information you need, so there is no reason to break the law. I am personally acquainted with some investigators who spent 18 months in jail for illegally obtaining social security wage information and then reselling it. It didn't seem like a big deal at the time … until they were arrested and prosecuted.

The customer service person will probably ask you to verify the last four digits of your social security number. Be sure and give him your subject's, and not yours by mistake. When he asks for your telephone number, tell him you just changed it and you don't give the new number out, but your address is such and such. He'll pull up the subject's account. Talk to him about the premium services available and their prices. After a few minutes, trust between the two of you will have been established. As the conversation winds down, you tell him you've decided not to make any changes. But oh, by the way, what telephone number do they have for you? He'll give it to you and you can tell him, yeah, that's the right number, you must have given it to them before.

If you can't find a friend who can get the nonpublished number for you, and you can't con it out of the cable company, then call your local PI. She'll go to her broker of telephone information and get it for you. It'll probably cost you about $125. If she wants a lot more than that, find yourself another PI.

Pay Phones: Location, Location, Location

My client's 16-year-old son ran away. Anybody who's dealt with a teenager would think my client should be ecstatic. The kid's finally out the door, but no, the client wanted him back. And the kid didn't even take the family car or his girlfriend with him. Go figure. This particular runaway is someone I've picked up and returned to his family four times in four years, so I knew the kid's friends and haunts pretty well.

This time, the boy apparently headed south to a city 200 miles away. The girlfriend cooperated with us to some degree because she was more mature than the boy and genuinely concerned for his safety, though she wouldn't rat the kid out entirely. She never told us exactly where we could find him. She did say he would routinely call her from pay phones and she would turn around and call him back because he didn't have any money.

I went to my phone source and got a list of all the calls the girlfriend made from her cell phone to the area code where the boy was suppose to be. That cost my client about $250 for the first 100 telephone calls on the girl's bill and a dollar a call for each call thereafter.

I then ran a reverse search on the numbers. Pay phones frequently have repeating numbers or a successive series of numbers in their phone number, such as 305-768-9999 or 305-768-3456. However, that's frequently but not *always* the case, so don't count on it. After running the reverse search, it was pretty easy to figure out which numbers were pay phones and which weren't. Next, we needed the physical address for the phones because we wanted to stake them out to find the boy. We'll talk more about how to find runaway kids in Chapter 20.

Sometimes the direct and honest approach works just as well as being sneaky. The locations and phone numbers to pay phones, while not published in the telephone directories, are not a secret. In this case, I called the telephone company business office and told them I was a private investigator. I explained the facts of the case and in a few minutes, after the customer service representative checked with her supervisor, she gave me the street address where the phones were located.

I took the street locations and plotted them out on a city map. They all fell within about a three-block radius in West Palm Beach, Fla. You'll have to read Chapter 21 to see if we found the runaway boy, but now you know how to find the location of a pay phone if you have the number.

There are websites that provide some lists of pay phones, the numbers for the phones, and where the phones are located. The lists on these sites are not very extensive. You can use any search engine to find the sites and check a number. You might get lucky. You can start by checking these sites: www.payphone-project.com, www.payphone-directory.org, www.geep.net/paydata. Be sure and check the links on those above. You'll find links to other sites with payphone lists.

Phreaking the Phones

Telephone phreaking is similar to computer hacking, only it involves breaking into the telephone system. A phreak is someone who wants to learn about the telephone system. Some phreaks take this knowledge and use it to make free calls from pay telephones and to circumvent paying long distance charges on private phones. Both are clearly illegal, constitute theft of services, and might land you in jail.

Elementary, My Dear Watson

In the 1960s and the early '70s, there was a proliferation of "black boxes." Black boxes used a variation in voltage to trick the phone company equipment into thinking that a telephone call coming into your phone with the black box attached continued to ring, when in fact you'd already answered it. Therefore, anybody could call you long distance and there would be no toll charges. When the phone company switching equipment went electronic, not to mention digital, it made black boxes obsolete.

Phreakers now have a multitude of different boxes, their functions known by the color of the box. There are red boxes, beige boxes, violet boxes, magenta boxes … the list of colors goes on and on. Also, some boxes have names, such as invisible box, stop box, Pandora's box, and soda-can box, just to name a few.

With long distance rates below 5¢ a minute and most cellular companies offering nationwide long distance service at the same price as regular airtime charges, it's difficult to understand why anybody would expend such effort trying to cheat the phone companies out of long distance charges.

However, there are other reasons to learn phreaking techniques. If you, as a PI, have the least bit of interest in telephones, telephone taps, the ins and outs of the telephone system, Caller ID, or call blocking, then you might find phreaking an interesting sideline.

A good place to start is the web-based newsgroups (usenet) alt.phreaking and alt.2600 You can find these by going to the alt. newsgroups provided by most Internet Service Providers. It's incredible how much you'll learn by lurking there.

You might want to look at two websites to get you started:

- www.artofhacking.com. They have a terrific write-up on all of the boxes that have emerged since the demise of the black box. They also have a lot of information on the Canadian telephone system and Canadian pay phones.

- www.nettwerked.net. Nettwerked has a good list of FAQs (frequently asked questions) and other information about phreaking and some good links.

Another interesting source is a magazine called *2600*. It's sold at most Barnes & Nobles and deals with hacking and phreaking. *2600's* website is www.2600.com.

A professional PI should have some knowledge of telephone systems and, short of going to a phone company school, the phreaking community is probably the best place to get it.

The Least You Need to Know

- To obtain telephone data from the phone company, one must bypass the automated directory assistance system.

- Directory information costs can be cut in half by asking a live operator for two listings at the same time.

- Directory assistance operators will verify a nonpublished address if you give them the address, but they will not give you the address outright.

- Phone numbers, pager numbers, and cellular numbers can be broken by use of pretext phone calls.

- Nonpublished numbers can be found in public record information and retrieved from sources other than the telephone company.

- The phone company representative will provide you with the locations of pay telephones if you convince him or her you have a good reason.

- Phreaking phones is similar to computer hacking, and there are phone-phreaking resources on the web.

Chapter 12

Techniques of Interview and Interrogation

In This Chapter

- Learning preparation techniques
- Getting the most out of a witness
- Handling informants
- Outsmarting the suspects into confessing
- Taking notes in the interview
- Principles behind recorded statements
- Digital cameras and the witness interview

Obtaining information from people is almost always the largest part of a private investigator's job. Attorneys ask investigators to track down witnesses and take statements from them. Insurance companies want accidents investigated. Businesses ask investigators to solve internal thefts. Parents need their runaway teenagers returned. Each of these types of cases involves interviewing witnesses and potential witnesses, and interrogating suspects.

A witness is an individual who may have testimony pertinent to an investigation. A suspect is an individual who may have committed or aided the commission of a crime that is under investigation.

Witnesses and suspects sometimes are very friendly, cooperative and willing to be interviewed. This is especially true in employee theft cases where the interview is taking place during working hours. This gives the employees a break from their regular routine.

Most other witness interviews are done under less-than-favorable conditions. The interview may be at the county jail or a state prison. It might take place on a busy street corner with horns honking every few minutes, or on a front porch during a heavy rainstorm. In addition to all of the outside distractions, the witnesses usually have no interest of their own in the case you're investigating. They just happen to have been present when the accident occurred and now you, the PI, have interrupted their busy schedule.

In this chapter, we'll examine some techniques and methods that will aid you in extracting the information from witnesses and make it possible for you to get those suspects who have the most to lose, the guilty ones, to reveal the details of their crimes.

Be Prepared

There has never been better advice for debriefing a witness or interviewing a suspect than to be prepared. Before beginning an interview, the PI has to be completely familiar with all of the facts of the case.

Attorneys and insurance companies will usually call with a new case assignment or fax the assignment to your office. It is a good practice to go to the client's office and review the entire file concerning the case before beginning the investigation. I made a practice of this whenever possible for two very good reasons.

First, you're the investigator. You know what will help you locate your witness much better than your client. There may be nuggets of information in those files that your client doesn't even realize are important, such as license tags, phone numbers, dates of birth, and social security numbers. Employment data for your witness may be in there, but the client didn't relay that to you. If you want to set up an appointment with the witness, it's usually easier to contact him or her at work first. Most people would rather be interviewed at home, but sometimes finding them is difficult. If you know where they work, you can at least contact them there and set up the interview for after hours.

Second, going to your client's office and reviewing the file gives you an opportunity to meet face-to-face. I can't tell you how many additional cases I've picked up by going to an attorney's office and walking past other attorneys in the practice. They see me going down the hall and invariably I hear, "Well, since you're here, I've got a case I could use some help on." It never fails. Even the attorney or claims adjuster you originally came to see will frequently find additional work or other files for you to review. Whenever it's feasible, go to the client's office.

In making your preparations for the interview, write a list of the items you need to cover. Sometimes the interview takes an unexpected turn; the witness reveals some information of which you were unaware, and in the heat of following the new lead, you forget to ask everything you needed to ask about the facts you had to begin with. That's why you should always make a list of the topics you want to cover. If the interview gets really exciting for some reason, be sure to go over your list before you leave the witness. That way you're sure to cover every topic you originally intended.

Just last week, I sent one of my investigators to a small town, a three-hour drive away. When I went over his report, I saw he forgot to ask some really pertinent questions. He didn't make a list before he left as I'd taught him to do, so he had to drive six hours round-trip to redo the interview on his own time and at his own expense.

Get Them to Like You

In conducting interviews, you have to give the person you're interviewing a reason why he or she should tell you what you need to know. Logical reasons why the witness should cooperate are actually the least effective. Emotion works better than reason. One of the best emotional reasons for him or her to cooperate is because your witness likes you and wants to help *you*.

If you're interviewing a driver who witnessed a car accident, she really doesn't care about helping some attorney win a case where the attorney is going to take 30 or 40 percent of the settlement. Most people don't like attorneys anyway. Her dealings with attorneys have probably always been negative and she considers them a subspecies of the human race. Her sympathies may lie with the other side. She certainly isn't interested in helping a big insurance conglomerate save a few bucks at the expense of some poor old guy who ran into another person's car accidentally. So why should she help you at all?

The answer is to make her like you. Become her friend. Once a friendship has developed, she's now invested time and emotion in this relationship. Now by helping you, she unconsciously feels she is helping to improve the relationship between the two of you.

When you knock on the door, greet her with a smile and genuine warmth. Once inside, survey your surroundings immediately. There are two reasons why you want to do this:

1. Glance around the room when you enter to make sure that there is no danger present—nobody hiding in back of the couch or behind the front door, for example, with a weapon, intent on inflicting serious bodily harm to you. You may think this is a paranoid thing to do, but you just never know what was going on in that house or apartment at the time you knocked on the door. You could be walking in on a drug deal or a violent domestic dispute and the couple stopped in order to answer the door. It is better to err on the side of caution.

2. People surround themselves with what's important in their lives or what's of interest to them. Look around to find some common ground or an interesting hobby that your witness has. If you can discover her passion, what really motivates her and makes her life worthwhile, then you are on the road to making a new friend.

Once you discover what makes her tick, find a common element with that part of her life. If you're a sailor and she has a picture of a sailboat on the wall, talk sailing. If the woman you're trying to interview is busy cooking dinner and the kids are screaming, pick up the screaming baby and keep her occupied while you talk to the mother. If you can make friends with the child, the mom will be your friend, too.

Talk about her problems, her life, what interests her. Be charming and witty if you can. Once she's told you what is going on in her life, you've succeeded in subconsciously tying yourself to that part of her life that makes life worth living. Now, instead of being an outsider, a representative of one of those "damn insurance companies," you're a real person with a tie to the better part of her life. And most importantly, she's now emotionally involved with you, even if she's not actually aware of it.

Once you've established that bond of trust, the witness will tell you everything you want to know, as long as your questions don't break that bond.

At one time during my career with the FBI, I was assigned to the Phoenix division. I had a road trip that covered three Indian reservations: the Pima, the Maricopa, and the northern part of the Papago. Early every Sunday morning, I'd receive a telephone call from the tribal police indicating that some federal crime had been committed, typically burglary, rape, assault with a deadly weapon, or homicide. I'd leave my bed and travel to the reservation. Generally, by mid-morning the crime would be solved, the perpetrator arrested, and the prisoner handcuffed with his hands behind his back and strapped into the front seat with the seatbelt where I could keep a close eye on him. I'd transport the prisoner, a two-and-a-half-hour drive, back to the Maricopa County jail in Phoenix.

Elementary, My Dear Watson

Crimes on a government reservation fall under federal jurisdiction. Military bases and Indian reservations are considered government reservations. Typically, on Indian reservations, misdemeanors between reservation inhabitants are investigated by the Bureau of Indian Affairs police and prosecuted in tribal court. Felonies or crimes punishable by more than six months in jail are investigated by the Federal Bureau of Investigation and prosecuted in the United States district federal court.

The suspect's rights would have been read to him and usually he would have waived those rights, signing a document to that effect. During this drive to the jail, I'd engage him in conversation. Invariably we'd talk about his life on the reservation and his frustrations with life in general. Before the trip was over, he would have told me how some part of his life made him commit the crime I'd arrested him for. It was never his fault, some outside force or inner demon made him do it, but he always confessed to the act itself. Because of the ironclad confession I obtained during the drive to the jail, I never had one of those cases go to trial. Every one of them pleaded guilty.

There was no rubber hose, no coercion, just concern for the suspect's troubles and his life. You know, some of these guys committed the most heinous of crimes, brutal, body-mutilating crimes, sometimes against their own mother. But during that drive I always found a redeeming side to each one of them. I never arrested a man I didn't grow to like during that ride back to Phoenix. And I think the feeling was mutual.

Informants

Working with *informants* has similarities to interviewing witnesses, but there are differences as well. You must first develop the same level of trust and rapport with an informant as we talked about in the preceding section. Informants usually have some motivating factor, something that drives them to help you besides the bond you develop with them. This could be a secret desire

Crime Scene Clues

An **informant** is an individual that cooperates, usually without the knowledge of others involved in the case, by providing information during an investigation. She may or may not be a witness or a participant in the particular case under investigation. Frequently, an informant may receive compensation, or other benefit, for her information, whereas a witness never should.

to be a private investigator themselves. It's good to kid with your informants about "putting them on the payroll." It feeds their need to live an exciting life vicariously through yours.

Forget what you've seen on television about police and informants. The tough-cop routine, slamming the informant against the wall, threatening him, and then expecting him to work for you is ridiculous and just pure fiction. You should never call an informant a "snitch." It's derogatory, and if you think about him in derogatory terms, your actions, mannerisms, and tone of voice when speaking will betray your true thoughts. He will sense your demeaning manner and you can kiss that informant good-bye. Remember, the informant is a friend first, an informant second.

When Does a Private Investigator Use an Informant?

An informant can simply be a neighbor of a subject in a domestic case under surveillance who will let you know when the subject arrives home. This informant may call you when your client's wife, who is supposed to be at the gym, just showed up for a different kind of workout. To motivate this informant, you must build the bond we spoke about. The chances are, however, that the two neighbors have some sort of ongoing dispute. It could be something as trivial as your subject's dog relieving himself on your informant's front lawn every morning. Regardless, whatever the reason, your informant is probably using you to get even with your subject.

How Do You Come by Informants?

An informant may have started out as a witness in a nursing home abuse case whom you've previously interviewed. You've established that sense of trust and now another case has arisen at that same nursing home. She may not know anything about the new case, but she is in a position to tell you who does know the facts and who was present, even though she has no first-hand knowledge about the current situation.

A smart PI will keep a list of people whom he has helped and have helped him in the past. Having good contacts, whether they are in the local police department, at the headquarters of the FBI in Washington, D.C., or a maid in a nursing home, makes the PI's job easier, and him more productive.

Can You Pay Informants?

Money and informants seem to go hand in hand. You can perform favors for informants. You can pay informants. But you can never pay an informant if that person may be a potential witness in a case. A witness may hint to you that for a little money her memory might improve. After all, her testimony might save your client, an insurance company, millions of dollars. Regardless, you can't pay her.

If a witness were to be paid by a private investigator and then actually be called to testify, her testimony would be thrown out. You may see witnesses paid on television. No matter. You can't do it. Now, with law enforcement and criminal cases, the story changes. Police can pay informants, but civil cases have different rules than criminal law. There's no quicker way to be embarrassed in open court in a civil matter, lose the case, and lose a very good client at the same time, than by paying a potential civil witness. Don't do it. The exception to that rule is the "expert" witness, who can be paid.

Interrogating the Suspects

Do private investigators ever get involved in criminal investigations? Absolutely. Some PIs make a career out of working criminal-defense cases. Even though our firm doesn't specialize in criminal-defense investigations, we usually have a homicide or suspicious suicide case going at any given moment. Frequently, in the defense of a *premise liability* case, we will be investigating rapes and assaults that were alleged to have occurred on our client's property. We'll talk more about premise liability cases in the next chapter.

When interviewing suspects in criminal cases, it may not be easy to establish a bond of trust. Most criminals are street smart and believe in their hearts that they are smarter than you, the investigator. For certain, they may have more street smarts than you do. A good investigator can turn the criminal's "smarter than you" self-image to his advantage in interrogating the suspect.

After a high-speed chase through downtown Phoenix, I arrested Daniel Black for interstate transportation of a stolen motor vehicle and assault on a federal agent. He'd assaulted my partner and fellow FBI agent who'd accompanied me to interview Black concerning his attempt to obtain false identity papers.

A week or so later, Daniel called me from the county jail and requested I come down to talk. He claimed concern for his wife who'd escaped during the chase, but whom we later identified

Crime Scene Clues

A **premise liability** case involves the allegation that a property owner was negligent by not curing some default in the premise or real property owned or managed by the defendant, and this negligence led to the harm of the plaintiff. An example of this could be the plaintiff alleging that the defendant failed to provide adequate exterior lighting and the ensuing darkness caused a rape or assault inflicted upon the plaintiff.

and charged as well. Previously, he'd had shoulder-length hair, but when he entered the interview room, I noticed he sported a completely shaved head. I ignored the change in his appearance and listened to his stated concerns about his wife, who'd made bail for herself, leaving him in jail. I think he actually called for the interview (he was represented by counsel, but since he'd initiated the contact, I could talk to him without his attorney present) to try to find out how much we knew about his numerous and varied criminal activities.

After a few minutes, he couldn't stand the fact that I'd asked nothing about his shaved head. In order to show how "smart" he was, he admitted he'd shaved his head so when he was put into a lineup, his appearance would be radically different and the witnesses wouldn't be able to identify him. That statement constituted an admission of guilt and I used it at his trial to convict him. He got eight years in the federal penitentiary because he just had to demonstrate how much smarter he was than the young FBI agent.

Whatever the case, if you can figure out what motivates your suspect, you can successfully interrogate him. A client called me just about a month ago. This client held a fairly high political office. His home had been burgled three days previously and a safe containing over $40,000 in cash had been stolen.

The facts were as follows: My client and his wife, the Smiths, returned home one evening to find a glass panel in the front door broken. A baseball bat lay on the front stoop. Wisely, rather than entering the house, they called the police. The officers arrived and found the door locked. They reached through where the broken pane had been and opened the door. When the police entered the home, the burglar alarm sounded. The police inspected the house and found the burglar was not present. The Smiths entered the home and discovered the safe, which had been in a hall closet, was now missing. They reported to the police the safe had held $20,000 in cash, but insisted to me the figure was really closer to $40,000.

Who committed the burglary? After interviewing my clients, the Smiths, I was convinced that there had indeed been a burglary, the Smiths were actual victims, and that this was not just an attempt at insurance fraud. The facts of the case and the burglar alarm being armed when the police arrived gave me three good clues as to the identity of the thief. Can you guess what they are?

- Whoever broke in and took the safe knew the alarm code, turned it off when he entered, and reset it when leaving with the safe.
- The reason he took the entire safe was, while he knew the alarm code, he didn't know the combination to the safe and hence couldn't open it on the spot.

- The psychology behind rearming the alarm when he left indicated to me the burglar had concern for the Smiths and didn't want anybody else to burglarize the house while the Smiths were out; that, or else the burglar set the alarm out of force of habit.

Evaluating those three reasonable deductions, I decided the thief was a regular visitor to the house and probably a family member.

We can make other deductions based upon the facts I've given you, but those are the important ones. I went through the list of possible suspects with the Smiths and pretty well narrowed it down to their 21-year-old unemployed son Luke.

Luke lived in a trailer park with his girlfriend, whom the Smiths did not approve of. I went to the trailer park to interview the prime suspect. Luke was a thin white boy, who was unsuccessfully trying to grow a mustache. A bare whisper of straggly dark hair grazed his upper lip. I showed my private investigator's identification to Luke and asked him to open the trunk of his car. He didn't balk at the request and didn't ask why. I knew then he was good for the burglary because if he'd been innocent he would have protested. Protesting wouldn't have necessarily made him innocent. A guilty man might have protested too, maybe even more, but not protesting, combined with the other facts certainly convinced me he did it. When he opened the trunk I also knew the money wouldn't be in there or he never would have opened it so readily.

I went through the motions searching the car, just in case he'd left some of the money hidden there. Nothing. Luke told me his girlfriend was pregnant but his folks didn't know about the pregnancy. Luke appeared vulnerable and I knew he wouldn't fare well in the state penitentiary.

Elementary, My Dear Watson

On occasion, a case may arise that lends itself to some sort of a percentage for a recovery rather than an hourly rate. In most civil cases, private investigators are prohibited from working on a percentage because they are suppose to be "finders of fact" and if their fee is dependent upon the success of the case it could lead to a conflict of interest. This is especially true if the investigator will be a witness in the case.

However, if the case is similar to the Smith safe burglary described in this chapter, then a percentage of the monies recovered would be an acceptable fee arrangement. Use the sample contract in Appendix B and modify it at the beginning of the case to delineate the fee agreement before you begin the case. The risk is though, if you don't succeed, you won't get paid.

I asked him if the police had been there yet. They hadn't. "The police are coming," I told him. "They'll be here shortly." I explained to him very graphically and in great detail what life in prison is like for young men of his slight build and complexion. Next, I put myself in a position to help him, to become a friend with his best interest in mind. I told him the only way for us to keep him from that fate was to get the money he'd stolen and return it to his parents before the police got there. Once the police had him, there was nothing his parents or I could do to help.

After my clear description of prison life and his alternatives, it took Luke about 30 seconds to step to the side of his trailer and begin digging with his bare hands. In a few minutes, he'd dug up a plastic container filled with bills. We took it inside and counted it together. I photographed him with the money, wrote out a receipt, and had him sign it. Together, we took it back to his parents.

> **Crime Scene Clues**
>
> **Results billing** is the practice of charging more than a standard hourly rate if the results achieved justify a higher bill or a higher hourly rate.

The police had a three-day head start in solving that burglary. It took me a little over an hour. Why was I able to solve it when they couldn't? First, the use of a little deductive reasoning. Second, I was able to read what would motivate Luke into confessing. Lastly, I was more motivated than the police, because I needed results to justify my rather large bill to my client. The police get paid whether they solve the crime or not. It's not unusual in a case like this to use *results billing*.

Copious Notes

When interviewing witnesses or suspects, always take copious notes. You should have a yellow legal pad or other type of notebook to record as much as possible of your interview. It's not necessary to write down the questions that you ask the witness, but you should record in a personal shorthand or scribble how the witness responds.

Next, you should initial your original notes, date them, and, after using them to write your report, the original notes should be placed in an envelope and maintained in the case file.

There are three very good reasons for this:

◆ Memories are not perfect. The interview will be absolutely clear in your mind when you leave the witness, but it may be a day or two before you write or dictate your report. In the intervening time, you will forget some of the facts the witness had related to you. Your detailed notes of the interview will refresh your memory and make the report you deliver to your client more accurate.

- ◆ A witness will change her story. Six months to perhaps four years later, you may be called upon to testify as to your interview with that person. The witness also will be called to testify. Her memory of the accident will have been colored by what she's read, or seen, or been told by other people. Sometimes a witness will change facts intentionally; sometimes she just can't remember.

- ◆ Your attorney, the opposing counsel, or the judge will ask you to produce the original notes. Your original notes are considered documents produced in the normal course of business, and as such, are admissible into court. They carry considerable weight in our judicial system. When the witness's story, four years later, conflicts with your reporting, your attorney or the opposing attorney may ask you to produce your original notes. If your notes have been dated and initialed and are clear on the point in question, your testimony will be considered factual, not the witness's. When a case is won because of your professionalism, charge the client more. You deserve it and he will pay it.

A successful resolution to a case makes the client happy, the attorney happy and you should be happy, too. The attorney who hired you will usually suggest that you get your bill to him right away so that he can submit it to client for prompt payment. If the case was a big win for the client, and you don't have a signed contract with him, you may at that time want to bump your rate up a notch. Nobody will balk because you're worth it. You may have just saved your client a million dollars. If you're a successful PI and produce winning cases for your clients, you should consider raising your rates anyway.

Recording the Interview

Attorneys use investigators to locate potential witnesses and interview them because it's cheaper for the client to pay the investigator than it is to pay the attorney. It makes no sense to have the attorney running around interviewing folks who may or may not have any information about the case.

Once the investigator finds a witness that has information germane to the investigation, then the attorney may schedule a *deposition* for the witness. Depositions are expensive and time-consuming and require that a court reporter be

> **Crime Scene Clues**
>
> A **deposition** is a statement made under oath by a witness, usually written or recorded, that may be used in court at a later time. If there is the likelihood that the deponent will not be available later, for instance, due to illness, it is not uncommon for the deposition to be videotaped. The deponent is the witness being deposed.

present to record the questions and answers. Also, the opposing counsel is present. An attorney would not want to be deposing everybody on the block where the accident occurred. He'd only want to depose the folks who actually witnessed the accident or had some first-hand knowledge of contributing factors.

For instance, you, the PI, might find a woman who can testify that the driver of one of the vehicles involved in an accident you're investigating was drunk when he left a party. Later, that driver caused the accident. The witness, although she didn't see the accident, could testify to the driver's condition shortly before the accident when he left the party. In addition, the attorney is not going to want to depose a witness that would hurt his case.

Sammy the Snitch

Unfortunately, the law in civil cases is not always about truth, but more about which side can present its view of the truth most effectively. The PI should not take sides in a case. He should report the facts accurately. If the facts are not good for his client, then that's too bad. Report the facts and let the chips fall where they may. If you start skewing the facts, your client will not be happy and you will tarnish your reputation and quickly lose clients. If there is information out there that is going to hurt your client's case, he needs to know about it because you can be sure the other side will bring it up. At least your client can be prepared for the worst.

You, the investigator, need to get all the facts, good or bad, to your client. But your client, the attorney in this case, doesn't want the opposing side to know there is a witness out there that will hurt his case. If he deposes a witness harmful to his case, the other side will be at the deposition and obviously know it.

In order to make sure you have all of the facts and don't omit anything from your report, you should consider recording the interview. I use a small microcassette recorder. The PI has to have the permission of the witness to record the interview. Getting permission is not always easy.

One approach that seems to work is to tell the person you're interviewing that recording the conversation would really save you a lot of the trouble of taking handwritten notes. Would she mind? Don't make a big production out of it. If the approach is low key and seems to be the normal thing that you always do, most people will not object. But if you make a big production out of setting up the recorder, the witness may change her mind.

Once you have the witness's permission to record, there are four items that have to be at the very beginning of the recording:

1. State your name and occupation.

2. State the date and location where the interview is taking place.

3. State the witness's name and indicate that she has given you permission to record this conversation. "Mrs. Brown, you are aware that we are recording this interview and I have your permission, is that correct?" Make sure the witness verbally says yes to that question. A nodding of the head can't be heard on the tape when you produce it in court two years later.

4. Indicate the subject matter of the interview: an accident that occurred on such and such a date at a certain intersection.

Don't give the original recorded statement to your client. See Chapter 23, for details on handling recordings and maintaining the chain of custody on the evidence. Some clients will ask for the original tape. Give them a duplicate. Besides violating the chain of custody on the evidence, attorneys are notorious for losing things. Produce the original tape when you go to court.

Photographing the Witnesses

It's the practice in my PI firm to carry a digital camera whenever we're going out to do an interview. Remember, in the preceding section on interrogating suspects I indicated I'd photographed the son with the money? It would be hard for him to later deny that he stole the safe if I had a photograph of him holding the money. In Chapter 17, we'll talk about why you always photograph evidence. Just as in that case, we also find it's a good idea to photograph the witness you're interviewing.

Many of my attorney-clients like to see what the potential witness looks like. Will he make a good witness on the stand? Will he appeal to a jury, if necessary? We always try to photograph the witness if he will allow it. Sometimes he'll refuse and there is nothing you can do about it. If the person you're interviewing is a victim, you may want photos of cuts, bruises, or other injuries.

I recommend digital cameras because then, if you have the proper equipment, you can embed the photograph in your written report. See Chapter 4 for more details on how to do this. You can also always print a hard copy onto photo paper if you have a good color printer. Flash the witness when you can. There is no downside to doing so.

The Least You Need to Know

- Never go to an interview unprepared. It's better to go to the client's office to review the file, because the investigator knows better what he needs out of the file than the client does.

- The best way to gain a witness's assistance is to befriend her. Have the witness invest in your mutual relationship and then you'll have her help.

- Informants should become your friends and be treated with respect. Do not be demeaning to an informant and then expect his complete cooperation.

- Successfully interrogating a suspect requires the PI to outsmart her and to understand what will motivate her to confess.

- During a witness interview, it is imperative to take complete notes and retain the original notes, as they may be called into evidence later at a trial.

- With permission, tape recording a witness interview is a good idea. Never give up the original recording unless you have to produce it in court.

- A digital photograph of the witness makes for better reports and allows the client an opportunity to evaluate the witness.

Chapter **13**

The Neighborhood Investigation

In This Chapter

- Learning the steps to neighborhood investigations
- Searching for the know-it-all neighbor
- Weaving neighborhoods with liability investigations
- Matching talents with assignments
- Fibbing to the neighbors
- Checking out the dirt … literally
- Finding other crimes, other times

At some point in your life as an investigator, you will inevitably have to perform what is termed a "neighborhood investigation," usually referred to in the trade as just a "neighborhood."

If you're investigating a burglary, for instance, and you are going to "do a neighborhood," you'll want to knock on every door in the immediate area and interview the neighbors. If you have the time and the budget, you should check with neighbors up to several blocks away. Why? Because burglars don't usually park their cars in front of the home or business they're burglarizing. If you want a description of the burglars' getaway vehicle, it's not going to come from the guy across the street from the victim.

There are several techniques and important methods to conducting neighborhood investigations. If the PI is going to go to the effort to do this type of investigation, he or she might as well do so effectively. A neighborhood investigation can be one of the best investigative techniques a professional can use, and yet the inexperienced PI or lazy law enforcement detective frequently overlooks it.

The Mechanics

A neighborhood investigation really involves several steps. The most obvious is to knock on doors in the neighborhood where the accident took place, or the home was burglarized, or from where the child was kidnapped. This should be done as shortly after the inciting incident as possible. If the case is a kidnapped child, chances are the police will have beaten you there. If it's a runaway teenager, the police probably won't be involved at all. In a number of jurisdictions, the police won't respond to a home burglary where the items taken amount to less than $5,000. If your case does have police involvement and the police have already done a neighborhood, do it again.

There are three steps required to conduct an effective neighborhood investigation:

1. Knock on doors.

2. Check out the vehicles.

3. Consider the getaway car.

Performing these steps on a neighborhood investigation will be the subject of the sections that follow.

Knock on Doors

The key to success in this type of investigation is to talk to every person who was home on the day and at the time of the incident.

Let's take burglaries as an example. Chances are that when the PI arrives on the scene, it is going to be some time after the burglary occurred. Remember the son in Chapter 12 who stole the safe from his parents? The police didn't do a neighborhood investigation in that case. Had they done one, they may have found that the neighbor across the street had seen the boy at the home during the time of the burglary. We'll never know, though, because the police didn't ask. I didn't do one either, in that case, but I would have come back and done it if the son hadn't confessed to the crime.

Obviously, you have to narrow down the time frame of the offense. You do this by interviewing the victims, their family, and the immediate neighbors to get a fairly specific idea of when the burglary occurred.

Once the approximate time has been established, you have to figure out the point of entry and exit. These two points are not always the same. If the burglars entered through the back door and there are neighbors across the back fence, then that should be the first door you knock on—not because they're suspects (although you need to keep an open mind), but because they may have noticed someone cutting through their backyard and climbing the fence to get into the victim's yard.

> ### Sherlock's Secrets
>
> Take good notes while you're talking to the neighbors. Keep track of whom you've talked to, what they saw, who was home at the time of the burglary, and who wasn't home at the time you knocked on their door. If a wife tells you she wasn't home when the burglary occurred but her husband may have been, make a note of it. You're going to want to go back and talk to that husband, even though the wife says the husband didn't see anything.

The only way to do a thorough neighborhood is to talk to each and every neighbor, not just a representative from each home, but every person who may have been home at the time of the burglary. That's a lot of work and will require multiple trips through the subdivision. A PI can cut a corner in a neighborhood investigation by getting the phone numbers of each home he talks to. Then, instead of going back to the residences to speak to those who weren't home on the first visit, he can call and conduct the interview over the phone. A face-to-face interview is better, but the budget may not allow for repeated trips back to do the neighborhood.

Don't forget the kids. Kids are all over the neighborhood, riding bikes, walking to friends' houses, inline skating, and skateboarding. Kids notice strangers and strange goings-on. Be sure to speak to all the children and not just the parents when you're conducting the neighborhood investigation.

Check Out the Vehicles

After the PI has talked to all of the neighbors and the kids, the next step is for him to plant himself in his car or on a street corner at approximately the same time of day as the burglary took place. He should write down the license plate number of every car that passes by. A lot of those cars pass by that location at about the same time everyday.

He should run the tags on the cars and then contact each of those drivers and inquire if they, by chance, saw anything that might give him a lead in the case. Obviously, he can't do this at a really busy intersection where a thousand cars an hour pass, but in a residential neighborhood, he'll find cleaning people, construction workers, and delivery people that pass by on a regular schedule. If the PI can do this on the same day of the week and same time as the burglary, then his odds of finding a good witness improve significantly.

A good PI must remember, though, to ask these folks about any unusual activity in the general vicinity and not just at the crime scene. A broken-down vehicle or a person sitting alone in a car a few streets away could be important. This degree of a neighborhood investigation requires a great deal of manpower, but if the case warrants it (such as a kidnapping or mysterious disappearance) and the client's checkbook is big enough, then he should do it. Neighborhood investigations can produce some very good leads.

Consider the Getaway Car

Most criminals use some sort of transportation to flee the scene of their crime. Certainly, if it's a planned crime, getting to and away from the scene of the crime is an important part of the plan. Now, we all know that criminals are not always the smartest folks, but usually they try to think a little bit ahead. In solving burglaries or property crimes, the PI has to put himself into the mindset of the criminal. If you were a not-very-bright criminal, how would you make your escape? Where would you have parked the getaway car?

Examining the list of items stolen can give the PI an idea of how far away the getaway car may have been. If the burglars stole a big screen television, they didn't carry it very far. If they only took jewelry and small items, the car might have been several blocks away.

Why do we care about the getaway car? In movies, the getaway car is always stolen and not traceable back to the criminal, anyway. In real life, most getaway cars belong to the criminal or to an associate. When the getaway car is identified and the license plate run, you'll probably catch the criminal.

Once the investigator has identified where the getaway car might reasonably have been parked, he knows how far out to conduct the neighborhood investigation. It's possible that the getaway driver, sitting in the car with the engine idling, was spotted by a neighbor who wrote down the license number.

Find the Nosy Neighbor

In almost every neighborhood there is some person, a little old lady or gossipy man, who just has to know what is going on all of the time. It's not unusual for that type of person to be peering out her window to see what the fellow across the street is doing. And if she's not sneaking glances at the neighbors, then she's on the phone catching up on all of the rumors—who is ill, who is pregnant, and who is sleeping with whom.

At one point in my PI career, we were moving the office from one rental space to a newer one. While waiting for the new space to be readied, I ran our operation out of my home. My wife, who worked in a medical facility, had to leave for work by 6:30 every morning. A female assistant, who drove a little red sports car, would come to the house around 9. After about six weeks of this, my next-door neighbor made a point of asking my wife if the cleaning lady, who drove that little red car and came to our house everyday, was any good. She needed somebody to clean her place, too, but not as often as we did. My wife, of course, knew we didn't have a cleaning lady daily and it took her a minute to realize to whom my neighbor was referring. Women have to stick together, you know, and my neighbor was just doing her duty, making sure my wife knew that after she'd gone to work, some strange woman came to our place and always left before my wife got home.

The FBI is big on neighborhood investigations, and so am I, because they work. Sure, they're manpower intensive, but they can produce good leads.

While I was still with the bureau, I had a case where I was doing a neighborhood where I had an interest in some people at a certain address. I went to the residence and noticed the house stood vacant. The mailbox by the front door was stuffed with letters. Don't tell the postal inspectors, but I thumbed through the mail, writing down the return addresses. After walking around the house and not seeing anything of further interest, I began knocking on doors and interviewing neighbors. Eventually, in doing this neighborhood investigation, I arrived at the house directly across the street from my subject's residence. I'd noticed that at this house, the drapes were drawn. I thought perhaps nobody was at home, but there was a car in the driveway. As I started up the walkway, I noticed the drapes in the front window moved a little.

I rang the bell and this little old lady came to the door. I identified myself and showed her my credentials. She opened the door and invited me in. Next to a chair by the front window was, no kidding, a pair of binoculars. When she saw my glance toward the binoculars, a sheepish grin spread across her face. After explaining the interest I had in her former neighbor's comings and goings, she produced a lined pad of paper. On it were written 45 license plate numbers. These 45 cars had all visited her neighbor across the street during the last month the house was occupied.

I've never found anybody that nosy, or that conscientious, since. But I have found a lot of very good neighbors who write down license plate numbers of suspicious cars they see in their neighborhood.

I have developed many, many excellent leads and solved numerous cases by executing the laborious and tedious task of a neighborhood investigation. If the circumstances warrant it, there is no better investigative technique.

Premise Liability Cases

In Chapter 12, we briefly touched on premise liability cases. These cases always involve an allegation of negligence on the part of a property owner and some sort of an injury to the plaintiff. The underlying incident that starts the whole case rolling may be an assault, a rape, a homicide, or something as simple as a slip and fall on a banana peel or a dog biting a neighbor.

If the inciting incident of a premise liability case is a slip and fall in a grocery store, then a neighborhood investigation is obviously not warranted. Hopefully, the store manager will have taken the names of a number of customers and store employees who witnessed the accident.

However, in most premise liability cases that take place outside of a commercial establishment, such as in a parking lot or an apartment complex, a neighborhood investigation is definitely warranted. Keep in mind that for our purposes, the neighborhood does not have to be residential. Employees of neighboring stores make good witnesses.

One such case I worked involved the alleged abduction and rape of a young girl from her residence. It was in the heat of a southern July, about 2:30 P.M. Julie, a 15-year-old girl living with her stepmother in a large apartment complex, was brought into the hospital emergency room. She had been beaten about the face and her bottom lip was swollen and bloody. She was alleging rape. Physical examination confirmed her allegations, and the sheriff's office began an investigation.

Julie stood only 4-feet, 10-inches tall. Her mother had gone to the store for cigarettes and told her daughter not to let anyone into the apartment while she was gone. Julie said that while her mother was out, someone knocked on the door. She thought it was her mother returning. She went to look through the peephole installed in the door, but the hole was too high for her to see through, even standing on the tips of her toes. She opened the door and an unknown male grabbed her by the hair, dragged her through the apartment complex to a wooded area behind the apartments, and proceeded to rape her.

Her father and mother, as her guardians, were suing the apartment complex, alleging that the peepholes were installed at such a height as to make the apartments unreasonably unsafe.

The crime scene in the wooded area indicated a struggle may have taken place there, and articles of the girl's clothing were still there, as well as a packet of spilled cigarettes. At the time we were called in, nearly six months after the incident, the crime was still unsolved.

I began interviewing neighbors and came up dry. Nobody had seen or heard anything. Several of the people I talked to had been home at the time of the assault. It seemed unusual that the girl had been dragged, kicking and screaming, past the swimming pool, through the apartment complex, and down a hundred yards or so through an asphalt parking lot, and nobody would admit to having heard or seen any of it. Perhaps this might happen in New York City, but I found it unlikely in this southern town.

Some of the people I talked to had been at the swimming pool, but were not there continuously. They had gone inside to get drinks and such, so the girl's story could have been true. Nonetheless, I smelled a rat.

In talking with the apartment residents, I had several tell me they knew the girl had been friends with a couple of boys who hung out at a certain corner market. They gave me a good description of those boys. I spoke with the manager of the market. Of course the boys weren't there, but the manager said they came in every afternoon between 2 and 5 P.M. It was already after 5, so I went back the next afternoon at 2 and waited. Eventually, two boys came in that matched the description I'd been given.

I spoke with the two youths and they admitted that they knew about the assault. In fact, those two and a third boy had been in the woods smoking pot with Julie at about 2 P.M. the afternoon of the rape. The third boy, let's call him Leroy, had wanted to have sex with Julie for a long time. When Leroy began putting the moves on Julie, these two told him to leave her alone, as they knew she was underage. Julie seemed mildly cooperative but my two informants didn't want anything to do with that particular scene, so they departed, leaving Leroy and Julie alone smoking more pot.

It's apparent that Julie probably got scared and changed her mind, but Leroy was determined and finally beat her and raped her. It was a terrible crime, but it didn't happen because the peephole was too high in the apartment door. It happened because Julie had some questionable friends.

The rape didn't actually occur on the apartment grounds, so my client, the owner of the apartment complex, was off the hook. I provided a copy of my report to the sheriff's office and Leroy was eventually charged with the crime. Why was a PI able to solve this case when the sheriff's office couldn't do it with all of its manpower and forensic evidence? Because the investigating detectives didn't perform a thorough neighborhood investigation. Remember, my neighborhood investigation was done six months after the incident and I still got a good lead from it. Suppose I'd been able to do it the day of the rape or the following day. Had the sheriff's office executed a proper neighborhood investigation, they probably would have found Leroy hanging at the corner market still bragging about what a good time he'd had.

Dress for Success

The issue of appearance may seem obvious to some, but it's clearly not obvious to most investigators. I have an investigator on staff who is a very good street man. Cliff is usually unshaven, smokes heavily, and could stand on a street corner with a cup in his hand and really fit the part. Cliff does well following people and is good with a video camera. I cringe every time he goes to court, because some people, well, you just can't dress them up. Cliff is one of those. Even wearing his best suit, Cliff just looks rough. If Cliff came knocking on my own door, I wouldn't open it. There is no way I could send Cliff into middle-class suburbia to do a neighborhood investigation. If I sent him out into the boondocks with his pickup truck to talk to the rednecks, he'd do very well. The point with Cliff is that you have to evaluate your assets and allocate them where they will be most effective.

I have a long-haired blonde female investigator. She doesn't do well in the inner city. The males she interviews are distracted by her appearance. They spend more time looking at her and coming on to her than they do listening to and answering her questions. She doesn't do well with the inner-city females she interviews, either. The women are mad at her because of her looks, are hostile toward her, and refuse to cooperate.

Put the blonde from my office in a yuppie sports bar or let her follow a wayward husband to a wine-tasting party and she does a marvelous job. She can do a good job on a neighborhood investigation because suburban residents will open their doors to her. They aren't afraid of her. She is one of them.

If you're performing a neighborhood, then you must dress the part: shirt and tie for the male investigators, pants suit or dress for the females. Don't wear ragged cuffed jeans and expect a woman who's alone in the house with her newborn to open her front door when you ring the bell. It's not going to happen. Dress the part and you'll have better success. Clothes shouldn't make a difference, but the reality of the situation is that if you believe appearance doesn't matter, you're in the wrong business.

Discretion with the Neighbors

Interviews are successful if you build the bond of trust with the person you're interviewing. Part of that bond of trust is that the interviewee is confiding in you and expects you to exercise discretion with the information he entrusts to you.

Almost without fail, during an interview the subject will say something like, "Well, I don't really want to get involved. I have to live in this neighborhood, even after your case is over." And that is very true. He knows that if he rats out the lady across the street, then she may try to get even with him at some point. That's a very real fear people have. You'll be long gone, but he's still living across the street from her.

Going to Court

If you promise the subject that what he says is "just between you and me," he won't believe it and he will know you've just lied to him. If you say that, you've just broken the bond you've worked so hard to build. He knows you've got to report the results of your interview to your client. He knows there is a lawsuit going on and he may end up in court testifying.

How do you handle that situation? By being completely honest—well, almost—with the interviewee. Tell him that most of these cases never go to trial. Ninety-nine percent of the time, these types of lawsuits are settled out of court. You, of course, have to share the information that you get from him with the attorney for your client, but you will not share it with anyone else. Unless the case actually goes to court, the other side will never know what your interviewee says. If it does go to trial, then he will likely be *subpoenaed* and will have to testify anyway. By cooperating now, he might help settle the case, which would prevent him from going to court and testifying.

> **Crime Scene Clues**
>
> A **subpoena** is a command from the judge of a court requiring that the person or representative of an institution named in the subpoena appear in court at certain time. A **subpoena deuces tecum** is a subpoena that requires the individual or institution to provide documents to the clerk of the court as outlined in the subpoena. A subpoena could require both an appearance and the retrieval of documents.

Keep in mind that some people might enjoy going to court and testifying. Your interviewee may get a big kick out of saying what he has to say about his neighbor across the street and doing it in front of her. If that is the case, then play on that. Encourage him to tell you all he knows now and if it is good enough, you can practically assure him of his day before the judge. In order to have success here, you have to evaluate who you're talking to, determine what motivates him, and manipulate him accordingly.

Arbitration

There are occasions where the interviewee's information might get reported back to the client without the case going to trial. In the settlement process, a case might go to arbitration. Arbitration refers to a process where the plaintiff and the defendant in a civil lawsuit meet with a third party, known as a professional arbitrator.

The arbitrator is skilled in negotiating, and it is his responsibility to try and help the two different sides come to an agreement. This process reduces the number of cases going to trial and helps clear the court calendar for cases that cannot be settled.

If your report contains some really hot stuff, a smart attorney will use those statements as leverage to encourage a better settlement. It's possible that those statements might be reported to the subject of the investigation, the neighbor of your interviewee, even though the case is settled before trial. It's not likely, but it's certainly possible. So, the neighbor might find out what was said by your interviewee, regardless.

Usually, if a settlement is not reached by arbitration, the case is scheduled for trial. This does not preclude a case from settling later, even though no agreement was reached during arbitration. However, some contracts provide that in the event of a dispute, the parties must submit to binding arbitration. This means that a settlement *must* be reached during arbitration. If the parties cannot decide upon a settlement considered fair by all, then the arbitrator, after being fully informed of the facts, will reach what he considers a fair conclusion. But his determination is binding on both parties.

Keep an Eye Out

One last major factor to consider in conducting neighborhoods is the "other crime" aspect. Be aware of your surroundings and what the folks you speak with are telling you. You have to be intuitive and sensitive to the meaning behind their words. Many times people will try to tell you something but are afraid to come right out and say it, so they allude to it rather than by being direct. You need to have your antennae up all of the time.

By listening carefully, you may become aware of other factors that have a bearing on your case. Remember Daniel Black from Chapter 12? He was the fellow who shaved his head in an attempt to fool the witnesses at a lineup. We later obtained a search warrant and conducted a search of his home. In his garage we found, in addition to the stolen motor home he was driving when we arrested him, a stolen Volkswagen and a stolen Porsche. In talking to his neighbors, they all mentioned that some items around their homes had gone missing. We were able to return bicycles, a lawn tractor, numerous personal items, credit cards, and traveler's checks, all belonging to the neighbors. Daniel was a thief. And it didn't matter to him who he stole from.

As a PI, most of your neighborhood investigations will involve some sort of criminal or fraudulent activity. You might be talking to neighbors about an insurance fraud case. Most investigators don't consider performing a neighborhood in those cases for two reasons:

1. They just plain don't think of it, or don't know how to do a neighborhood investigation.

2. If they do consider it, they're afraid that the neighbors will alert the subject to the investigation and this will spoil any chance they have of getting "good" video of the subject's activities.

We spent a lot of time trying to catch a man who was the subject of a workman's compensation fraud case. We knew he was physically capable of working and had been told that people saw him performing all sorts of physical feats that he'd told his employer he could no longer do, yet we rarely saw him leave his house.

We decided to do a neighborhood investigation. We talked to his neighbors on either side of his house and the ones across the street. Those interviews were all negative. Finally, I went around the block and spoke to the family that shared the back fence line. It seems they would see him through the fence nearly every morning chopping firewood. You can guess where I was the next morning with the video camera.

In working any case, you have to use your judgment as to whether or not a neighborhood investigation might bear fruit. Put the neighborhood in your toolbox and put it to use when appropriate. A well-done, thorough neighborhood investigation, although possibly labor intensive, is a good technique. If the FBI is fond of it, you know it has its merits. Most investigators don't like doing them because they don't want to spend the effort or have never been taught how. Now you know more than they do.

The Least You Need to Know

- ◆ A good neighborhood investigation requires not only talking to the families nearby, but also finding vehicles that regularly drive by, interviewing those drivers, and being alert as to where the getaway car may have parked.

- ◆ Every neighborhood has a resident that is nosy and knows everything going on in the area. Find and interview that person.

- ◆ Conducting a neighborhood can further your investigation on a premise liability case, rape, assault, or slip and fall.

- ◆ Assigning investigators who will "fit in" at that particular area can enhance a neighborhood investigation. Be aware that you're asking people to open their doors and their homes to you.

- ◆ Be honest with the people you interview. If they feel you're lying to them, they will not be forthcoming. You can promise them anonymity only to a certain degree. Cases most often settle out of court (sometimes using arbitration), and usually their identity is between you and your client.

- ◆ Neighbors who take care of their yards usually make good witnesses. If the PI is getting doors closed in her face, she should look for the house that has the neatest yard and try there.

- ◆ Be aware that your subject may be guilty of other crimes besides the one you are investigating. His neighbors may know about his other activities. Or, in speaking with the neighbors, you may piece together facts that implicate your subject in additional criminal behavior.

14

Stationary Surveillance

In This Chapter

- Choosing the type and picking the site
- Planning the cover story
- Handling the nosy neighbor
- Staying cool if you're busted by the cops
- Keeping your secrets to yourself
- The price of goofing off

If there is one aspect or technique most people associate with the professional private investigator, it is surveillance. An investigator's entire practice may be criminal-defense work, which almost never requires surveillance. But let him be introduced as a private investigator at any cocktail party or business luncheon and the first statement made is something like, "I suppose most of what you do is following husbands and wives, that sort of thing, huh?"

Depending upon an investigator's clientele, that may or may not be true. Many PIs spend a good deal of their time doing surveillance. For example, there's always the insurance company that doesn't believe the workers' compensation claimant is really injured. Those cases are 99 percent video surveillance, with maybe a little judicious neighborhood investigation thrown in, like we talked about in Chapter 13.

Number 2 on the PI's list of FAQs, after it's learned that he's former FBI or other law enforcement type, goes like this: "I suppose being a PI is not as exciting or as challenging as being a cop, is it?"

Crime Scene Clues

Being made means that a covert operation like a surveillance has been exposed and its presence made known to the subject of the operation. It's a clue you've been made when the person you're following gives you the finger.

Nothing could be further from the truth. When the FBI tails a subject, they frequently have eight men in six cars doing the surveillance. Plus, it's not at all unusual for the bureau to also use an airplane. It is the rare—very rare—client that would pay for that much manpower.

It is much more challenging and rewarding to conduct a one-man surveillance and not *be made*, than to utilize eight men, six cars, and an airplane. In this and the next chapter, you're going to learn how to conduct a successful one-man surveillance, and how to most effectively utilize additional manpower, if it's available.

Picking the Site

There are two methods of stationary surveillance:

◆ Fixed surveillance

◆ Fixed-mobile surveillance

In a fixed surveillance, the location used by the surveillance team is usually an apartment or house that has a clear view of the subject or the subject's property. In a domestic case, the PI is more interested in what the subject does after she leaves her house than her activities at the residence. In that case, then, a fixed-surveillance site might be set up some distance from the subject's location, but along the path of the subject's egress in order to alert mobile units that the subject is on the move.

By far the most common in the PI business is a fixed-mobile surveillance. This is a surveillance set up in a temporary fixed site, such as a surveillance van or other vehicle. In this case, while the surveillance takes place from a mobile vehicle, the purpose is to gather evidence at one specific location.

Fixed Surveillances

An attorney for a department store chain contacted us and explained that a man who claimed to have slipped and fallen in one of their stores had filed a lawsuit. Because of the fall, he alleged he'd hurt his neck and could not work. The plaintiff was, by profession, a commercial underwater diver. He'd been working on drilling rigs off the Louisiana coast. It was a coincidence that the slip and fall occurred about the same time as the oil drilling business hit a new low and the diver was scheduled to be laid off.

The diver was supposed to be living temporarily with his folks. We spent a little time watching the parents' house but never saw the guy there. We did a pretext (see Chapter 16 for a full discussion on how to do a pretext) on the man's father and learned that the diver was flying out the following day to Grand Cayman to work on a dive job down there. We hurriedly consulted with the client, who approved the trip, and I was off to Grand Cayman the next day. Ah, the life of a PI.

Sherlock's Secrets _____

If you only learn one thing about surveillance, learn this: The key to obtaining successful surveillance video is to get as far away from the subject as your video equipment will allow and still get good quality video. The client, and possibly a jury, has to be able to recognize the claimant's face in the video. If you get too close, you'll get burned every time. Amateurs always begin a surveillance too near to their subject. You can always move closer, but once you've been burned, the gig is up. Explain to a client how he paid for a round-trip plane fare to Grand Cayman, only to have you get burned on the first day—and not sunburned, either. That requires a different explanation. At any rate, stay as far away from your surveillance subject as possible.

We weren't sure what job he was working on, except that it was some sort of underwater pipe construction. The job could have been on land as well as in the ocean. The water table there is pretty high; you can dig a hole 6 feet deep and hit water, so a diver might be needed even if the pipeline was on land. After settling in, I stowed my camera equipment in the rental car and went looking. There was construction along Seven Mile Road and it looked like they were laying some type of pipe in a ditch alongside the road before repaving. It didn't take very long to spot the subject dressed in his dive gear, dropping into a hole filled with water. I guessed he was probably securing the pipe connections.

It was impossible to sit in the car anywhere close to the construction site and get good video. Construction vehicles blocked the view from the other side of the road and any attempt at setting up a surveillance from the rental car would certainly have resulted in being burned. "Getting burned" has the same meaning as "being made"—the subject has become aware of the surveillance.

In a situation like this where surveillance seems impossible, as we discussed in Chapter 1 you have to think outside the box. You have to step back, look around, and search for other alternatives. A PI cannot be successful and have tunnel vision. Be creative.

I studied the surrounding area and noticed a two-story hotel directly across the street from the construction site. It looked promising, so then I explored around the inside of the hotel and figured out which room numbers would give me the view I needed. I rented the room, explaining I wanted the roadside view instead of the ocean side because it was less expensive. In a few minutes, I had the camera set up on the tripod and was rolling tape. Two days later, the pipeline had moved further down the road and so did I, into another hotel. After four days of watching our diver working 10-hour days, I consulted with the client, and we decided we had enough. I took the next day off to do some diving (after all, it was Grand Cayman) and headed home with the goodies.

The diver's attorney dropped the lawsuit just as soon as he saw some of the videotape.

If you can get a fixed-surveillance site, do it. Sitting in an air-conditioned room is so much better than sitting in a car, suffering from heat exhaustion in the summer and hypothermia in the winter. And room service is a lot better than trying to use your cell phone to persuade a pizza place to deliver to some guy under a bush behind a lamppost.

Sammy the Snitch

One caution on fixed-surveillance sites: If you're using a hotel room or other facility that has regular cleaning people, you have to hide the surveillance equipment before the cleaning people enter. The maids or the cleaning folks will report unusual equipment, like your long-range video lenses, to the management, who will in turn report it to the local authorities. There is no better way to get burned than to have a squad of police cars come roaring into the parking lot and storming your room to see what you're up to. Spending a night in a foreign jail, for working without a permit, is no fun either.

A fixed-surveillance site does not have to be a hotel room or rented apartment. In my firm, we've even climbed trees and sat in them all day long to obtain videotape of allegedly injured people. I have hidden under bushes in the rain at 4 in the morning to document a newspaper delivery person unloading, folding, and bagging stacks of newspapers. My guys have hidden behind sea oats at the beach to catch surfers who could surf standing on their heads, but couldn't work because of neck injuries. All of these—trees, bushes, and sea oats—constitute fixed-surveillance sites, because if the subject moves, you can't take the site with you.

Fixed-Mobile Surveillance

Private investigators universally use fixed-mobile surveillances for workers' compensation, slip and falls, automobile accident claims, and other types of surveillances where obtaining video tape of the subject's physical abilities and range of motion are important. Not surprisingly, the most commonly used method is the surveillance van. However, we find that pickup trucks with a cab over the bed work just as well if the investigator can squeeze through the small window that separates the inside of the truck and the truck bed.

Surveillance vans come in all configurations. We always constructed our own from a bare, two-seated delivery van. Customizing your own surveillance van is fairly straightforward. The windows, except for the windshield, should be tinted. We always have this done professionally because too often, the do-it-yourself tinting leaves bubbles in the window that tend to distort the video, which is hard to explain to the client.

> **CAUTION**
>
> **Sammy the Snitch** _____
>
> Some states only allow a certain degree of darkness in vehicle window tinting. Always comply with the state law in that regard. The last thing a PI wants is to have some policeman stop to write him a ticket in the middle of a surveillance. Typically, the reduced-tinting laws only apply to the windshield and the driver's and front passenger's windows. Vans are not required to have any other windows anyway. These laws were passed to allow the police to see better into a vehicle when they make a stop.

The entire interior of the van, the floor, sides and roof, should be carpeted in a dark color. You'll probably want to affix plywood to the floor, sides, and roof of the van first. This makes it easier to install the carpet. The plywood and carpet insulates the van for heating, cooling, and most importantly, sound. When talking on two-way radios, the PI doesn't want his voice to carry outside of the vehicle where people walking by might hear him.

In addition to tinting the windows, each window should be covered with a very thick black curtain. Use Velcro-type fasteners to hold the material close to the windows. The idea is to let no light into the back of the van. Likewise, a heavy black curtain should be hung to separate the back of the van from the driver and passenger area. Again, Velcro-type fastening works well, making a light-proof seal, top to bottom and all around the sides. The Velcro strips will have to be screwed into the top and the sides of the van and around the windows. Glue will not hold the Velcro in place with the heavy weight of the coverings, especially in warm climates.

During the surveillance, the PI can remove one of the window coverings or pin one of them half way up for viewing and videotaping. The interior of the van will be substantially darker than outside on the street and nobody will be able to see the inside. Even if a curious onlooker presses his face right to the uncovered window, his vision should not be able to penetrate through the darkness to see the investigator inside, unless the investigator makes some sudden movement.

Crime Scene Clues

A **repeater** is a radio tower that receives the signal from a mobile radio, such as a walkie-talkie, and repeats the broadcast signal over a larger area than a 5-watt walkie-talkie could cover. The signal may bounce from one repeater to another to another, and possibly could be received over an entire state. This is common with the FBI radios. An agent in the field should be able to reach her division headquarters from almost anyplace within the geographical boundaries of her division's area. Most commercial repeaters, set up for business purposes, do not have such a broad area of coverage.

Some investigative agencies install periscopes disguised as roof vents in the vans. A good periscope will cost several thousand dollars. They work to some degree, but a van set up properly with tinted windows and black curtains works just as well.

Twelve-volt fans wired directly to the van's battery with on and off switches are necessary. They allow the investigator in the van to remain longer during the warmer-temperature months. In addition to the fans, a small 12-volt color monitor is good to have. Looking through the camera eyepiece while kneeling or sitting for extended hours can be very difficult. The camera should be on a tripod most of the time anyway, so the PI might as well hook it to a monitor and then he can see what he is taping without ending the day with a crick in his neck.

The exterior of the van should be painted white or blue. Unusual paint jobs will call attention to the van, as will red and green paint. There are more white and blue work vans on the streets than any other color. If the PI ends up following the subject, then her white van will look just like all the others in the subject's rearview mirror.

If the van is a little beat up, all the better. It should not be a total junker, though, or you may find yourself being towed away after a call from an irate neighbor.

One more consideration with surveillance vans is the communication factor. The PI will have to evaluate his needs in his own locale. If all of the surveillance is done in downtown or major metropolitan areas, then perhaps Nextel, which combines cell phone and two-way radio communication, would be the best bet, if it's available.

Relying strictly on cell phones for communication between surveillance team members has two drawbacks. First, it can be very expensive. Second, you can only talk to one person at a time. Frequently, fixed surveillances turn mobile and end up with two, three, or up to five persons on the street at the same time. The best solution is to have handheld walkie-talkies that share a common channel as backups to whatever primary communication device you use. Why? Things do go wrong. Your subject may lead you out of a coverage area for cell phones or away from radio *repeater* sites. A backup is always a good idea.

Sherlock's Secrets

When setting up the surveillance van, try to think like your subject for a minute. If he sees a van pull up nearby, park, and no one gets out, he's likely to be suspicious. In fact, many subjects have been warned by their attorneys that insurance companies often use surveillance people.

To overcome this, have your video investigator safely out of sight in the back of the surveillance van while another investigator drives the van into the subject's neighborhood. The driver parks the van on the subject's street, with a clear view of the subject's residence. The driver then exits the van and walks to where she parked her car, a block away, out of the subject's line of site. If the subject is observing any of this from his house, hopefully he will assume that the van is now unoccupied and not be suspicious of it. The driver could raise the hood and fool around in the engine compartment, giving the impression the vehicle has broken down.

After the driver walks away, it's not unusual for us to see the subject come out of his house and inspect the van to assure himself that it is unoccupied. Of course it is, but if done properly, he can't tell. Be sure and have the camera running, because your client will have a good chuckle when he sees the videotape of the subject walking, unaided, to check out the van. But when you videotape him going to the doctor, he is limping heavily and using a cane, or crutches, or even a wheelchair.

Setting Up the Cover

In a typical insurance claim, the surveillance van is placed in a strategic location close to the subject's house, but not too close. Stay as far away as your video equipment will allow. If the subject starts mowing his yard, roofing his house, cutting down trees, or working on his car, the woman in the van can get the video. It's not unusual to use a surveillance van in conjunction with another chase vehicle.

In the event the subject leaves the house, the investigator in the van radios to the chase vehicle that the subject is leaving, giving a good description of what the subject is wearing, which vehicle he is leaving in, and which direction he is headed. The chase car, which should have been parked with a clear view of where the subject would most likely leave the subdivision, picks up the surveillance. The van sits quietly until the subject is well out of sight. The van then follows behind as the second vehicle in a two-man surveillance team.

The PI should purchase several sets of magnetic business signs to place on both sides of the van. A safe telephone number that can be answered by the business name should be on the signs. South East Survey and Oasis Carpet Company were two names that we employed for a long time.

Sherlock's Secrets

Many times, suspicious neighbors will call the number on the sign and report that one of your vans is parked in front of their residence. A good PI will be able to explain why the van is there. One suggestion is to thank them for the call and explain that the van broke down on your driver, but he will be back in a few hours to retrieve it. That explanation seems to pacify almost everyone. If you receive a call like that, be sure to park somewhere else next time. We had one of our insurance subjects call us from his mobile phone, while he walked around the van, trying to peer into the windows, and tell us he thought he'd located one of our stolen vans, because it was parked in the driveway of a deserted house across the street from him. We thanked him for the call and told him we were going to be doing some work at that house over the next few days and would he mind keeping on eye on the van for us. He did a very good job safeguarding our van in this crime-riddled neighborhood, and we got hours of videotape on him.

Sometimes it may be necessary to park the van directly in front of the subject's residence. Try to avoid this at all costs. Look for alternatives. If there is a vacant lot across the street and the undergrowth is thick, perhaps you can hide in the bushes instead.

As a last resort, if the subject is outside of the house and you must get the video, then put survey signs on the sides of the van and park directly across the street. This time, instead of the driver leaving the area, have him set up a surveyor's tripod and go about the business of appearing to survey the street, or a ditch, or the vacant lot. Wear the typical orange safety vest and take strings and stakes and spend a few hours tromping around.

Another good cover is to do the other type of survey. Take a clipboard and walk around the neighborhood, knocking on doors, filling out a questionnaire while the man in the back of the van is getting the video.

Sammy the Snitch _____

Be careful about talking directly with the subject of an investigation, even if it is to do a phony questionnaire-type survey. Most claimants in insurance investigations are represented by attorneys. It is unethical for a PI to have direct contact with that claimant unless his attorney is present. This includes any casual conversation or any contact whatsoever, unless the contact is initiated by the claimant himself. In Chapter 16 we'll show you one way to get a subject out of the house without violating that rule.

Pesky Neighbors

If the PI specializes in insurance fraud, workers' compensation, and slip-and-fall defense cases, then most of his surveillance will take place during daylight hours. Success here requires videotaping the claimants in some activity that they have previously sworn they can't perform. This type of activity usually takes place outdoors, and most people don't mow their lawn at night. This is an advantage to the investigator, because more than half of the neighbors will be at work and their houses are unoccupied. That means fewer people to become suspicious.

If the man in the chase car has to park on a residential street, you can be guaranteed that at least one neighbor will wonder what he is doing there. Wouldn't you, if you saw some stranger sitting in his parked car in front of your house for several hours?

What's the best way to handle that without blowing the surveillance? When the PI notices a resident peeking out the window at her, she should leave the car and approach the neighbor in a nonthreatening manner. She shouldn't hustle to the person's door just so she can get back immediately to her car. That'll just scare the day-lights out of the poor folks. Instead, she should walk up to the front door, in a professional manner, with her identification displayed in her hand. Then she can explain to the inquiring fellow that she is a private investigator conducting a surveillance. The surveillance is not on anybody in this block, but she is just waiting for the subject to leave the subdivision.

Now, the inquisitive neighbor usually gets excited and will ask the PI who she is watching. Obviously, she can't tell him that. The PI needs to be careful here. You never know who knows whom in the subdivision. It is possible that this person and the subject are friends.

Sherlock's Secrets

The best way to get nosy neighbors off your back is to tell them something. I suggest that if your female PI is working a potential insurance fraud case, she should tell the nosy guy that she is just working on a divorce matter. If she's working a divorce case, she should tell him she's working an insurance fraud case. Reverse the cases and the sexes. If the subject is a male, tell him you are watching some wayward wife. If the subject is female, tell him you are watching some cheating husband. Of course, that will make about 75 percent of the men in the neighborhood more paranoid about their own activities, but that's okay, too.

Many times, I've had women who are out for a late afternoon walk stop at my vehicle and ask me why I was parked on their street. If it's a woman asking, I always tell them that I'm trying to catch a wayward husband. They almost always say, "I hope you nail the son of a bitch" and then go on with their power walk.

Sometimes, despite all of your precautions, somebody walking by the van will realize that you are inside. They may have seen the van rock slightly as you changed positions. Or they may have heard you talking, or your two-way radio *breaking squelch*.

Crime Scene Clues

Breaking squelch is not related to bodily functions. It refers to the sensitivity adjustment on a radio receiver. The squelch is the point where the receiver is tuned to its most sensitive setting. If tuned beyond this point the radio makes a loud, piercing sound similar to a screeching parrot.

Once they're sure your inside, they will pound on the side of the van, or knock on the door and even call to you. This is not good. You're busted big time. All you can hope is that your subject does not become aware of this commotion. If you're parked far enough away from the subject's house, chances are he'll never know you were there.

The question then becomes, how do you get out of this situation? The easiest solution is to lay the camera down and cover it with a towel. Then open the side door, exit the van, and shut the door immediately so nobody can peer in to see what's inside. Confront the people knocking on the van and tell them you had problems with some equipment "back there," and had to stop and make adjustments. It took a little longer than you thought it would, but it's fixed now, and you'll be on your way. Proceed to the driver's side door, get in, and leave.

PIs sometimes find themselves in confrontational situations. This can happen if you've been made by the subject and he's not happy about it, or if you're conducting an investigation in a crime-ridden neighborhood and the residents make you for a cop. Maybe you're knocking on a door to do an interview and a crime has just been committed inside and you don't know it. Whatever the reason for the confrontation, don't let it escalate. Don't let your ego, your right to be there, or anything else exacerbate an already potentially dangerous conflict. Just leave. Don't get argumentative. Don't answer any questions. Just turn around and leave. Leaving the area always defuses any situation you might get yourself into. This technique will save you grief and may save you from being physically harmed.

Rousted by the Cops

There is going to come a time in every PI's life when he is sitting on a surveillance and a neighbor calls the police about this suspicious man parked in front of her house. Most of the time this can be avoided, if the PI approaches the neighbor as we discussed in the preceding section. This aborts the call to the police. If that's not done, the call is made and the police will respond.

Another method to keep this from happening is for the PI to actually advise the police himself that he will be doing a surveillance. The PI should call the police department from his cell phone as soon as he sets up, then ask the dispatcher to alert the patrol units in the area that a licensed PI is working on a surveillance on such and such street. He gives them a description of his car and the dispatcher passes the word to the police cars in that zone. However, you can count on at least one patrol car coming by just to see what is going on. Wave at them as they pass. Some of the less clever patrolmen will stop to chitchat, which does wonders for your cover.

CAUTION

Sammy the Snitch _____

If you're not a licensed PI and you are rousted by the police, then you have a problem. The best you can do is explain to the police why you're out there, trying to catch your husband with his girlfriend or whatever, and hope you've found a sympathetic ear. Remember, there is no law that says you can't be sitting in a parked car. However, if the police ask you to move, then you must obey a lawful order. If you don't, you risk spending the night in the pokey, and it's really hard to do any surveillance from there.

Only once, in 20 years, have I ever had a problem with a beat cop. In that case, the cop asked me to move on. I was sitting in the only place possible, several blocks from my subject's residence, where the subdivision exited onto a main thoroughfare. I told him I was on a public street, I was licensed by the state to be there doing what I was doing, and had just as much right to be on that public street as the neighbor who complained had a right to park her car on that same street. He relented, but said if he received any more complaints, he'd make me move. I told him that was fine, I would move then, but before he asked me to move again, he should check with his sergeant. I didn't see him the rest of the day.

Don't Ask And Don't Tell

If the pesky neighbor situation is not diffused, or goes unnoticed by the private investigator the police will arrive. The PI now has a little bit of a problem. In a second, the blue lights will flash and the cop will bleat her siren once to let the PI, and the entire neighborhood, know that he's there. All the residents in the vicinity will come out to watch and then the cop will ask him to put his hands out the window where she can see them. In the midst of all that, there are three very important points the PI must keep foremost in his mind:

1. Attitude: Don't have one. Don't panic. And definitely be polite. Make this a conversation, one professional to another. Remember, the state has given you, the PI, a license to do what you are doing and to be where you are. Explain that calmly to the police. Don't fall into the TV cliché of the PI hustling the cop.

2. Despite the cop's repeated questioning, the PI is not compelled to reveal the identity of the subject, nor his client. In most states that license PIs, it's a violation of state law for a PI to reveal anything about the case he is working on, even to law enforcement, unless there are exigent circumstances.

3. In this situation, again, use the reverse-sex, reverse-case-type fib. Tell the policeman that, as she knows, you can't really give her any details of the case … but if she promises not to tell anybody, you're just watching some woman who is a claimant in a workers' compensation case (when you're really watching a man in a divorce case). I don't recommend lying to the police, but the officer shouldn't be asking, anyway. This will satisfy her curiosity and she'll go away and leave you alone.

Why fib? You can bet that the officer will go right out and relay to the rest of her squad what type of case you're working on. Why would she do this? A beat or patrol cop just doesn't come into contact with private investigators all that often. A PI is something of a novelty to her. Also, many cops are already thinking that when they retire they might try their hand at being a PI. So when she's talking shop, taking a break with the other cops in that zone, she'll tell them where you are and what you're working on. So, let her talk—just not about your case.

Eternal Vigilance

Working a stationary surveillance leaves little time for reading, daydreaming, or taking care of bodily functions. As soon as you pick up that book because nothing is happening, the subject will come out of the house carrying a load of bricks and you will miss it. You can't read and do an effective job at the same time. You may think you can, but you can't. Nobody can. And that includes reading this book on surveillance. Put me down now and focus on the surveillance.

It's not unusual to only have one chance of obtaining videotape on some crucial activity. The activity may only last 15 or 20 seconds. By the time you put the book down and get the camera rolling, the important stuff will be over. You might have taped the 20 seconds of case-winning video had you not been reading. It might be the one time all day that the claimant comes out of his house, and you just missed it. The line between being a jerk and an outstanding investigator is very thin. About 20 seconds thin.

Plan the surveillance. Know in advance how long you're going to be in the back of that van, or in front of the window at the hotel, or under the bushes, or in the tree. Take food and drink with you. Have a large-mouthed cup to pee into, and don't forget the lid. Be sure and pour it out later and not leave it to ferment in the van. Forgetting to take it with you won't make you very popular with the other investigators on your surveillance team. And for heavens' sake, don't spill it in the van. This is the advice I give both my male and female investigators. If you're going to be a successful surveillance PI, you have to do it. So think twice before slurping down that 64-ounce iced tea.

Stationary surveillance may not be quite as much of an art as a moving surveillance, but it requires patience, planning, fortitude, determination, and good luck to be successful. The use of a fixed-surveillance van is much more physically demanding than a moving surveillance. Give me an air-conditioned car traveling 70 MPH down the highway anytime over the 150° sweltering heat inside a stationary van during a summer surveillance.

The Least You Need to Know

- ◆ There are two types of stationary surveillances: fixed and fixed mobile. Both are designed to obtain information from one specific point. The fixed mobile may be a van that can be brought in and out as needed, but the surveillance should be conducted from as far away as possible while still capturing good-quality video or photographs—good enough to recognize faces.

- ◆ Surveillance vans should be insulated for sound and temperature. Circulating fans and a 12-volt television monitor should be installed. The vans should look like work vans and be painted white or blue.

- ◆ One method for setting up a surveillance in a residential neighborhood is to have the driver pretend the van is broken down and walk away, leaving a second PI in the back to get the video.

- ◆ Pesky neighbors are best dealt with directly. Introducing yourself and showing them your PI license will avoid a run-in with the police.

- ◆ If you are busted, make an excuse and leave the area immediately. Being rousted by the cops requires that you maintain your demeanor and speak to them as a professional. You must maintain your statutory obligations and not reveal, even to the police, the identity of your subject or the nature of the surveillance.

- ◆ Success in a stationary surveillance requires a constant alert status. The surveillance investigator cannot read a book, watch television, or leave the site. Have appropriate food and drink available and use a wide-mouth jar or cup with a lid to pee into.

Moving Surveillance

In This Chapter

- ◆ Five tricks to a one-man surveillance
- ◆ Learning the principles of foot surveillance
- ◆ Preparation techniques that ensure success
- ◆ Using additional manpower to maximum advantage
- ◆ Winning and losing with traffic lights

Coordinating and running a successful mobile surveillance requires experience, luck, and a sense, almost a mental gift, of knowing what your subject will do. Famous FBI criminal profilers talk about putting themselves in the criminal's head. Likewise, a good surveillance man will have the gift of putting himself or herself in the subject's head. There is no rational explanation of how that is done. Hopefully, this chapter will put on paper the esoteric sense of surveillance that a private investigator develops with enough time and practice.

Not all private investigators are good at surveillance. Just as some people have a talent for playing the piano by ear, others have a natural talent for sensing how people are going to drive their cars or stop at yellow lights or run the red ones. But you can always take piano lessons and learn the piano. Likewise, this chapter is a lesson in moving surveillance. The more piano practice you have, the better you play. There is no difference with surveillance. It's an art, but every art—be it painting, musical composition, or novel writing—has its craft that must be learned and is perfected through practice.

Going It Alone

Unfortunately for private investigators, most clients will not foot the bill for more than one man on a surveillance. Thankfully, there are a few who will. A few months ago we were looking for a runaway teenager. We had six men on surveillance in multiple locations around the city, staking out this spoiled kid's haunts. The father had the checking account to cover that heavy of an expense. Usually, you're lucky if you get a client who will pay for a two-man surveillance team, not to mention six.

So how do you run a one-man moving surveillance? Well, it's not easy. The sections that follow describe five tricks you can use that will make it go a little more smoothly.

Know in Advance Where the Subject Is Going

So now you're supposed to be clairvoyant? Not really. If this is a domestic case, your client may know where and when his spouse is meeting with her lover. Men in particular are adept at tapping their own telephones. We'll talk about the nuts and bolts of tapping phones in Chapter 21. In most states, tapping calls on your home telephone, if you're not one of the parties involved in the call, is illegal. I never suggest to a client that he tap his wife's phone calls. But if it comes up, I do let him know that he can go to Radio Shack and for less than $65 he can get the proper equipment and they'll tell him how to do it. It's very simple.

> **CAUTION**
>
> **Sammy the Snitch** _____
>
> Learn the wiretap laws in your state. Never suggest to a client that he break the law. If you do, your client may take the suggestion, tap his own phone, and later tell his wife what he's done. She'll go to her attorney and tell him you suggested it. The next thing you know, the state will be prosecuting you or taking away your license. They might not prosecute the client, because he didn't know any better, but you're the professional—you're supposed to know the law.

If it's your husband that is cheating on you, a tap on your own phone line may save you thousands of dollars in PI expense. Of course, if your husband doesn't use the phone to talk to his lover, then it won't do you any good. But you really don't know if he does or not until you find out for sure. If he's using his cell phone, read Chapter 18, for tips and tricks about using a cell phone.

If you're following an insurance claimant, talk to the claim adjuster and find out when the claimant's next doctor's visit is scheduled. Scout the location of the doctor's office before the day of the visit. If you lose him on the way to the doctor's visit, no sweat. It's not good to lose him but at least you know where to find him again and at what time. Claimants frequently run other errands en route to and from the doctor's office. It always makes for good theater in the courtroom when the claimant can climb ladders, cut the grass, or pump the gas without help until he gets to the doctor's office. Then, when he arrives, he can't even walk without assistance. And what an amazing cure rate these doctors have! The poor fellow limps on his crutches to his truck as he leaves, but at his next stop on his way home, he seems just fine again.

Follow the Yellow Brick Road

We call this the Yellow Brick Road Technique. Usually, the client will know who the other woman is. She's been told by friends or the husband has said flattering things about this woman at work or has tipped his hand somehow. If you've tried to follow the husband and he has a lead foot, runs yellow lights, pushes the red ones, and makes lots of U-turns, he may not be a good candidate for a one-man surveillance. So don't follow him. Follow the other woman instead. She won't be suspicious. She won't be looking over her shoulder, and nothing is going to happen until the two of them get together anyway.

We worked a domestic case recently. The husband was a doctor. He was difficult to follow, so we followed the girlfriend. It wasn't long before he showed up at her place. She had him out in her yard doing chores, taking down shutters after a hurricane scare, and raking the yard. We had a good laugh at that. He could have done chores at home and it wouldn't have cost him a divorce.

Plan Your Exit

Working alone means working smarter, because you don't have the luxury of being able to cover an entire subdivision or company parking lot. If this is a domestic matter, talk to your client. She'll know which exit her husband usually takes. She can advise on which way out of the neighborhood from his house he always travels. The easiest time to lose the subject is when he's leaving a location. If the husband is at home, have the wife call you on your cell phone the minute he leaves the house.

If you've followed your subject and he stops at a business location and leaves his car, use the time to survey your situation. How many exits are there? Which way is he likely to go? Is there a median in the street so he can only exit one way or could he come out and turn right or left? Plan your exit. You don't want to be right on his bumper when he leaves. That's the best way to get made. You don't want to be too far behind him, either. That's the best way to lose him, because the car in front of you won't hustle out into the traffic and your subject will have made the next turn and be gone while you're still stuck in the parking lot.

You have to anticipate his exit strategy and put yourself in the best possible position to see him coming out (without him seeing you) and to be able to resume the surveillance. If there is only one way out and he can only turn one direction, go down the block and wait for him.

Don't Play Follow the Leader

Your subject has just made a left turn into a service station or a fast food restaurant. What do you do?

Do not follow him into the restaurant parking lot. You continue traveling past the restaurant he turned into. Keep your eyes on the rearview mirror in the event he is making a U-turn. When you're sure he's parking and going to enter the establishment, just reposition yourself and figure out his most likely exit and direction of travel. Take into account the traffic flow. When the subject exits, can he make a left across the traffic or does he have to make a right and continue in your direction?

This is the nuts and bolts of a one-man surveillance. Watching the traffic, and anticipating what the subject's next move will be based on traffic flow, concrete medians, stopped buses, and one-way streets. Be prepared for any harebrained moves he might make. Don't lull yourself into thinking he's going to do what you would do. Count on his actions being something entirely different from what any reasonable person might attempt. When he exits the drive-through with his hamburger in one hand and a chocolate shake in the other, he is concentrating on not spilling his lunch all over his pants before he gets to his honey. Be ready for sudden illogical driving patterns. After all, do you think he's got his mind on traffic, or something else?

Do Play Follow the Leader

Now you're two cars behind your subject (good, you've put some cover between him and you) and he's signaling a right-hand turn into a large regional shopping mall. What action do you take?

You follow him in. I know we just said don't follow him into a business lot. That's true. But with a large mall lot, there are four reasons why you'd want to follow him right on in:

- It is very easy to lose the subject in a large mall lot. Don't be fooled into thinking you can cruise the lot later and find his car. It probably won't happen.

- He may just be cutting through the lot to get to the highway exit on the other side.

- The subject may be meeting his girlfriend in the lot and could leave in her car. If she's on time (I know, not likely), he'd be gone before you ever found him. If you do find his car and they left in hers, you will have missed the big show. Or they may meet in the lot and leave in separate cars headed toward the motel. She didn't want to be sitting in front of a motel waiting for him, and since he's going to pay for the room, they arranged to meet in the mall lot first.

- He may be meeting his girlfriend inside, where she works at one of the stores. You may find his car but you probably won't find him in the mall.

Watch which aisle he takes in the parking lot. Once he's pulled into a space, park in a different aisle where you can see his car. You have to hurry here. Don't lose him now. You'll want to follow him into the mall and continue the surveillance inside, on foot. Any purchases he makes may be significant. Who he meets may also be of importance to your client.

The Effective Foot Surveillance

Following a subject on foot is fraught with difficulties. You must stay close enough to see whom he comes in contact with, but remain discreet and unobtrusive so the subject is unaware of your presence. Easier said than done. Holding a newspaper up to your face when the subject looks your way is overdone in the movies. How many people do you see walking through a mall reading the paper? Okay, no newspaper ... so how do you do it?

Here are three basic principles of conducting moving surveillances that applies to all forms, whether you're on foot, in a car, or have multiple people working the surveillance with you:

1. You should always keep something between you and the subject. In a mall, that means stay behind other people who are walking in the same direction. We're going to harp on this idea of having cover throughout this chapter. It's a very important principle, but don't overdo it. No lurking behind pillars and tiptoeing

between kiosks type of stuff. Most malls have pretty good surveillance security cameras hidden throughout, and if you make a spectacle of yourself, the next thing you know, two security guys will be hauling you down to their office to ask you a few questions.

2. Change your appearance. A good surveillance person always has a couple of extra hats and jackets in the car with him. When you follow your man into the mall, grab a hat and coat, even if it's during the summertime in Florida. By varying those two articles of clothing, you can look like four different people. If you're a female, keep a scarf in the coat pocket and now you can add five additional appearances for a total of nine. And don't forget the sunglasses or regular glasses. Use anything you can to change the way you appear to the subject. (Anything except streaking. It might call too much attention to yourself.)

3. Don't get in front of the subject. This third principle is particularly important if you are working by yourself. If you're with a partner, it's still a good idea to adhere to this, but you can make an exception if the situation demands it. If you're driving and he's behind you, he's looking at your tag, any bumper stickers you have, and how you part your hair. If you accidentally get in front of him again, he'll remember all of those things and will become suspicious. If you're on foot and you're in front of him, he'll notice how you're dressed and how you walk. If he sees you again, you're dead meat.

The preceding three principles of moving surveillance, if put into practice will go a long way toward making your surveillance successful and keep you from getting burned.

A Bird in the Hand

All clients want photographs. The wife who wants to catch her husband cheating can read your report. She already knows in her heart that her husband is unfaithful to her. None of that makes any difference. Remember, her husband will come up with some logical explanation of why he went to the mall, bought that watch, gave it to some lady, and followed her to a hotel.

The explanation? The lady was a client, the watch was a gift for her because she can get him a big account, and the two of them had a business lunch at the hotel. If the PI she hired says they went into a hotel room, he must be mistaken or he's lying to justify his bill. PIs are a sleazy lot anyway, and …. Now he gets mad at his wife for having doubts about him and wasting the mortgage money on a keyhole peeper. That's what he'll say to his wife.

Get the photograph of him and the other woman kissing, holding hands, walking through the mall arm in arm. Your client needs to be able to throw it down on the coffee table in front of her husband when he comes up with excuses and gets defensive. "There, buster," she'll say, tossing the photograph at him. "Let me see you explain that."

The problem here for most investigators is they're not properly prepared for that unexpected moment. When the good stuff happens, a kiss between lovers, or an insurance claimant going into a handstand to impress his 4-year-old child, the PI must be ready, camera in hand, to grab that shot. Sometimes it's the only shot she'll get, and she'll miss it if she's not ready. The lovers won't kiss again until they're behind closed doors and the claimant's wife will remind him he's out on disability and he'd better stop with the gymnastics. You've got to get the bird in the hand, because there might not be two in the bushes later.

I flew from Arizona to Florida recently. Seated next to me was an older lady. We talked some, exchanged histories. I fended off the usual questions about PI work and explained to her how a lot of PI cases were insurance-related. Catching claimants roofing their houses, that sort of thing.

She turned very pale and questioned me quite thoroughly about why the insurance company would hire a PI to spy on a claimant. Finally, she admitted that her son was home on workers' compensation and was at this very moment using his free time to install a new roof on his house. She picked up one of the in-flight phones and called him to warn him to be on the lookout for PIs sneaking around his house.

If your subject is an insurance claimant and he's roofing his house, you'll have plenty of time to set up, get the video rolling, and capture days worth of tape. But if it's a domestic case and you want to capture that hug and kiss at the airport as the subject's girlfriend comes through the gate, you'll only have that 20 seconds that separates the jerk PIs from the hero PIs, as we talked about in the last chapter.

Two's Company

Say your client's a big spender, not some adjuster working for a tightwad insurance company, and he wants you to catch his philandering wife. If it takes two men to follow her, no problem, use whatever resources you need. He doesn't care what it costs, just get the job done. Hmm, he doesn't care what it costs ... that's music to any private investigator's ears.

Running a two-man surveillance requires skill and practice to know how to use the extra resource wisely. Remember, if you mess up the surveillance now and lose your client's wife with two men on her, you're going to have one unhappy client. There are three areas to focus on with a multiple person surveillance team: communication, positioning, and information. Each of these areas will be discussed in the sections that follow.

Communication

Obviously, if there is more than one person working the surveillance, there has to be good communication between all members of the team. That's why we previously suggested having multiple forms of radio communication and relying on cellular only as a backup. Each team member should always carry a minimum of two radios that have the ability to bounce off a repeater and to talk car-to-car. The equipment you have will depend greatly upon what is available in your geographic area. Keep in mind that a surveillance will sometimes take you to areas not covered by cell sites.

Crime Scene Clues

A **point man** on a surveillance is the investigator that actually has "the eyeball," or has physical sight of the subject.

My firm uses a primary and two backup types of communication. The primary is a radio that works off a repeater. The backup is a handheld walkie-talkie. The third is the cell phone.

Having the means to communicate and actually doing it are two different things. All the investigators on the surveillance must first be taught to talk. Seems simple, right? It's not. Talking means the *point man* must give a detailed running commentary on the subject's actions if he is on the move.

The running commentary means that the point man must alert the rest of the surveillance team when the subject moves, changes directions, turns a corner, stops at a red light, or runs a yellow light. It doesn't mean that he keeps his microphone keyed the entire time. He must be short and clear in his comments. As the point man indicates a change in direction or speed, the other surveillance units should acknowledge it so the man on point knows he's been heard. The radios are not devices for idle chatter and the only communication during a moving surveillance should be pertinent to the surveillance itself.

Even with the best equipment and excellent organization, there will come a time during a moving surveillance that the lead vehicle will be separated from the rest of the surveillance team. The team might be stopped or slowed by traffic lights, crawling freight trains, automobile accidents, raised drawbridges, or the highway patrol. It doesn't take long for that distance to grow to half a dozen miles going down an interstate at 75 MPH.

When this occurs, the point man should continue the surveillance and should broadcast his position *in the blind* even though he can't hear the rest of the team. Just because he can't hear their radio traffic doesn't mean they can't hear him. Radio transmission and reception are dependent on a number of variable factors, such as height of antennae, inclement weather, and even sun spots. As the lead car climbs a hill or bridge, he should report to the other cars his position. The increased height in his location of broadcast may be sufficient enough to allow what he says to be heard by the other units, even though he cannot hear them respond.

Crime Scene Clues

Broadcasting **in the blind**—when the members of a surveillance team have been cut off from one another—is something that must be taught. It means that the broadcaster may not receive acknowledgment that his message was heard, but he's putting it out there anyway because it might be heard by his surveillance team members. It's a valuable technique used by those in law enforcement. Add it to your tool bag. Many a surveillance has been saved by an investigator smart enough to broadcast her position in the blind, thereby allowing the balance of the surveillance team to catch up to her and the subject.

Positioning

There are two purposes for having more than one man on a surveillance. First is the ability to cover more than one possible point of egress by the subject. In a subdivision or an apartment complex, there is frequently more than one exit, and the subject may some days use one and other days use another. Having two cars available helps eliminate the possibility of losing the subject before he's even left the immediate area.

The second main purpose for a surveillance team composed of two or more people is to "confuse the enemy." A good set of surveillance investigators will change off the lead so the subject is not seeing the same car in the rearview mirror for hours at a time. Likewise, if the subject makes a turn into a business, shopping mall, or another residential area, the lead car, which has been behind the subject for a while, can drive on past as the subject turns and the next car becomes the lead car and makes the turn following behind the subject. The former lead car makes a quick U-turn as soon as the subject is out of sight and plays catch-up.

> **⚠ CAUTION**
>
> **Sammy the Snitch** _____
>
> The subject lives in a subdivision with multiple entrances and exits. Also, it is impossible to park discreetly and have a clear view of the subject's residence. In this case, it is tempting to drive by the residence periodically to see what is happening and to make sure his car hasn't moved. Resist the urge. The same car passing by the subject's house multiple times may alert him, or, at the very least, make him suspicious.
>
> If there are two cars available and you can't resist the urge, then alternate each time you make a drive by. Keep the drive bys to a maximum of one per hour. If there is only one car available, perform the drive bys once every two hours, but you will probably be skunked anyway. According to Murphy's Law, if anything can go wrong, it will. And at the worst possible time. This has never been more true than on a moving surveillance.
>
> If it is after dark and the house is not in a cul de sac, then indulge yourself all you want.

Information

My client, the wife, was handing her 3-year-old over to her soon-to-be ex-husband. The husband was supposed to bring the child back to the mother later that same night. The father had been taking the child to the new girlfriend's house and sleeping over. The mother didn't approve, thinking it set a bad example for her older children as well. She wanted proof, somebody who could testify to the judge, that yes, the husband was indeed cohabiting and had the child with him when he did it.

The handoff was to take place after dark. This was a fairly busy residential area with major hotels and shopping areas along the street just before the security gate. Due to the heavy foliage, the gate itself could not be seen from where I had to park. My client was supposed to call me from her cell phone as the husband approached so I could creep out of my parking space and follow in behind him.

She didn't call until after he'd left (lack of communication), and informed me he'd taken a turn through one of the shopping areas instead of driving past where I had parked. I scrambled up to where he turned and saw his vehicle making the turn onto the main thoroughfare a quarter mile down the road. I broke more traffic laws than I care to enumerate, but eventually caught up and followed him the rest of the evening.

The key objective in this case was to follow the husband to the new girlfriend's apartment and get her identified. Once we had her name, we would run basic background checks to include criminal and civil records. As it turned out, he did not go to the girlfriend's, but instead, returned to his own apartment after picking up pizza. He parked his car in the garage assigned to his apartment, but left the garage door open. Since it was dark, I waited about 30 minutes and drove by the apartment again. There was another car now parked directly behind his.

I wrote down the tag on this other car and ran it on my laptop computer equipped with a wireless modem. In a few minutes, I had our mysterious girlfriend identified. With just a few more minutes of database searching, I had her full name, her date of marriage, her social security number, date of birth, her maiden name, her current address, plus five or six previous addresses, the address of her soon-to-be ex-husband, and the fact that she held a professional license in the health-care field.

Sherlock's Secrets

A PI has to make his own luck. Getting into gated communities requires luck, talent, or knowing somebody who lives in the area who will give you a gate pass or the gate code. In the example about the father and the 3-year-old, the father lived in a gated community. There was no security guard at the gate, just either magnetic pass cards for residents or a combination keypad for visitors.

You can tailgate another car through the gate. Cars do it all the time, and if there's no security guard, it's nothing to worry about. The only problem is you can't always get in when you want to, because there may not be a car entering when you need to enter. If there is an exit separate from the entrance, I don't recommend entering through the exit as a car leaves, because that is a dead giveaway that you don't belong there.

In this instance, I was waiting for a car to enter so I could tailgate my way in, when I noticed a visitor trying to punch in the code at the visitors' gate. I drove right up behind her, got out of the car in the rain, and in my friendliest voice, said, "This damn electronic pad always does that when it rains. What combination did they give to you?" "Pound, one, two, three, four," she said, giving me the combination. I hit the star key a couple of times to clear the pad and put in the combination. The gate opened. Now it opens on command for me whenever I want it to. No more waiting to tailgate through. The lady thought I was doing her a favor but really she did one for me. A good PI is always on the lookout to improve his luck.

The father returned the child to my client on time and went back to his apartment where the girlfriend waited. Now that I knew who she was, I didn't have to stay out there late into the evening to attempt to follow her home. She probably stayed all night anyway. I saved my client the cost of five or six more hours of surveillance, and I could hightail it on home, all because I had information available to me when I needed it.

If you're a professional investigator and you're doing surveillance, you need to have the ability to run license tags and other online database searches while you're in the field. Either make sure somebody is at the office while you're out so you can call it in, or be able to run searches from your car.

There are several methods available that will allow an investigator to run tags and data searches from his vehicle:

- **Cell phones.** Cellular telephones can access wireless application protocol (WAP) websites. The state of the art hasn't quite arrived to the point where the WAP allows you to access the databases with your cell phone to get the vehicle information you'll need. But it will soon—or some similar technology will.

- **Personal digital assistants (PDA).** PDAs, such as the Palm Pilot, are wireless-enabled, have their own browsers, and should enable you to access the right databases. However, the small screen size on the PDA makes retrieving the information problematic.

- **Laptop computer with a cellular, or wireless, modem.** There are a number of companies across the nation, including GoAmerica, which provide Internet service through the use of wireless modems. Wireless modems use one of several networks. The bad news is the data transfer rate of these networks is slow, about 14.4K, which is one-fourth the speed of a regular 56K telephone modem. If you need nongraphic downloads such as vehicle tag information, then it's not a bad way to go. The good news is that a new wireless protocol called 3G should be arriving on the scene in North America soon. This will allow access at about 256K, four times as fast as the phone lines. 3G is available now in Europe and some other countries.

Sherlock's Secrets _____

Billing clients is also something of an art. A new laptop computer, wireless modem, and cigarette lighter adapter can run between $1,500 and $3,000 or more. I use a Sony Vaio with a Sierra Wireless modem. Total cost, including carrying case and sales tax, was not quite $3,500. GoAmerica wireless service runs about $60 a month. An investigator has to recoup those costs. The only way to do that is to pass it along to his clients. If he doesn't, he'll be closing his doors quickly. When the PI bills the client, he should bill the database charges at between two and three times what the database services charge him. For the wireless access, a smart PI will add an additional charge on the invoice. At our firm, we just call it "wireless database access charge." I've had clients question me about it but never complain. Do you think the mother we discussed in this chapter is going to complain about a $25 access charge when it saved her $420 in investigative time?

The importance of having the necessary information at your fingertips is magnified if there is more than one person conducting the surveillance. Had the preceding surveillance been a two-man gig, my client would have been paying twice the rate. Having the ability to run that tag and secure the database information saved her 10 man-hours.

Red Light, Green Light, Duck for Cover

This is the one tactic of running a moving surveillance that an investigator must learn. If you're going to follow your own spouse, or help somebody follow her spouse, read this section. If you don't learn anything else in these two chapters on surveillance, I hope you learn this.

There are two rules you have to follow in order to be successful in following someone and not being made; each is described in the sections that follow.

Keep Cover Between the Subject and Yourself

Try your best to use two to four cars as a cover screen. If the subject keeps seeing the same car in his rearview mirror, you will get burned sooner or later, and probably sooner. If your cover turns off or passes the subject, leaving you naked, slow down until the guy behind passes you. If your subject changes lanes, don't change lanes with him unless you're sure he's going to make a turn. Even then, it's better not to make the turn with him. Let the rear surveillance unit make the turn and you come back from the other direction.

If the subject pulls into a grocery store parking lot, don't park out in the open where you have a clear view of him, because he'll have a clear view of you, too. It's best to put a light pole and a whole bunch of cars between you and his car. Also, don't back into a parking space in order to see better out the windshield and make a fast getaway. This is a common mistake made by inexperienced surveillance investigators. Don't do anything that will draw attention to the fact that you're sitting in your car. If you smoke, don't stand around in the middle of the parking lot next to your car and smoke. If you have to smoke, stay in your car, but it's best if you wait until you're moving. Why? Because if you're holding a cigarette, then you're not holding the camera ready to pounce on that unexpected meeting or that quick kiss. You don't know who he is going to walk out with or who he is buying groceries for.

Play the Lights

This is absolutely a must. If you don't learn this trick, you'll lose your subject every time. "Play the lights" means to evaluate not when the next light is going to turn from green to red—you should already know that—but to figure out what the one ahead of that is going to do. Why?

You have two cars as cover. You're approaching a traffic light that's been green for a while. It turns yellow and your subject guns it, racing through the intersection. The two cars you're using for cover stop for the red light. You can pull around them and try to run the red light (not advisable), but if you know that the next light up is going to turn red before your guy gets there, then there is no rush. Save your own life by sitting through the light and then moseying on up to where your subject is patiently waiting for his light to turn green. If you don't know what the next light is going to do and when, then you're up a creek. You should always, always be aware of what the traffic light situation is two or three blocks ahead if you can see that far. If the first light is going to turn yellow and the next one up is red now, you know it's going to be green when your guy arrives at that intersection. You'd better ditch the cover cars and hustle through with your subject, then lay back and get some more cover.

Playing the lights and keeping good cover are the two most important aspects of being successful with moving surveillances.

The Least You Need to Know

- Know in advance where your subject is going by talking to the client or finding out from the insurance adjuster when the subject will be visiting the doctor. If a husband is impossible to follow, then follow the other woman. She won't be looking for a surveillance.

- Plan how your subject is going to exit from wherever he is, whether it's a subdivision or a grocery store parking lot.

- Don't follow the subject into a small business parking lot, but do follow her into a major mall lot and the mall itself, if she goes in.

- To conduct an effective foot surveillance, always keep some cover between you and the subject. Alter your appearance by adding and removing clothing and glasses. Don't get in front of your subject.

- You may only have one chance to get the photograph you need, so always be prepared to take it. There are only 20 seconds separating a jerk investigator from a hero.

- Multiple-person surveillances require good communication, the ability to position the rest of the team to maximum advantage, and the capability of obtaining license tag information during the surveillance.

- The most important aspects of a moving surveillance are keeping cover between yourself and the subject, and evaluating the traffic lights ahead of the surveillance so proper decisions can be made when the subject runs red lights.

Part 4

Working the Cases

Okay, you've done your homework and you're ready to hit the street. What's your first case? This section takes you to the places where the PI works, and we'll teach you how to get the job done.

You'll learn professional tricks such as trash covers and getting information from airline personnel without them even knowing it. You're taught, in fascinating detail, how to work an actual crime scene investigation on your own. You'll be there, dusting for prints and bagging and tagging the evidence. Sifting for clues of an unfaithful spouse and setting up Nanny Cams for home surveillance are also part of a PI's caseload. After studying these chapters, you'll be up for all the challenges.

Chapter 16

Tricks and Treats

In This Chapter

- ◆ Bypassing Caller ID
- ◆ Using the garbage to get the dirt
- ◆ Learning legal pretexts
- ◆ Enlisting an airline ticket agent's help
- ◆ Tricking the subject out of his house
- ◆ Getting forwarding addresses for 50 cents
- ◆ Obtaining the elusive hotel statement

Every profession has tricks of the trade. These tricks are shortcuts to help the professional achieve successful results more rapidly than "traditional methods" might allow. In the investigative business, the case is considered successful if the client is happy with the work performed and the investigator gets paid. That is not to say that the PI is not emotionally involved with some of his cases. He cannot, however, let his emotions dictate his actions or color his reporting. If he becomes biased and loses his objectivity, then he has lost the case, regardless of the legal outcome.

It's not really an accurate description to call the techniques presented in this chapter "tricks." Actually, they are advanced and sophisticated methods for obtaining information necessary for a successful resolution of a case, keeping in mind our definition of what constitutes "a successful resolution."

Fooling Caller ID

Caller ID has invaded North America. For the private investigator, it can be a blessing. More often, though, Caller ID is a curse to the PI. It's a curse because the telephone is one of the greatest tools in our toolbox and sometimes it's better to keep the tool a secret.

For example, one of my assistants, Gretchen, was given the job to track down a potential witness in a case that we needed to interview. She ran this witness's name through all the different databases we discussed in Chapter 9. All she had was a name and a former address. In just a matter of minutes, Gretchen had identified the woman and obtained her social security number, date of birth, Florida driver's license number, and several former addresses, but no current address or telephone number. Databases are great, but they don't necessarily answer every question about a person that a PI might need answered, especially important ones such as where is this person right NOW.

In reviewing the information that the databases spewed out, I noticed an active phone listing at one of her former addresses that was listed to another person with the same last name. Figuring it was probably a relative, I picked up our best tool, the telephone, and called. It was the witness's brother. He wouldn't give me her phone number, but did give me her father's number. I called the father in another state and he promised to have his daughter call me. She did shortly thereafter. I could have spent hours searching directory information in the various states trying to locate her and might never have found her. But after just two phone calls, I had her interviewed and got the information my client needed. You can't beat a PI who is talented with a telephone. Maybe all those hours your teen spends on the phone will train her for PI work.

Part of that talent includes knowing how to keep the party he's speaking to from knowing that the call originates from a private investigative office. It's a growing challenge, since Caller ID comes standard on almost all cellular telephones, and many, many residential telephones are equipped with it as well. An astute investigator has to assume that every telephone number he dials is going to show the recipient the calling telephone number, and probably the name as well. It's a fact of life now that the private investigator has to deal with and be prepared to circumvent.

How Caller ID Works

For the techies in the audience, here is a good explanation of how Caller ID works. If you've always wanted to know what a Caller ID data stream looks like, now's your chance.

Caller ID is a data stream sent by the phone company to your line between the first and second ring. The data stream conforms to Bell 202, which is a 1200-baud half-duplex FSK modulation. That is why serial Caller ID boxes run at 1200 baud.

The data stream itself is pretty straightforward. Here's an example:

```
UUUUUUUUUUUUUUUUUUUUUUUUUUUUUU '^D
032415122503806467x
```

The first thing to note are the 30 Us. Those are actually sync pulses. A "U" is 55 hex, or 01010101 binary. This is called the "Channel Seizure Signal." After that comes 130 milliseconds of 1200 Hz (the Bell 202 "mark" frequency) which usually shows up in the data stream as a character or two of garbage.

That is followed by the "message type word," which is 04 hex for standard Caller ID, 07 hex for name and number. A word, by the way, is 8 bits for our purposes. That is followed by the "message length word" which tells us how many bytes follow.

The next four bytes are the date, in ASCII. In the example above, the date is 0324, or March 24.

The next four bytes after the date are the time, also in ASCII. In the example, the time is 1512, or 3:12P.M.

The next 10 digits are the phone number that is calling. In the example, the phone number is 250-380-6467. The number is also in ASCII and doesn't contain the hyphens. Some phone companies will leave out the area code and only transmit seven digits for a local call, others will always send the area code as well.

If this were a name-and-number Caller ID data stream, the number would be followed by a delimiter (01h) and another message-length byte to indicate the number of bytes in the name. This would be followed by the name itself, in ASCII.

If this call originated from an area that doesn't support Caller ID, then instead of the phone number, a capital "O" is transmitted (4F hex).

If the call was marked "private" as a result of the caller using *67 or having a permanent call-blocking service, then instead of the phone number, a capital "P" (50 hex) would be sent.

The very last byte of the data stream is a checksum. This is calculated by adding the value of all the other bytes in the data message (the message type, length, number and name data, and any delimiters) and taking the two's complement of the low byte of the result (in other words, the two's complement of the modulo-256 simple checksum of the CID data).

Thanks to The Clone at www.nettwerked.net for the detailed explanation.

How to Get Around Caller ID

There are three easy ways to circumvent Caller ID:

- Use a pay telephone.

- Dial *67 prior to dialing the phone number (or use an Automatic Number Identification service).

- Use a prepaid calling card.

When you use a pay telephone, the Caller ID may display the words "pay phone." In making a pretext call, it'd be difficult to pretend you're doing a survey, when the Caller ID reads pay phone. The advantage to using a pay phone is that there is no way the call will be traced back to you.

> **Sammy the Snitch** _____
>
> A word of caution about pay phones. They are not usually tapped by the government, but they can be with a court order, just like any other telephone. Likewise, if you're using the same pay phone repeatedly, there will be witnesses to that fact. We put an employee of a major cellular company in jail for making repeated bomb threats to her employer from a pay phone located just down the street from her house. We tracked the location of the pay phone and developed witnesses who saw her making calls from that phone at the appropriate time the bomb threats were received. Be aware that the use of pay phones can be compromised.

Most Regional Bell Operating Companies allow a person to dial *67 prior to dialing the phone number. Dialing *67 blocks the transmission of the Caller ID information to most telephone numbers. A *67 blocked call will be reported to the receiving party's Caller ID as a "private call." There is usually no additional charge for this service if it's available within your area.

Another service provided by the phone companies is Automatic Number Identification (ANI). Some telephone companies call it Automatic Identification Number (AIN) instead of ANI. ANI is typically used with toll-free numbers, 911 emergency operations, and large companies, but anybody willing to foot the expense can have the service. ANI is sending different data over different lines than Caller ID and cannot be blocked by dialing *67 first.

If you call any subscriber to the ANI service, he or she will be able to see your number. Not all ANI subscribers have "real-time ANI," which gives the recipient the caller's phone number at the time of the call; 911 relies on real-time ANI to locate callers. Toll-free subscribers usually get their list of callers at the end of the month, along with their bill. ANI service is usually combined with more sophisticated telephone equipment and lines like a T-1 line. Expect to pay over $1,000 a month to get it started.

When someone phones our agency and refuses to identify himself, or we see some other need to know who a particular caller was, we write down the date and time of the call. When the toll-free bill comes, we compare it to our list of suspect calls by date and time, and usually are able to identify the caller. If the unknown call is particularly important, we can wait one day before calling our toll-free provider, which can then provide us with the phone number for the call. Remember, calling a toll-free number and blocking the Caller ID by using *67 doesn't work for ANI subscribers. You'll end up as naked as the emperor in his new clothes. You can run, but you can't hide.

If you're regularly making phone calls and you don't want your number to show on Caller ID, then you might try using a prepaid calling card. In dialing the 800 number to access the prepaid calling card's call center, the Caller ID information is passed to the call center, but is not passed through to the final recipient.

This is not true of all prepaid calling cards. We find that Sprint cards pass the Caller ID information right on along. We have found only one prepaid calling card that does not pass the Caller ID data stream on to the final recipient, and that is World-Com. For the most part, AT&T cards don't pass it either, although we've noted that for some reason, calls going to Texas seem to get the Caller ID data stream passed through from the AT&T card. So be careful. The best way to check is to purchase a card and try it by calling your cell phone or other phone with Caller ID. If the incoming call shows "out of area," you're probably all right. If you have a need to make discreet calls to Texas, I'd find a friend there and try it first.

Trash Covers

If you really want to get to know a person up close and personal, collect his garbage. Collecting another person's trash is called a "trash cover." This is a perfectly legal method of digging up information about a person. The law is pretty well established in most states that once a person has set his garbage at the front of his property for collection, it is considered abandoned property and fair game for anybody who wants it.

CAUTION

Sammy the Snitch

State laws on picking up garbage that belongs to a third party vary from state to state. Most state laws agree that it is abandoned property and, as long as you don't trespass, there is no problem in conducting a trash cover. In the past, a few states argued in court that until the trash was commingled with other trash, it was still the property of the original owner. Before conducting a trash cover, check your state's statutes. Most attorneys have a complete set of the statutes in their offices. If a client requests a trash cover, ask the clients attorney what the applicable statutes are in your state. If they don't know the answer, they'll look it up.

If your spouse is nagging you to take out your own garbage, why would you want to go digging through someone else's? Because it's ripe. Not just with smells, but with very detailed information, such as bank account information, bills, credit card statements, and new and expired credit cards themselves. You'll know what kind of liquor the person drinks and how much. Rough drafts of letters written to friends, cards from lovers that he doesn't want his wife to see, payroll stubs, and empty prescription bottles will all be found in the garbage. You name it and you can find it by performing a trash cover.

There are several techniques utilized in trash covers. You'll have to evaluate your particular situation and decide for yourself which would work best. First, call the local sanitation company or the city, if it's city run, and find out what days of the week the garbage is collected at the particular address in question. Next, scout your subject's house and look at his or her garbage cans.

Most people set their garbage out the night before the collection. The most professional technique is to purchase garbage cans identical to your subject's cans. About 3:00 in the morning, drive to the subject's house in a van and swap cans. Be sure that there is garbage in the cans that you leave behind so nobody gets suspicious.

If you don't want to do that, the next easiest method is to drive to the residence in the early morning, take the garbage out of the cans, and place it in the back of a pickup truck or a van. I strongly suggest putting some plastic sheets on the floor of the van or truck, or repackaging the garbage into clean plastic bags as you collect it. In addition to the paper products, there will be a lot of rotten food, dead animals, dirty diapers and messy stuff of undeterminable origin.

Latex gloves are a must. A mask to breathe through is not a bad idea, either. Murphy's Law applies to trash covers: The papers with the information of most value will be the soggiest. Be sure to have a large, well-ventilated room to lay out the trash and examine it. You will also need a drying rack or some way to spread out mushy paper so it will dry and hopefully be readable.

Trash covers are disgusting, but we've always found them to reliably produce important information. You may not get what you're looking for the first time out. For a trash cover to be productive, you should plan on grabbing the garbage regularly for several weeks. Follow the rules of evidence that we will discuss in the next chapter. You never know what you might have to produce in court. Hopefully, not the dirty diapers. It's probably safe to just toss them.

> **Elementary, My Dear Watson**
>
> Speaking of diapers .... When Khrushchev was the Soviet premier of Russia during the era of the Cold War, one of the Central Intelligence Agency's greatest coups was snagging one of Khrushchev's bowel movements. By analyzing it, the government had an inside view into the premier's health. And you thought it was just government waste.

The Pretext

A pretext is a subterfuge or a ploy used by private investigators to encourage an individual to reveal information about himself, or another party, without giving away the true reason for the conversation. In the course of responding to what appears to be a normal, everyday query, the individual releases the information the investigator actually is seeking, without ever suspecting a thing.

Basically, a pretext is a lie. It is not a mean-spirited lie designed to injure. It is a clever lie designed to scam a person into providing information. Surprisingly, the hardest skill for many private investigators to develop is the formulation of good pretexts. Being deceitful seems to come naturally to some people. For those who never lie, developing good pretext skills will be difficult ... but not impossible.

Identifying the Subject

Suppose you, the private investigator, are trying to locate Steve Brown. You think you have him located, but you're not sure that you have the right Steve Brown. Whatever you do, you do not want him to know a private investigator is on his tail. Why? Because if he is the right one, you're going to begin surveillance and you don't want him to be watching for you.

You call him from a safe telephone and ask if Steve Brown is there. Be sure and use both first and last names. If you just ask for Steve, you could get any old Steve. There might be more than one Steve at that phone number, or you might have dialed the wrong number. The person answering will either say yes or no. If he is there, ask to speak to him.

When he comes to the phone, you employ the pretext. Assuming you know the background on the right Steve Brown, ask him if this is the Steve Brown whose date of birth is such and such. Give him the right Steve Brown's date of birth. Normally, he'll answer yes or no. If he answers no, then you have the wrong Steve Brown, so keep searching. If the answer is yes, you must now give him a reason for the call that will not alert him. A good pretext to use in this case is to say that you are looking for the Steve Brown, born such and such, for a high school reunion. The Steve Brown you're looking for graduated from Coral Gables High School in 1965. He'll say no, you've got the wrong Steve Brown, and hang up.

Now you know, in fact, you do have the right Steve Brown, and you also know where he is at this very movement. You can begin your surveillance whenever you please and be assured that you're on the right man. I know investigators who've spent days following the wrong person with the same name as their subject because they didn't do a simple pretext telephone call to verify they had the right guy.

Finding the Employment

Suppose you need to know a person's employer. This one works most of the time, but not always—no pretext works every time. This is one of those pretexts that sometimes works just as well if you're talking to a spouse as to the subject himself. Telephone the subject from a safe phone. Tell him you are (make up a name) from (make up a bank name) and he has been preapproved for a credit card with the low introductory rate of 0 percent guaranteed for 12 months, no annual fee, and the preapproved credit limit is $9,500. Not everybody wants or needs a new credit card, but most of the people a PI deals with would kill for a card with a credit line of over $500.

Explain that you only need to have him verify a few items and he'll have his new card within two weeks. If he's gone with you this far, he'll go the rest of the way. Here is the important part of this pretext. You start giving him details about himself to make him feel comfortable that you are legitimate. Say, "Let's see. You were born on Oct 10, 1972, correct? You reside at" (give him his address) "and your telephone number is" (supply him the telephone number).

Now you have to get him to start giving you information. You say, "I'm going to give you the first part of your social security number, to verify that I'm actually talking to Steve Brown, then I need for you to verify the last digit for me." You give him the first eight digits of his social security number (so he knows you already know it) and he verifies the last one. Now he is starting to give you information. Next you ask him for his mother's maiden name to use as a code word for his account. Nobody ever balks at that question and he's still spitting out information you didn't have.

Next ask him how many cards he'll need, and does he want his wife's name on one of them? He is giving you even more information. It's not important information. It's not information you care one whit about, but he is growing accustomed to giving you information. Now you say to him, "The only thing left to verify is your employment. We're not interested in your salary, but we need to have in our records your current employer." He has time and emotion involved in the relationship with you and he wants that card. If he has an employer, and he's come this far, he'll give it to you. Get the employer's name, telephone number, and address. Bingo! You've got what you wanted.

> **CAUTION**
>
> ### Sammy the Snitch
>
> The Gramm-Leach-Bliley Act made it illegal to use pretexts to obtain another person's financial information by making false, fictitious, or fraudulent statements to financial institutions. The Federal Trade Commission regularly conducts sting operations on private investigators who advertise asset or bank account searches. Typically, those types of searches involve pretext calls to the banks and also the subjects. Be warned: Don't do that. If you need financial information on a subject, try using a trash cover at both his residence and office, if appropriate.

If you've developed a friendly rapport with this subject on the phone, you can push this pretext a little further. If you're going to do surveillance on him, it might be helpful to know what his work hours are. Say something to him like, "Oh, that sounds like an interesting job. Do you like that?" Chat with him for a minute about his job and then slide in a question about his hours. Does he have to be to work very early or does he work a night shift? Ask whatever seems reasonable. If you're friendly with him, and chatty, you'll end up with his entire life story.

Where Is She Going?

A client wanted us to follow his soon-to-be ex-wife to Bermuda. I told him to twist my arm a little and maybe I'd take the case. He thought she would drive from Florida to Atlanta, their home, and leave from there. The client was flying into our local airport to pick up his 8-year-old and spend two weeks at the beach. We had to follow the wife from the moment she turned over the boy, because nobody really knew for sure where she was going. Bermuda was the client's best guess, and I was rooting for it, too.

He informed us that his wife had just undergone several different plastic surgeries, including a tummy tuck, liposuction on her thighs, and breast implants. He thought she probably had a lover, and in Georgia, at that time, adultery was not only grounds for divorce, it also figured big time into alimony settlements or lack thereof, according to the proof that was given.

I told the client we would need a two-man surveillance team for this. He said fine; he didn't care what it cost. Got to love the sound of that. I chose one of my investigators to go with me. We had our carry-on luggage crammed with surveillance gear, radios, binoculars, and cameras.

The wife met our client at the airport and turned over the child. He left, and she got into her car, left the airport grounds, made a U-turn, and pulled back up to the curb of the terminal. She took two suitcases out of the trunk and gave them to a skycap. She then took her car to long-term parking.

I gave the skycap $10 and asked him where the lady with the bags was going. He took my $10 and then said he couldn't remember. Thanks a lot, bud. He did add she was flying out on Continental, but he wasn't sure which flight because she didn't have her ticket yet. He'd set her bags down near the Continental ticket counter.

Continental had two flights that left within 20 minutes of each other. One went to Los Angeles, the other to Houston. Nothing to Bermuda. Bummer. We needed to know where she was going so we could get on the same flight. Our only chance was to arrive with her and follow her from the airport. If we lost her here, or at the other end, we were out of luck and we'd never find her. The pressure was on.

When she came back into the terminal, I've got to admit, she looked like a million bucks. She was wearing a filmy silk dress and, it appeared, nothing else. As she got into the ticket line, I stepped in right behind her. I didn't want to talk to her because if she saw me in LA or Houston, I didn't want her to recognize me.

The line moved slowly, but eventually it was her turn to approach the counter. My only chance was to get to the same ticket agent she was talking to. Other agents became available and I pretended I was looking for my ticket in my carry-on luggage and let several people behind me go ahead. Eventually she bought her ticket. As she left the counter I hustled right up to the same agent, who happened to be a man. As my subject was walking away in her nearly see-through dress, I said to the ticket agent, "Man, what a fine-looking woman. Where is she going?"

He responded, "Houston."

"Well then," I said, "Give me two tickets to Houston."

He couldn't believe it. "Really, you want two tickets to Houston?"

"Yeah, really. I've got time. Maybe I'll get lucky," I said.

As he was printing the tickets, I inquired about seat assignments.

"Not to worry," he said. "I've put you right next to her."

What a nice guy.

I had him change the seats so that I was two rows behind her and my other investigator was a row in front of her.

What's the point to this story? Do you think that nice guy would've been as nice if I'd rushed up to him, pulled out my state-issued private investigator's license, and demanded to know where that woman was going? Not on your life. He would've started spouting company regulations about the privacy of their records and the need for a court order or a subpoena, and a supervisor would have appeared out of nowhere. I would've drawn attention to myself and been made. Instead, I got exactly what I wanted and had the agent on my team, giving me more help than I needed.

You can get information from almost anybody. You just have to find a reason for that person to give it to you. You cannot coerce it from people. You usually can't pry it out. It has to slide out easily so they don't even know they gave you what you wanted. This trick can be used at any airport. Just adjust the facts to the particular case you're working on.

The Outhouse Routine

Your client is a workers' compensation insurance company. Your assignment is to get some productive videotape of the subject who is currently not working due to an alleged injury on the job. The problem is the subject never seems to come out of his house when you have him under surveillance. How do you get him out of the house?

This little trick takes two people and a dog. The dog is optional. It can't be used on every case, but if the situation is right, adapt the facts to the neighborhood where your subject lives and go for it. One surveillance investigator is already set up with the video camera on and ready. The other, who needs to be a female, is walking her dog or jogging. She approaches the subject's front yard and gets down on her hands and knees on the lawn and begins searching carefully through the grass. This continues for as long as necessary until the subject can't stand it any longer and comes out of the house to see what is going on. The camera should be rolling.

The female explains that she was walking her dog and her $6,500 engagement ring, which her boyfriend just gave her last night, slipped off her finger and is somewhere on your subject's front lawn. She tells your subject she was going to get it resized today but hadn't gone to the jewelry store yet (it helps to mention a local, high-priced store) to have it done. What is she going to do? Her fiancé will kill her if she can't find the ring. By now, if she's a good actress, she'll be in tears.

One of two things will happen. Your subject may get down on his hands and knees and begin combing through the grass to help her. This makes excellent video for a workers' compensation case. Or he won't. She can look all she wants by herself. If the subject retreats to the house again, she should look for a while longer and then approach the door, ring the bell, and give the subject a name and phone number, asking him to call her if he finds the ring.

![CAUTION] **Sammy the Snitch** _____

> There are some things you cannot do to your subject under surveillance. Some investigators will flatten a subject's tire in order to videotape the subject changing the tire. Not only is this not fair, it's malicious mischief and against the law. The worst part is how you, the professional PI, are going to respond when the subject's attorney asks you in court if you have any knowledge of how the tire became flattened. Are you going to lie and thereby be guilty of perjury?
>
> So you lie. Then the attorney produces the subject's neighbor, who saw you let the air out of the tire. Now you've ruined your client's case and run afoul with the court, all at the same time. Good move, huh? That story will spread so fast, you'll never get another case from an insurance company or any local attorney again. Play smart, play fair, and don't break the law.

After she's been gone for a while, the subject will come out of the house and begin combing through the grass by himself, with no intention of telling her he found the ring.

If the subject doesn't come out of the house at the beginning of the pretext, he may not be able to see your female investigator from where he is in the house. After a few minutes, she should ring the bell and tell him what has happened to her ring, to get the plot moving along.

This little maneuver usually works really well. At worst, you'll get a little video of the subject and know what he looks like. It's not unusual to get a lot of video of your subject and his wife and everybody else in the house, out on the front lawn looking for that $6,500 ring after the girl and the dog have left.

Postal Tricks: Getting More from a First-Class Stamp

The U.S. Post Office forwards more than two billon pieces of mail a year. Most everybody is aware that you can put "Please Forward" on a first-class letter and the post office will forward it, if it has a forwarding address. Frequently, when searching for somebody, you might have an old address, but can't find the current one. You could write your subject a letter and hope he or she will respond. I wouldn't hold my breath, though. There is another option.

You can physically go to the local post office that covers the subject's old address and request the forwarding information, but usually they won't give it to you. They used to give it to you and charge a dollar, but there's been a rule change in the last couple of years. However, if it's a small post office in a small town, I still have pretty good luck getting the new address from the postmaster.

When that doesn't work, or the old address is in another state, there is an alternative. Address an envelope to the subject at the last known address. Above the subject's name and address, in the middle of the envelope, type in bold print, "Address Correction Requested." Be sure and put your return address on the envelope. Now, when the letter goes to the post office that covers the old address, the clerk there will see the "Address Correction Requested." Instead of forwarding the envelope to the subject at his new address, he will return it to you with a yellow label that has the new forwarding address on it. This will normally work for up to a year after the subject has moved and left a change of address with the post office. The only cost is the original first-class stamp. Why the post office will give it to you that way, when they won't give it up when you ask directly, beats me. Some bureaucrat somewhere dreamt that one up. Nevertheless, it's a good way, for less than 50¢, to get a forwarding address.

Proving the Hotel Stay

Working domestic cases has lots of entertainment value. There are some PIs that turn up their noses at domestic cases. We've always made them one of our specialties, for several reasons. One, we collect a retainer up front and put the money in the bank before we start the case. We don't have to wait for some insurance company to pay us in three or four months, or whenever they get around to it. The other reason is that these cases can be a lot of fun.

PIs often get asked to prove that a client's spouse stayed in a particular hotel during a certain time frame. This is kind of like the ticket agent in the earlier section in this chapter, "Where Is She Going?" If the PI asks the hotel directly for a copy of a bill, the hotel will steadfastly refuse. Before I worked out this little trick, I even tried to bribe a hotel clerk, offering her $1,000 for a duplicate bill. She refused. I developed this trick I'm about to reveal to you here and got the invoice anyway. The next day, she was kicking herself for not taking the $1,000. She told me herself how stupid it was for her not to take the money, since I "tricked" them out of the bill.

Let's make up two names, call them Gary Fielding and Sheila Smith. Sheila Smith is the wife of my client and had a fling with Fielding at a certain hotel on May 5. My client wants the bill for two purposes. He's hoping the invoice will show there were two occupants to the room. He also wants any long-distance calls charged to the room as additional proof that his wife was there. Here's how you can get it.

This works even if you're on the case several months after the hotel rendezvous. Call the toll-free number for the hotel chain and make a reservation for the next day. Tell the operator there will be two of you in the room. Give the reservation clerk the name of Gary Fielding as the primary name and include your own name, Steve Brown, as accompanying Fielding, and use Brown's credit card to guarantee the room.

The next day, check into the hotel. Use your own name, Steve Brown, to check in, and tell them Fielding hasn't arrived yet. This is important: Make sure the registration says Fielding on it.

An hour or so after you've checked in, ring down to accounting and identify yourself as Gary Fielding. You're in room such and such. You stayed here last month on May 5 but seemed to have lost your copy of the statement and you need it to attach to your expense report. Ask them to drop another copy by your room. They can just slip it under the door sometime today, if that's not inconvenient. In a few hours, you'll have delivered into your hot little hands exactly what your client wants, and it'll only cost you (or your client) the price of the room.

If your client really wants to nail Mrs. Smith, there's more you can do while you're there. Once you get the statement, you'll know she and Fielding occupied, say, room 502. Call the front desk and tell them you'd like to move to room 502 if possible, if not today, then tomorrow, when it becomes free. In your spare time, snap some pictures of the door to room 502. Make sure the room number shows in the photos.

When you get the room reassigned to you, unmake the bed. Toss some bathroom towels around on the floor and make the room look recently used. Take lots of pictures of the unmade bed and the room and bathroom. Forward the pictures, with your report and generous invoice, to your client.

At a pretrial hearing, your client can toss a copy of the room bill across the table to his wife's attorney. Next, he flips copies of the photos, one by one, (very dramatic moment here) to the attorney, saying the pictures were taken of the room Mrs. Smith and Mr. Fielding shared after they checked out of the hotel. That's a true statement. It just so happens they were taken way after they checked out ... like a couple of weeks after.

Sounds sneaky, you say? Not as sneaky as committing adultery and then trying to wring your spouse's wallet for all it's worth.

That combination works very well and has saved my clients hundreds of thousands of dollars in alimony payments.

The Least You Need to Know

- Caller ID can be bypassed by dialing *67 before the number, utilizing a pay telephone, or using a WorldCom prepaid calling card as of this writing.

- Pretext telephone calls can be used to prove identity and obtain a subject's employment.

- While attempting to obtain flight information on a subject under surveillance, a PI can enlist a ticket agent's help without revealing his status or real intentions in the case.

- A good method to encourage a subject under surveillance to leave his residence is to make him believe something valuable has been lost on his front lawn.

- The post office provides an address correction service that can be utilized at the cost of a first-class stamp and will provide the PI with a forwarding address, which cannot be obtained by requesting it in person.

- The elusive hotel bill proving an overnight stay can be obtained by registering at the hotel, on a later date, under the name of the subject and then requesting a copy of the previous bill. Accounting will provide it with no questions asked.

Conducting Your Own Crime Scene Investigation

In This Chapter

- ◆ Making the decision to do it yourself
- ◆ Keeping the dirt out
- ◆ Going slow and being thorough
- ◆ Learning the value of photographing the scene
- ◆ Bagging and tagging the evidence
- ◆ Understanding what to look for at the scene
- ◆ Raising fingerprints
- ◆ Learning the rules of evidence

You've come home from a night out. Your keys are in your hand and as you start to put the front-door key into the lock, you notice the glass panel on the door is broken. If you're smart, you'll back off, call the police, and wait until they arrive before entering. The burglar may still be inside.

The police walk through your house and verify that nobody is inside. You enter. Right away, you notice an empty spot on the wall where the stereo, DVD player, and your new HDTV television used to be. Strange—in the bedroom, you notice one of the pillows is missing a pillowcase. You later learn that the burglar used it to carry off the sterling silver from the dining room. The drawers in every room are opened and contents spilled on the floor. Your 35mm single-lens reflex camera and all your zoom lenses are probably nestled with the sterling in the pillowcase.

One policeman trudges along behind you, surveying the mess, while the other one sits at the dining room table, writing the report. "What's the value on the missing articles?" he asks.

You start adding it up. The camera was new 10 years ago. You paid a lot for the DVD player but you saw one at the wholesale club last week for $100. You guesstimate the replacement value of the missing items to be approximately $7,500.

> **Crime Scene Clues**
>
> Conducting a **crime scene investigation** entails the collection of evidence or possible evidence toward the goal of placing suspects at the scene of the crime. The evidence must be collected according to the rules of evidence that have been established by law and judicial precedence.

"When will the crime scene investigators arrive?" you ask.

"Oh, we're sorry, but the department won't dispatch a crime scene unit unless the amount missing is over $15,000. They're just too busy working larger crimes to come out here," the officer replies. "But your homeowners policy should cover most of your loss."

The two patrolmen leave, and you and your wife are surveying the mess left behind. Before you start cleaning up, you should think about doing your own *crime scene investigation*.

Can You Do It?

The answer to "Can you do it?" is, unequivocally, yes—after you finish reading this chapter. First, we have to get rid of all those notions about "doing a crime scene" you picked up from the O. J. trial, and from watching Court TV and *CSI* on television. Aha, there's another benefit of reading this book: no commercials.

You can find the fingerprints and save evidence that later down the road might directly connect a suspect to your burglary. I've seen it happen. A month or even six months after your burglary, a potential suspect pops up, and the police department that was too busy to send a crime scene unit to your house will sit up and take notice of the evidence you've collected, as long as you've followed the instructions in this chapter. And how, you ask, are you going to come up with a suspect? A neighbor may tell you he saw another neighbor's son climbing your back fence with a pillowcase over his shoulder. Or your camera may show up in a pawnshop. We will discuss pawnshops in Chapter 22.

One of your children may be in another child's house down the street and mention to you that Johnny's dad has a television just like the one you had stolen. Remember Daniel Black from Chapter 12? Daniel stole whatever he could, from whomever he could, including his neighbors across the street (actually, on both sides) and from his landlord.

Even the police might eventually get lucky and come up with a suspect by accident. Police frequently arrest somebody for one crime, and the suspect admits to several dozen burglaries. Yours may be one of them. If you have the evidence, all the better. In addition, the police often find whole houses or warehouses full of stolen property. When that happens, they have to sort through it all and try to find the original victims. Your property may be in there. The police may have suspects, but no evidence. If you follow the directions in this chapter and have collected the evidence yourself, suddenly you become a hero, and can help the police convict the burglar by providing them with the evidence that they wouldn't come out and collect themselves.

Don't let the responding patrolmen talk you out of collecting the evidence yourself if they're not going to send out a crime scene unit. The truth is that, by the end of this chapter, you'll know more than the responding patrol person does about the evidentiary value of the crime scene. What they learn in the police academy is more geared toward preserving the crime scene than conducting one.

Contamination

In this chapter we use residential burglary as a method for discussing the approach and techniques of crime scene investigation. The techniques discussed in relation to burglaries also apply to any crime scene you may be called upon to investigate. This includes murder, rape, assault, robbery, kidnapping, automobile accidents, and hit and runs. Each crime scene will be different, but the techniques for one are similar to the others.

A crime scene has to be initially examined, as we discussed in the beginning of this chapter, to ensure that the subjects have fled and the immediate area is safe. This will require some walking around the scene, opening doors, and performing an initial assessment. In doing this, be observant. If it is a murder scene and there are bloody footprints, don't walk in the blood. Step around it. Get down on your hands and knees, shine a flashlight across the floor, and see if there are any footprints that you can't identify as your own.

If it's a murder, you probably won't be doing the crime scene yourself. But maybe it's your dog that was shot or had its throat cut by the burglars, and there are bloody footprints and handprints all over the house. Or the burglar might have cut his hand breaking the windowpane where he obtained access to your home.

If it's been raining and your shoes are wet or muddy, take them off. Leave the umbrella on the porch. I know it's difficult, when you come home and find your house has been burglarized, not to run from room to room, examining your treasures to see what the burglars took and what they left behind, but don't do it. Your examination has to be careful, controlled, and systematic. Don't let your hysteria lead to contamination of the crime scene. If you do, then you might as well forget this chapter and go on to the next.

Are there any beer cans left around the scene? The natural inclination is to pick up foreign objects and examine them. Don't. Leave them where they are. By picking up a can or a cigarette butt or a drinking glass with your bare hand, you've just contaminated the object. You haven't necessarily made it useless as evidence, but you have made the later examination of it more complicated than it needed to be.

There are certain techniques we're going to learn concerning retrieving, marking, and handling the evidence. So for now, secure the scene, and make sure your immediate environment is safe.

Slow-Crime Scene-No Speeding Zone

Once you're sure the burglar has gone, the next thing to do is to carefully and slowly examine the crime scene. If it's a house, walk around the exterior and look for anything out of the ordinary. Criminals frequently drop things while they're trying to gain entry. It may be a cigarette, maybe an entire pack of cigarettes. Beer and soda cans are commonly left behind by thieves. Criminals have been known to leave their tools behind, and even to have dropped their wallets with their driver's license and other identity papers.

Figure out how the burglar gained entry to the house, and then very carefully examine the area around the entry site. Look for footprints in soft dirt or anything else. Maybe a snagged piece of cloth on a rose bush or a handkerchief that fell out of a pocket. We obviously can't list all of the many possibilities, but just be very, very observant.

Next, inside the house, with your shoes off, walk carefully through the entire house and look for evidence. Stop and analyze how the criminal moved throughout the house. He came through the back window, so picture yourself coming through the window. What did he have to touch to get through the window? Did he have to reach inside and unlock the window? There may be a thumbprint on one side of the lock and a fingerprint on the other.

Reenact the crime, be it a burglary or something worse. Figure out where the players were and who did what to whom. Don't forget the kitchen. Burglars frequently raid the refrigerator while they're making themselves comfortable in your home. Always be thinking fingerprints. Will there be fingerprints and palm prints on the handle of the refrigerator door? Probably so, if they helped themselves to the Ben and Jerry's you keep in there. Many folks store valuables in the freezer section of the refrigerator. Burglars know this, and usually check it out. Chances are, they looked in your freezer.

How about the bathroom? Was the medicine cabinet ransacked? They were looking for prescription drugs. Did the perpetrator open a mirrored door to the cabinet? Unless she was wearing gloves, there's a good chance her prints will be on that mirror. If not on the mirror, then on the back of the cabinet door. If it's a metal door or the back of the door has a smooth finish, the chances of getting prints off of it are excellent. Did he pick up some pill bottles and drop them because he wasn't interested in your blood pressure medicine? There's another source of likely fingerprints.

Elementary, My Dear Watson

A favorite trick of the FBI when processing stolen cars (the crime is officially known as interstate transportation of stolen motor vehicles) is to dust behind the rearview and side-view mirrors. Car thieves will often wipe down the areas in a car that they figured they've touched, but will forget about the back of the rearview mirror they adjusted when they first drove the car off. Hundreds and hundreds of car thieves have been put in jail because they didn't think about that mirror.

The bedroom was certainly ransacked. Burglars regularly take pillowcases from their victims' beds, using them to haul away the loot. Was a pillowcase half full of stuff left on the floor? That means the thief had to make a hasty exit. He probably heard you coming in the front door and went out the back. His fingerprints are probably on the pillowcase as well as on the loot left inside of it.

Right now, some of you are saying, "You can't get fingerprints off of cloth."

That's wrong. You'll be surprised to learn from what materials fingerprints can be raised. Even on pages of books. So don't steal this book. Your fingerprints are already all over it.

Documenting the Scene

Get your camera out, if you still have one. If the burglars made off with your camera gear, borrow one from your next-door neighbor, or run to a 24-hour discount store and buy a disposable.

Photograph each room. You want to do this for insurance purposes as well as for evidentiary reasons. If there are footprints, photograph them as well. Take pictures of the entry and exit points, the ransacked bedroom, and any other areas the burglars were in.

Before you're finished, to properly document all of the evidence, you're going to need a good 35mm or digital camera, if you know how to use one. If not, call a friend who does. The photographing of the evidence is very, very important.

In your photographs, take some wide shots that show the entire room or area, and then tighten in and take several shots of each piece of evidence. Do this before you touch or pick up anything. When you're taking the tight shots, put a ruler or a dollar bill, or some object of known length, next to the object you're photographing, so that later the relative size of the object can be easily determined.

Let me explain the value of photographs. When my son, Kerry, was four, he was riding his bike around the neighborhood where we lived. A modified Volkswagen dune buggy came tearing around the corner and ran over him and his bicycle. Later, the kid driving told me he wasn't sure he'd hit anything until he looked in his rearview mirror and saw Kerry and the bike sprawled across the curb.

The driver picked Kerry up and carried him the 100 yards to our house, deposited him on the front steps, and, being late for work, took off without a word. I met my wife at the hospital. A thorough examination showed no permanent injuries, but there was bruising across Kerry's chest, and up the left arm and shoulder. The bruising was in the exact shape of tire treads. It appeared one wheel ran over the left side of his body, scraped the side of his face, and missed squashing his head by literally a fraction of an inch.

The police took a report, but since there were no witnesses to the accident other than my son, they indicated there wasn't much they could do. I knew better.

I took out my trusty Cannon 35mm camera and shot a roll of film, including close-ups of the tire-tread marks on his body. On the close-ups, I put a ruler parallel to the tread marks. I also took shots with the ruler perpendicular to the tread marks, and running across them. This would enable me to get an accurate measurement of the tread width and the length of each cut in the tread.

Determined to find the driver of the dune buggy, I conducted a neighborhood investigation on my own block. None of my neighbors had seen the accident, but finding witnesses to the accident was not the real purpose of the investigation. I was hoping to get some leads that would help me identify the vehicle and the driver responsible. Several neighbors said they'd seen that Volkswagen cutting through the area before, apparently to avoid a traffic light a block away. One person thought the driver was a young man about 20 years old, and remembered seeing the vehicle parked in a residential area a half mile south of ours.

I moved the neighborhood investigation to that other subdivision. In a quarter of an hour, after knocking on a couple of doors, I had the driver's residence located. I had his identity, and had determined his employment to be at a body shop a few miles away.

I went to the body shop with my photographs and found the dune buggy parked out front. There were paint scrapes that appeared to match the paint on my son's bike. Naturally I photographed them. Then I examined the tread on the Volkswagen tires, and compared them to the photos of the tread marks that ran up my son's arm. They appeared to be an exact match. I took photographs of the tires still on the car, close-ups of the tread, and wider shots including the license plate, just in case the owner decided he needed a new set of tires before the day was out.

With the investigation pretty well finished, I wrote a complete report, as you'll learn how to do in Chapter 23. The report detailed everything that happened. I took the report, with copies of the photographs, to the local police department. The next day, the driver was arrested for hit and run. I wasn't vindictive, and I didn't really wish any ill toward the young man; accidents happen. But I was mad as hell that he hadn't stayed around to identify himself and to see if there was anything he could do to help, instead of just laying my son on the front porch and running off because he was late for work.

That's one case that never went to court because the evidence was so overwhelming, the driver pled guilty. See what a good crime scene investigation can do? And it doesn't have to be done by the police department, either.

Bagging and Tagging

The whole purpose of conducting a crime scene investigation by yourself is to be able, at some future point, to testify in court that you collected this evidence. You have to be able to prove to the court, and the defendant's attorney, that the evidence you present in court is, in fact, the same evidence you collected at the time of the incident. How do you do that?

You document every piece of evidence you collect. Carefully pick up each pill bottle that may have fingerprints of the subject, and write your initials and the date on the label. Then, put each bottle in a separate plastic bag. Using a permanent marker, initial and date the bag as well.

When writing your initials and date on potential evidence, you want to leave a permanent mark. It might not be possible to write on a beer can, so take a sharp instrument, like an ice pick, and scratch "your mark" on it. The mark should be something that you can later recognize and testify to the fact that, yes, that is the mark you scratched on it. If you can't scratch it, then stick a small piece of white adhesive tape to it, and initial and date the tape, but a permanent mark is better.

Although I have processed dozens, if not hundreds, of crime scenes, I don't claim to be a forensic expert, and neither should you. You have to use common sense and good judgment. If marking an item will obliterate the evidentiary nature of it, then don't do it. Put it in a bag and mark the bag.

Get a notebook or writing pad and keep a written log of each item. Number each bag, and on your written log, write down the bag number and a description of what is in the bag. Also note the time that the item was bagged. If family members or friends are helping, then also note on the log who collected the item. If there are several of you collecting, then it's a better practice for one person to keep the log and the rest to collect the evidence. I know this may seem tedious. Nobody ever said it was easy. But if you want to be able to prosecute the culprit, this is the way to accomplish it. Why so much paperwork?

Three months after your house has been burglarized, the police notify you that some of your stolen property has been recovered. They can't prove who took it, but they have a suspect in mind. You advise them that you have a beer can that was dropped by the burglar, and that you collected and preserved it. You believe it may have the burglar's fingerprints on it. You provide the can to them and get a receipt for it when you give it to them.

They match the print on the can to their suspect. Bingo. You've got him. Now the case goes to trial. You're on the witness stand testifying about how the can was collected. The defendant's attorney takes the can in his hands and turns his back to you.

Next he turns back around, facing you, and holds up two cans, one in each hand. He asks you, "How, Mr. Homeowner, do you know which can had the defendant's fingerprint on it? How can you be sure? The defendant lives just a few blocks from your residence. Perhaps you rifled through the defendant's trash one evening and stole beer cans, knowing they would have the defendant's fingerprints on them. Later, you provided this can to the police, tricking the authorities into believing my client would be so stupid as to leave a beer can at the scene of the crime."

First, you produce your log, which shows that a specific brand beer can was bagged by yourself at say, 8:06 P.M. on such and such date. Then you ask him to show you the two cans. You, following these instructions, had scratched your initials on the can at the time you bagged it. You hold up the can to the judge and say, "I can say without a doubt that this is the can I found on my living room floor because here are my initials I scratched into it when I collected this can as possible evidence."

This particular scenario has embarrassed many a defendant's attorney in court, and it makes you look like a hero.

Clues Are Where You Find Them

Before beginning to conduct your own crime scene investigation, you need to know what you're looking for.

Here is a list of potential items of evidentiary value that you might find at a crime scene:

- Glass—Shards of glass found on or in a suspect's pants cuff could be positively matched with the broken pane at the entry point in burglary. Bag and tag a piece of the broken glass for possible comparison purposes later.

- Broken headlights—Fragments of glass from broken headlights, or plastic from a taillight lens, can be positively matched to a perpetrator's car. Also, the type and manufacturer of the headlights, as well as the year and make of car, can usually be determined. Turn-indicator bulbs and headlight and taillight bulbs on a car can be examined and a determination made if the light was on at the time it was broken. This is important in accident investigations when one person says he signaled a turn and the other says he didn't. Or it was dark and one driver says her headlights were on and the other says they weren't.

- Cloth—Cloth fragments torn from a larger piece can be fitted and positively matched to the larger piece. Also be aware that buttons ripped off during a struggle frequently have small pieces of the shirt or clothing still attached to them. That piece can also be matched to the garment it came from. Broken buttons can be matched to the rest of the button that may still be attached to the garment.

- Tape—A piece of tape, such as duct tape, can be matched to the roll it came from if additional pieces of tape have not subsequently been cut from the same roll. Don't wad the tape into a ball, as this can distort the ends. Preserve it flat. Fingerprints frequently can be raised off of tape.

- Rope—Officially called cordage, this includes twine and string. If the ends are not too frayed, it sometimes can be matched with the rest of the rope it was cut from. Also, the manufacturer of the cordage can sometimes be determined.

- Typewriters—Typewritten letters may be matched to the typewriter that produced them. Also, photocopied material can sometimes be matched to the specific photocopier that was used.

- Handwritten materials—Handwritten materials such as letters and checks, with enough sample writings, can sometimes be matched to an individual.

- Serial numbers—Serial numbers that have been scratched or etched off of guns and automobile body parts may still be of value. Frequently, these numbers, although gone to the naked eye, can be raised and recovered. When the number is stamped onto the metal, the crystal structure in the metal below is changed. Consequently, through the use of chemical activity, these numbers can be brought back.

- Tools—If tools were used to cut or punch through metal items, then it may be possible to match the tool to the item cut. If a person's wrists were bound with bailing wire, the wire should be preserved for possible later matching with the tool that cut the wire.

Body Fluids and Hair

Some body fluids—semen and blood—can be positively matched to a specific individual through DNA testing. Other body fluids have to contain cells in order to utilize DNA testing. Cigarette butts will usually have saliva stains on them. Saliva itself does not contain cells, but saliva stains frequently do. Urine also is generally considered sterile, but may contain cells suitable for DNA testing.

About 80 percent of the population excretes the same blood group factors as their blood type (O, A, B, and AB) into the body fluids of semen, saliva, and urine. Therefore, an examination of these fluids may determine blood type, even if there is not ufficient DNA material available in the sample for testing. A person who has this characteristic is called "a secretor."

Elementary, My Dear Watson

If a crime against a person occurs, such as an assault, it's not unusual for the criminal to leave some trace fibers from his clothing, or hair from his body and/or head on the victims clothing or body. Likewise, you'd also expect some of the victim's hair and clothing fibers to be found on the assailants clothing or body. This is a hair/fiber exchange. For this reason, in rape cases, even where there are no body fluids present, pubic hair combings of the victim and the assailant (if arrested) are taken to find any loose hairs that may have been exchanged. This is good evidence and will help convict the assailant.

In collecting wet material like a blood-soaked shirt or sheet, let it dry first. Don't expose it to direct sunlight, as the harsh sun will degrade the blood. Lay the material over a makeshift drying rack in a well-ventilated room. Once it is dry, place it in a plastic bag for later examination. If it's not dry when you store it, putrefaction of the blood will occur, and the sample will be useless.

If the blood to be collected is already dried, such as on a car bumper or crusted on carpet or sand, scrape it gently into a container, like a pill vial or a pint-size cardboard or Styrofoam ice cream–type container. If the blood is dried on a piece of glass, leave it on the glass, and save the glass fragment for later examination.

These collection techniques would basically be the same for other body fluids as well.

Hair pulled from a person's head, perhaps in a struggle, will probably have cellular material attached, and would be suitable for DNA testing. Cut hair would not be suitable for DNA testing, but a hair and fiber examination may provide circumstantial evidence to place a perpetrator at the scene of a crime. There may have been a hair and fiber exchange between the victim and an assailant's clothing. A laboratory examination can determine if the hair is animal or human, and what species of animal. If of human origin, race can be determined and from what part of the body it originated. The fact that the hair had been altered by dye, bleach, or other method will also be known. An examiner can tell if the hairs match microscopically and have the same characteristics or came from different sources. This is not a conclusive match, but is very powerful circumstantial evidence.

The Possibilities

The possibilities of what might be of evidentiary value are almost limitless. Remember to think outside of the box. Look at the big picture.

The first crime I ever solved with the FBI was solved because of a good crime scene investigation. A local electronics distributor in Phoenix was losing goods from railroad cars parked on the track behind his warehouse. Somebody would break into the cars, open cartons of televisions, and pull the sets out of the boxes, leaving the empty boxes alongside the railroad cars. This was happening so regularly that I asked the Phoenix police to call me at home the next time it occurred, and to not disturb the crime scene until I got there.

They cooperated, and a few nights later after getting their call I was walking along some dusty tracks at 4 in the morning. There were about 40 empty television cartons lying around. I backed my car up close and proceeded to cut the flaps off all of the cartons. The cops were very amused at this young FBI agent who thought he could get fingerprints off of cardboard. Everybody knew that wasn't possible. These cops were still thinking of raising fingerprints only by dusting, and didn't have a clue as to how they could be raised chemically.

I initialed and dated each of the 160 flaps, packed them up, and sent them off to the FBI laboratory. In a few weeks, the lab reported they had found numerous prints on the inside of the flaps. It seems the perpetrators had reached in the boxes with their fingers to rip them open. We had palm prints on the outside edges of the flaps, and more sets of the same fingerprints than you could count on the inside of the flaps.

Now, once I had a suspect, I could match his prints with the latent prints found on the boxes. The problem was, I didn't have any suspects. How do you suppose I came up with the suspects? Right, the faithful neighborhood investigation played a big part. But also, there was another burglary a couple of days later at a car rental agency in the same area. One of the burglars had placed his hand on the copy machine and photocopied his hand. Why? Who knows. He left the photocopy in the trashcan next to the machine. We matched that photocopied hand to the prints from the boxes, grateful he hadn't copied his rear end. Imagine that lineup ....

Elementary, My Dear Watson

Crimes can often be prosecuted under federal statutes or under state statutes. For instance, stealing televisions from a railroad would be a theft from interstate shipment, which is a federal violation. It also would be a violation of the state's grand theft statute. It could be prosecuted in either court, depending upon who claimed jurisdiction originally, who investigated the case, and who wanted to prosecute it.

In doing the neighborhood investigation with the Phoenix Police Department, we came up with two young suspects who lived in the general area. I went to interview those two, and took another agent with me. The boys' parents allowed us to enter the home. Guess what? Every room had a television in it. I read the serial numbers off the televisions and compared them to a list of the stolen items. Every television in that house was stolen. We confiscated the stolen property. The U.S. attorney didn't want to prosecute in federal court, but the local county attorney prosecuted the case in state court.

Neither one of those two boys wanted to plead guilty, so we went to trial. A laboratory examiner from the FBI laboratory came to Phoenix to testify as to the matching fingerprint evidence. I testified as to how the evidence was collected. If you walk into my office today, you'll see framed and hanging on my wall the red, white, and black comparison exhibit prepared by the laboratory for trial, showing, side by side, the *latent prints* from one of those boxes and an *inked print*, with the points of identification clearly marked.

Fingerprints, Tire Marks, and Shoe Leather

Everybody knows that fingerprints can be used to positively identify a person. Also, palm prints, toe prints, and footprints are unique to each person and can be positively matched to the original source.

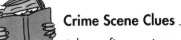

Crime Scene Clues

A **latent fingerprint** is a print that is not immediately apparent to the naked eye, but can be made visible by dusting, or fuming with chemicals. Latent prints can then be compared to inked prints of suspects. An **inked print** is a fingerprint taken in a controlled environment where the pads of a suspect's fingers are covered with ink and rolled onto a fingerprint card.

Dusting for Prints

There are four steps to collecting fingerprints by the dusting method:

- Dusting—Fingerprints can be powdered and lifted during your crime scene investigation on nonporous and nonabsorbent surfaces such as glass, polished metal, varnished woods, ceramic tiles, and plastics.

  A fingerprint powder that contrasts with the material on which the print is found should be used. Usually, the powders come in gray or black. On highly polished reflective surfaces like mirrors, I'd recommend using gray powder.

  The suspect area is powdered lightly with a few brush strokes of fingerprint powder. If a print is present, it will appear.

- Photographing—If you find a fingerprint after you've dusted, always photograph it. Do that before you do anything else. A good 35mm camera or a high-quality digital will do nicely.

  Why photograph a fingerprint? Because sometimes, when you go to lift the tape, you can screw it up, smudging the print beyond usefulness. If that happens, you'll still have the photograph, which can be used for identification purposes. The

Sammy the Snitch

If you use a digital camera to photograph fingerprints, be sure to archive the data on a compact disc or a floppy disk, and not just on the hard drive of your computer. Hard drives crash, and you don't want to lose these shots.

photograph should be taken as close as possible to the latent print. An external light source would be preferable to using the flash on the camera.

♦ Lifting—After photographing, the print should be lifted and mounted on a card. Take a wide strip of clear cellophane tape, and lay it sticky side down on top of the dusted print. Carefully peel the tape off and place it sticky-side down onto a white, 3-by-5-inch card. Congratulations. You have now dusted, photographed, and lifted a fingerprint.

♦ Initialing and Dating—Lastly, place your initials and the date on the other side of the 3-by-5-inch card, along with a description of where the print was lifted. Then log the print into your crime scene log. If you are going to lift a number of fingerprints, I'd suggest a number and a letter for each of them. For instance, all of the prints from the living room might be numbered consecutively, but append the letter L behind the number. From master bedroom, number them and add the letters MB. This will make for easier identification later.

Prints on Porous Materials

Fingerprints can be obtained from porous materials. When you place your finger on a smooth surface, oils from the ridges of your skin are left behind on the surface. When you brush the area with fingerprint powder, the powder sticks to the oils, making the ridges visible.

Sherlock's Secrets

Not everybody keeps a fingerprint kit in the closet with brush, powder, and lifting tape. If there is no rush, you can go to a local law enforcement supply store (a cop shop) and buy fingerprint powder. If you can't wait for that, you can use a good quality ladies' makeup powder and brush. Remember, though, fingerprints won't disappear overnight unless they are outside and exposed to weather. So there really shouldn't be any hurry to process the suspected area. For lifting tape, you can use 2-inch-wide, clear package tape.

The surface of the skin contains other chemicals besides oil, such as salts, proteins, and amino acids. These acids, proteins, and salts, along with the oils, will be left on porous materials. Dusting them doesn't work because the fingerprint powder will cling to the porous material also. But the prints can be raised by exposing the material to sprays of silver nitrate and ninhydrin, or fuming them with iodine and/or super-glue.

Spraying or fuming is probably beyond the scope of the "do-it-yourselfer." You can, however, preserve any papers, cigarettes, cardboard, or other porous materials that you think the suspects probably touched.

In a corner of the material you want to preserve, place your initials and the date. Then bag the item, and tag the bag as we've already discussed. Down the road, when a suspect is identified, notify the authorities that you have potential evidence that needs to be processed by the crime lab. They may laugh at you, but carefully explain to them what you've done. A conscientious detective will go ahead and take your evidence and send it in for processing.

Tire Marks and Shoe Prints

Tire marks and shoe prints should be photographed. If the prints are in dirt or sand, a plaster cast could be made of the marks. Frankly, I've never had any luck making casts of tread marks and boot prints. If you're good at that sort of thing, then go for it. I'm not going to give you my recipe, because mine always crumble. I've found that taking good, detailed photographs of the prints works much better than my attempts at casting them. If you do attempt to cast them, be sure to photograph them first anyway. This is true of every piece of evidence you might collect.

Rules of Evidence

There are a couple rules of evidence that you should learn. We've talked about initialing and dating every item you collect. I can't stress enough how important this is.

Next, you should maintain the evidence in a locked cabinet or closet, where only you have access to it. The reason this is so important is because there is this rule of evidence called "maintaining the chain of custody on the evidence."

Maintaining the chain of custody means that when you go to court, you have to be able to testify that the evidence has been under your care, control, and custody since it was collected. Now, in your case, you will turn the evidence over to the police at the proper time. You need to get a receipt for the evidence. It should be a detailed receipt, too. If there's not enough room on their form, attach your own list of all of the evidence that you are turning over.

The police will need a copy of the list as well, because they now have to maintain the chain of custody on the evidence. They do this by logging the evidence into their evidence room, which is a controlled-access facility. When the material is sent to their laboratory, they log it out of the evidence room, and log it into the laboratory. It has to be signed for and accounted for all along the way. If there is a failure in this chain, then the evidence can't be used in court, because it may have been tampered with. It is much like sending a registered letter through the U.S. Post Office. Each person who handles that letter signs for it, and a record is kept of each transfer from one person to the next.

Conducting your own crime scene investigation can actually be fun and interesting as well as productive. For it to be of any use in future court proceedings, though, the basic rules of collecting evidence must be adhered to, and the chain of custody on the evidence collected must also be maintained. If those two standards are met, then you'll likely have a successful experience.

The Least You Need to Know

- Following the instructions in this chapter, a civilian can conduct his or her own crime scene investigation if the police department refuses to do so due to the small dollar amount of the crime or the department's lack of ability to conduct a competent crime scene investigation.

- Upon initially discovering that a crime scene exists, care should be taken not to contaminate the evidence at the scene.

- A slow and thorough examination of the crime scene should take place before any collection activity begins. The sequence of how the crime occurred should be carefully thought out so as to include all areas of potential evidence in the processing of the scene.

- The crime scene should be photographed, using both wide-angle and close-up lenses. Each item of potential evidence should be photographed, showing its relation to the rest of the room. The close-up photographs should include a ruler or other common item, such as a dollar bill, to give size and perspective to the item.

- Every item of potential evidence collected should be initialed and dated by the person collecting it. It should then be placed in a plastic bag (unless it needs to be dried first) and recorded on a master log sheet.

- Knowledge of what items might constitute evidence, and how to process or package these items, is necessary for a successful crime scene investigation.

- Fingerprints can be revealed by dusting or through chemical means by spraying with silver nitrate or ninhydrin, or by fuming with iodine and super glue. Tire-tread marks or footprints should be photographed before attempting plaster casts.

- Maintaining chain of custody on the evidence includes keeping the evidence collected under lock and key until it is turned over to the police department. If this is not done, and the chain of custody is broken, then the evidence is probably no longer admissible in court.

Chapter 18

Clues to Infidelity

In This Chapter

- Diagnosing infidelity
- The most common symptoms
- Gathering the evidence
- Presenting the facts

You have a runny nose, a cough, your sinuses are congested, and you feel feverish all over. What do you have? Probably the flu, right? Almost every human condition has signs or symptoms associated with it, whether it's illness, well-being, depression, or joy.

Likewise, the unfaithfulness of a spouse or partner is manifested by a number of symptoms or clues. A good private investigator is aware of these signs. In this chapter we spell out clues that point toward cheating in a relationship.

Just as a runny nose by itself may not signal the onset of the flu, any of these clues, with the exception of the last one in this chapter, may have another explanation. But add enough of them together and you should be able to make a diagnosis.

Trust Your Gut

Two weeks before Halloween, a new client, Becky, came into my office. She'd called because she "had a feeling" something was wrong in her marriage and perhaps her husband was having an affair. She couldn't put her finger on why she felt that way; she just knew something was out of line.

It'd be impossible for me to count how many Becky stories I've heard. Some were longer, some shorter. Some involved lots of money, sometimes money never came up. Some included children. Others focused on drugs, alcohol, and physical abuse. Each one is different, but if you cut to the core, they all have the same basic genetic makeup.

Some call it instinct, others might say it's intuition that brought Becky to the realization something was wrong. But it really wasn't instinct or intuition. It wasn't magic, either. She hadn't had her palms read or her fortune told.

Becky came to see me because her subconscious recognized the symptoms of a foundering relationship, even though she couldn't consciously identify them herself.

Just like a doctor, it's a private investigator's job to be knowledgeable of these symptoms and make a correct diagnosis.

If you screen out the paranoid schizophrenics that frequent my office, only twice in 20 years and hundreds upon hundreds of cases has a client's gut feeling been wrong.

Sherlock's Secrets

Private investigators don't discriminate against persons afflicted with paranoia. They'll sometimes be your best clients. "Just because you're paranoid doesn't mean that there is nobody following you" is one favorite axiom of private investigators.

If you think about it, having lived with another partner for a year, five years, maybe twenty, you know that person, his or her habits, quirks, agenda. Your clients may not know how it is they're aware their partner is cheating, but they can feel it in their gut. It's your job to analyze the situation and point out the clues. If they "feel" their spouse is cheating, 99 percent of the time they'll be right.

Next you have to prove it to them, their family members, their spouse (who will deny it to the end), and perhaps to an attorney and a judge.

Behavioral Changes

Your client has lived with the same man for 15 years. All of a sudden the husband joins a gym and starts lifting weights, stops eating ice cream and French fries. His biceps are getting some definition. The abs aren't washboards yet, but the waistline is trimming down. He's going to live longer and his cholesterol, triglycerides, and blood-sugar levels are into a steep decline. Great. She should be pleased, right? But she still feels something's amiss. He's not paying much attention to her, so who is getting the benefit of all that exercise?

Almost all women and most men make an effort at improving their body image when a new love interest enters their life. They start—and this time stick to—a diet. The pounds melt away and new clothes appear in the closet.

A man's behavior changes in more obvious ways than a woman's. Besides getting more fit, he's working later, wearing cologne every day when before he hadn't worn it … well, since being single, anyway. He's more aloof and less affectionate with his partner.

A woman is frequently happier because now someone is paying attention to her, telling her how attractive she is and making her feel desirable again. She is more pleased with herself because she is trimming up and has a better self-image of her body.

Both men and women involved in extramarital affairs will have blank spots in their days or evenings, periods when they don't answer the cell phone or return the page. If they do communicate during those times, they will be short and curt with their speech and evasive as to their current whereabouts.

None of these behavioral changes necessarily signals a cheating partner. But keep a scorecard. Let's see what other clues we might look for.

Hang-Up Telephone Calls

Everybody receives hang-up calls. Why? Some may be rude misdialers who just hang up when they realize their mistake without apologizing to the person on the other end. But there's also a technological reason. Telemarketing and collection firms use computers to dial your home. When you answer the telephone, the computer connects your call to the next salesperson in line. If there is no salesperson available at that moment, then the computer hangs up on you. Presto, a hang-up call.

Naturally then, hang-up calls or numerous out-of-area calls are not necessarily indicative of any nefarious doings on the part of your client or your client's spouse. However, as in every other symptom, they may be.

Kathy's husband taught history at the university. When the calls first started, a female always asked for the professor. It seemed to Kathy that it was always the same student, the same voice. After she mentioned it to her husband, the student calls stopped but the hang-up calls began.

Elementary, My Dear Watson

In most telephone areas, it's easy for the caller to block his or her number from appearing on your Caller ID. The person at the originating phone simply dials *67 and then the number. Your Caller ID will then show "Private Call."

Hang-up calls will frequently show up on your Caller ID as "Out of the Area" or "Unidentified" or "Unknown."

This does not indicate that the person calling you blocked the call. One reason the call may read "Unknown," etc., is that it is a long-distance call and coming from an area or phone system that does not yet support the Caller ID function. The second, more common reason is that many telemarketing and collection companies use T-1 lines instead of standard phone lines. T-1 lines don't have to transmit the caller identification information as do Bell Company lines.

Kathy rarely received hang-ups during the day when her husband was at the university. Usually she only received them in the evenings or the weekends, when he might have reasonably been expected to be home. Sometimes immediately after a hang-up her husband would go into his study or run down to the corner store on some errand. Which brings us to our next symptom, the need for privacy.

Need a Little Privacy?

Everybody needs a little alone time, but the desire for privacy may indicate a problem. The key here is the change in the behavior, not necessarily the behavior itself.

CAUTION

Sammy the Snitch

Many clients will ask you to tap their telephones for them. It sounds like easy money, but don't do it. It is illegal in every jurisdiction for you, a professional private investigator, to do this and you would be prosecuted, even though the client probably would not. You would also lose your license. It's not worth it for a few hundred or even a few thousand dollars.

Samantha awoke at 2 A.M. and realized her husband was not by her side. They had two phone lines in their home and she noticed that one line was being used. She assumed her son had failed to disconnect the upstairs computer from their Internet service. As she climbed the steps, she heard her husband talking in the spare bedroom. When she got to the top of the stairs, he hung up the phone.

Brian went shopping with his live-in girlfriend at the mall. They separated, each searching for something in different stores. He needed some advice from her and went back to the store where he'd left her. She was talking on her cell phone. As soon as she spotted him walking toward her she ducked behind a rack of clothes, quickly finished her conversation, disconnected, and stuffed the phone into her coat pocket. You can bet she wasn't getting advice from her mother on choosing between the pink or the blue dress.

Sarah's husband began to take long walks alone. He'd be gone for two or three hours at a time. "I just need to be alone. Time to think some things through," he'd tell her. Actually, he was hoofing it over to a girlfriend's apartment.

If your spouse hangs up the phone when you walk into the room or goes to another room to take a call, or waits until you've hung up the extension before she starts talking, or wants more time alone, you may want to see if she exhibits any of the other indicators in this chapter.

Reviewing the Bills

There are two major sources of bills that provide dead giveaway clues to infidelity: credit card charges and cellular telephone statements.

Credit Card Charges

Gretchen had a nagging feeling that just wouldn't go away. Her husband, Rod, a physician, attended a medical convention in Denver for a few days and then came home. Gretchen, following her suspicions, wanted to check the credit card charges but didn't want to wait until the bill's usual arrival near the first of the next month.

She called me while her husband tended to patients at his office. After some discussion, I suggested she boot up his computer at home and bring up his credit card statement online. Rod used *Internet Explorer* as his web browser and had the *AutoComplete* feature turned on.

Gretchen had an idea what his user name might be and typed in the first letter at the prompt. The rest of the name popped up and the password, which she wasn't certain about at all, automatically inserted itself at the appropriate blank.

A few more clicks of the mouse and there on the computer screen lay all of her husband's charges for the previous week at the Colorado medical convention. There were several charges in the $60 and $80 range from the hotel gift

Sherlock's Secrets

If your client doesn't have access to his or her partner's credit card records, competent private investigators have sources that can obtain the list of charges. The cost will range between $200 and $300.

shop, and another from a national lingerie chain. The only gifts she received when he had come home were some free pens bearing pharmaceutical company logos and two refrigerator magnets. There was no $80 item from the gift shop and certainly no lingerie.

In searching through credit card charges, look for lingerie shops, sport shops, jewelry store charges, and the hotel gift shop. Large, unexplained dinner invoices or bar tabs are clues as well.

Crime Scene Clues

Microsoft **Internet Explorer** is a web browser that comes standard with Microsoft Windows operating system. **AutoComplete** is a function that can be turned off or on in Internet Explorer. As a user enters a secure website, he or she is prompted for a user ID and a password. Once the computer user has entered that ID and password the first time, AutoComplete will remember the ID and password as long as it's on. The next time you visit that website and begin to enter your user ID, AutoComplete will recognize where you are on the web and enter them for you if you want. Utilizing AutoComplete means you don't have to type in your user ID and password at every visit. AutoComplete is handy, but not very secure.

The AutoComplete option is found in MS Internet Explorer by clicking on tools, then Internet Options. Under Internet Options click on Content. The third listing under Content is Personal Information. There you'll see the AutoComplete button. Click the AutoComplete button and make sure "User names and passwords on forms" is checked.

Cellular Telephone Calls

Many people use cell phones as their primary means of communication and don't even have a regular phone line to their home. That number is growing every day.

Most cell-phone-bill printouts reveal the phone numbers of dialed, completed calls, and the duration of each call. These bills previously reported the phone number of incoming calls as well, but I don't know of any that do that currently, although the records are in the cell phone company's system and retrievable. How long they keep them is anybody's guess but you'll need a subpoena to get them.

If the spouse suspected of cheating has his own cell phone, I'll guarantee you that calls have been made to the alleged girlfriend or boyfriend, if there is one.

Vicki's husband was always on the cell phone. He never turned it off and it was always at his side. I suggested she bring in his bill and we went over it together. The last month's bill showed calls of 30, 40, and up to 90 minutes in length, at all times of the day and night, to a number which Vicki didn't know. The bill also included a mix of shorter calls to other numbers.

We ran a reverse search on the telephone number of the lengthy calls and discovered the number went to the residence of an office assistant he'd hired six months earlier.

You can run a reverse search on phone numbers yourself. To learn how to run a reverse search, see Chapter 11. Obtaining the subscriber information to a particular telephone number is called a *telephone break*.

> **Crime Scene Clues**
>
> A **telephone break** is the process of obtaining the subscriber name and billing address that corresponds to a particular telephone, cellular phone, or pager number. If you desperately need a break on a cell phone, nonpublished number, or pager, find a fellow PI who has a good phone source. Not all PIs can get this for you.

If you try the methods outlined in Chapter 11 and can't come up with subscriber information, then it is probably not a listed home telephone number but likely another cellular number, a pager, or a nonpublished number.

Vicki had access to her husband's cell phone records because he kept them at home. If you don't have access to the bill, a good private investigator should be able to get you a list of all the calls made during any particular billing cycle.

At the time of this printing, the wholesale price of cellular subscriber information (cell phone number break) is running at about $55. This price only includes the name of the subscriber to a particular cell phone and the billing address. It does not include the phone calls made from that number. Most professional investigators will double that price and charge the client from $110 to $125. That is a reasonable, common practice.

To get a list of the phone numbers called by a particular cellular phone, a PI will pay his source about $125 for that information and should charge you $250 for the first 100 phone numbers on the bill. After the first 100 phone calls you will be charged about $1 to $1.50 for each additional call. If he charges a little more, I wouldn't quibble because cell phone details are not easy to get. However, if he wants a lot more than that, find another PI.

Missing in Action

It's not unusual for persons engaged in the romance of an affair to have unaccounted time or to not be where they've told their spouse they were going to be.

Philandering doctors, male or female, frequently use the excuse of being called out on an emergency or making rounds at the hospital. They may be making the rounds, but not the kind their spouse expects. Just like doctors, nearly every profession has emergencies or provides its own brand of excused absences. Even private investigators are out late working surveillance or doing a *drive by*.

Amy fulfilled her obligation to her country one weekend a month in the Naval Reserves. This required her to fly from Florida to a Midwest location. Her normal flight would leave on a Friday evening. Amy, being enamored with her old boyfriend, told her husband the flight left on Thursday so she could spend the night with the boyfriend before she left town.

> ### Crime Scene Clues
>
> A **drive by** is performed by private investigators to make a casual check of a subject's residence to see if he or she is home, or to observe what activities are taking place at a particular location during a specific time.

One Thursday evening, a couple of punks broke into her van, which she'd parked on the street, and stole the stereo out of it. A passerby noticed the break-in and the police responded. They checked the vehicle's ownership and called her home.

Imagine her husband's surprise when the police told him their van, instead of being parked in long-term parking at the airport, had been broken into on the other side of town in front of Amy's "old" boyfriend's home. Busted.

Listen Up

An anonymous caller rings you up and informs you that your spouse is having an affair with his wife. Do you believe him?

You ask your spouse directly and he says, "No, of course not." Which one do you believe? Here are some other examples:

- Your friend tells you that your husband is cheating. Then someone from your church says she thought you had the right to know that your spouse was seen coming out of another woman's house.

- You're at your husband's office and his secretary pulls you aside and says, "We need to talk sometime."

- Your best friend, or your sister, says your husband came on to her or kissed her.

- You have a party at your house and your 3-year-old asks why daddy was kissing that lady in the hallway.

Do you believe them even though your husband or wife denies it? You'd better. Without exception, every one of my clients who'd been told something like that had an unfaithful spouse.

Nine out of ten times, family, friends, or co-workers will know about it before you do. Unfortunately, most of the time they "don't want to get in the middle," "don't want to see you hurt," "don't want to be responsible for breaking up your family," and on and on and on.

If they finally pulled up the courage to tell you about your spouse's illicit behavior, check it against the other indicators in this chapter. What they've told you is probably true. Listen. Sooner or later, you'll have to.

> ### Sherlock's Secrets
>
> Most clients still require proof, even after friends and family inform them of spousal infidelity. Their spouse will frequently deny it until the bitter end. This is the opportunity for the professional investigator to suggest surveillance be placed on the spouse. It increases revenues, and with satisfactory photographic evidence, puts your client in an emotionally superior position. Depending upon the state where the divorce proceeding is filed, it may make a substantial difference in any monetary settlement.

Diseases of the Body and the Heart

Infidelity in a relationship breaks the heart. Your client may know intellectually that his or her partner is unfaithful but finds it difficult to accept it in the heart.

There is one sure sign of an unfaithful partner, short of laying the photographs on the table in front of him or her as we discussed in Chapter 15. That sign is a sexually transmitted disease (STD). Even when confronted with having acquired an STD, some clients attempt to make excuses for their spouses.

Joe had a casual affair without his wife knowing. After the affair ended, Joe began to experience symptoms of gonorrhea. He visited a urologist, was treated, and the disease left—or so he thought.

> ### Sherlock's Secrets
>
> As a private investigator, your clients will be discussing with you the most intimate parts of their lives. The tales are sometimes bizarre and wild. Treat them with respect and sympathy and they will refer you to their friends and associates and help you build your business. And try not to snicker.

Ten days later, the symptoms reappeared. The urologist informed Joe he'd caught it again. Although he'd been treated and cured, he'd apparently infected his wife, and then she'd reinfected him. Serves him right, huh?

He dragged his wife down to the doctor's office with a story of an infected prostate. The doctor treated them both and the symptoms were gone for good. That time.

Did she believe his story? She wanted to believe, so she did. Believing Joe was easier than facing his unfaithfulness and its consequences.

> **CAUTION**
>
> **Sammy the Snitch**
>
> Medical records are considered confidential and it is not advisable to call the doctor, pretending to be the patient, to obtain the spouse's records. Having those confidential records might backfire in court at a later time. Once a divorce action has been filed, your client's attorney can subpoena the records if necessary.

Her refusal to see all of the symptoms didn't change the facts. Joe and his wife are still together. Joe still cheats on her.

If your client has developed an STD and has been monogamous in a long-term relationship, then the client's spouse is unfaithful. And it's probably not the first time. Ask your client if he or she has been suspicious on earlier occasions and the answer is almost always yes.

This is a plain simple fact, but one that is often ignored or passed off as some other benign type of infection.

Counseling the Client

With domestic relation cases such as we've discussed in this chapter, you have an obligation to your clients (or to yourself, if you're the client) to help them put together a plan of action.

The diagnosis of an illness has no value if you can't help with a cure. Likewise, in relationships, as a professional, once you point out the symptoms and identify the illness, you must solve the problem.

Ask clients direct questions. If you ask something general, such as what they want to accomplish, they won't have a clue. You have to guide them. Be specific: If you prove that their spouse is involved in an affair, will they divorce him? Some will say yes. Others will say no. Some will say they don't know.

Children, and the upheaval of their lives, have to be taken into account. The financial repercussions of a divorce or separation are usually monumental. I counsel clients not to make a decision either way until they have all the available facts at their command.

Elementary, My Dear Watson

The divorce laws of the United States vary from state to state. Many states are no-fault divorce states. In these states fault is not assigned to the divorcing parties and the rules for property settlements and child support are set by statute. In other states, blame is laid to the party committing adultery and generally, property settlements and alimony can be greatly affected if proof of adultery is submitted in court.

Not to be forgotten are health considerations. We touched on those lightly in the previous section, but as we all know, there are life-threatening and life-altering diseases spread through promiscuous behavior. Your client has to know and has a right to know the facts of the partner's secret life, if there is one.

At this point, explain to her that she needs to know what the real facts are before she can make a decision. This is a momentous occasion in most relationships.

Most partners will not admit to their infidelity. The next step is to gather enough irrefutable proof so that the partner can no longer deny his actions, and gather it in such a way that it is admissible in a court of law, even if at this time your client does not intend on pursuing any legal remedies.

Follow the techniques in Chapter 15 and you should get the proof your client needs.

Sherlock's Secrets

A professional investigator gives a full accounting to his client of the work performed. This accounting should be in a written report prepared in a professional manner. Clients who perhaps originally don't want to pursue legal remedies later change their minds. If your investigative work is done in a legal and professional manner, then you will be prepared to testify in court or be subpoenaed for a deposition.

The Least You Need to Know

- Infidelity has certain identifiable symptoms. These symptoms include changes in personal behavior.

- There are two major sources of bills that provide dead giveaway clues to infidelity: credit card charges and cellular telephone statements.

- Tangible evidence of infidelity can be found by examining credit card charges and cellular telephone bills.

- Once the symptoms have been identified and supporting evidence gathered, a plan for resolving the problem should be formulated.

Surveillance in the Home

In This Chapter

- Making your own hidden camera and its two cousins
- Tapping your own phone line
- Legalities and technicalities of phone taps
- The bible on wireless cameras
- Peeping Toms, vandals, and intruders

Private investigators are routinely asked about using some sort of surveillance equipment in private homes. Frequently, it pertains to the need to know what is going on in a teenager's life. The teenager is coming home late, skipping school, and spending a lot of time with friends who don't have the standards the parent would hope they'd have.

Or perhaps you've employed a new babysitter, and you can't shake that nagging feeling that all is not right when you're not there.

It may be simple paranoia, but it's not unusual for a female client to request a camera in the home because an ex-boyfriend who claims he's returned her keys, enters the home when the client is not there. He denies that he comes in, but she thinks items are moved around while she's at work.

A tenant may want to catch a nosy landlord. Also, we've had cases where the rental apartment's handyman made unwarranted entries into a client's apartment to snoop around and steal our client's underwear. There are many good reasons why a person may want some sort of surveillance set up within his or her own home.

Cameras in the Home

There are three approaches to using hidden or disguised cameras in your own home. We call them the Camera in a Bag, the Nanny Cam, and finally, the Installed Camera. They each have their advantages and disadvantages. We'll talk about wireless cameras later in this chapter, but using a wireless camera or transmitter and receiver is an option to consider with all three of these camera installations.

Camera in a Bag

This is a fairly simple technique that works very well for a constant time frame of about two hours, and it's mobile you so you can move it from room to room. It's portable, is easily constructed at home, and good for the do-it-yourself PI.

To make a Camera in a Bag, you'll need:

1. A battery-operated video camera.

2. A gym bag.

3. A small piece of fine, thin, black see-through material.

Cut a hole in the end of the gym bag and remove a square patch of material. A gym bag that is ventilated on both ends works best; if you can get one, just remove one of the ventilated screens.

Replace the material you've removed with the black see-through material. This material can be purchased at any fabric store. Before purchasing the material, hold it up to a light at the store or to the front window during daylight. You should be able to see through it fairly easily. Stitch this material onto the bag where you've removed the ventilated strip or cut the patch.

Place the video camera in the gym bag. Make sure the battery is fully charged. You may want to buy a longer life battery, depending upon your individual needs. Use the longest-play tape that will fit in your camera.

Pad the camera with a towel or some clothes to keep it from shifting. When placing the camera in the bag, be sure to turn off the auto focus feature. Some cameras, with auto focus on, will focus only on the black cloth screen you've sewn into the bag and that's all you'll get in your picture. Other cameras that can't focus on something that close to the lens will continuously, unsuccessfully, adjust the focus because the screen is so close to the lens and nothing will be in focus at all. Turn auto focus off and focus it yourself.

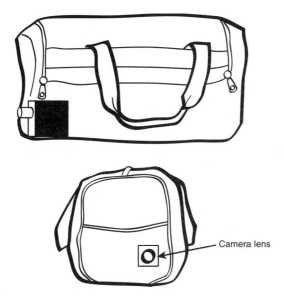

A Camera in a Bag is easily made at home.

Camera lens

Set the bag wherever you expect the action to take place. Turn it on just before leaving. Remember, the camera will only run until the tape ends or the battery is depleted. I recommend adjusting the camera settings so that it does not automatically rewind when the tape ends, because the rewinding would make some noise that could cause your subject to wonder why your gym bag is purring. You'll need to read your instruction manual about this feature, since each camera is a little different.

After you've made the bag, try it out a few times before setting up to catch whatever it is you expect to happen. Make sure you have the focus where you want and the zoom on the lens adjusted to get the coverage of the area that you want.

We use this setup frequently when we're trying to catch action indoors and the bag would not raise any suspicions. We nailed an aerobics instructor once with this camera trick. We sent one of our investigators to take her class. He turned on the camera, set the bag down, and we got an hour tape of her and my investigator doing aerobics. She was claiming she couldn't work because of injuries sustained in an automobile accident. She not only was teaching aerobics and dance classes, but also had taken out a new business license for a dance studio she was planning on opening with the money from the insurance settlement. We hated to rain on her parade but, hey, that's what we get paid for.

The Camera in a Bag would work fine to check up on a babysitter if you're going to the movies or just out for a while. If you have more than one video camera, you could make several units and place them throughout the house. If you do that, you should probably use different styles of bags.

Nanny Cams

You can go to any search engine on the Internet and type in "Nanny Cam." You'll find hundreds of websites that talk about Nanny Cams, and dozens that actually sell them. If you're a little bit electronically oriented, you can make your own.

A Nanny Cam basically is a covert, or hidden, camera. Typically, the camera is hidden behind a "smoked glass" plate or plastic faceplate of a clock radio or a boom box. You can put this covert camera in any room, and usually the radio will still function as it should, in case the nanny decides to turn it on.

The boom box has an advantage in that it can run off of batteries if there is no convenient electrical outlet. The problem with Nanny Cams is they do not include a video-cassette recorder (VCR). In order to use it, you must either connect a transmitter to the video output of the camera, or run a cable from the video output of the camera to a VCR. If you can't hide a cable, then you'll have to use a wireless transmitter.

You can buy these converted radios on the web for about $350. Of course, cameras can be placed and camouflaged in almost any household item that you might desire, and you'll find them hidden in motion and smoke detectors as well as wall clocks, VCRs, and videocassettes themselves.

If you do run a cable to a regular household VCR or use a wireless transmitter, then you are limited to six hours of record time, as long as you set your VCR to the longest play time available. Some VCRs are labeled differently from others but usually the setting for the longest play time will read "super long play" and be abbreviated SLP or "extended long play" (ELP) on the front of your VCR. Instead of buying and using normal 120-minute tapes, you can purchase the 160-minute tapes. Using those on the SLP setting will provide eight hours of recording time.

The Installed Camera

Some private investigators install covert cameras for their clients on a temporary basis. The typical installation will include a *pinhole-lens* camera and a time-lapse VCR. An advantage of utilizing a time-lapse VCR is you can record from 2 to 24 hours, up to multiple days of activity, on one videocassette.

Typically, when a time-lapse recorder is used, the images are recorded from about four images every second to one image per second, depending upon the length of recording time needed. Even with one image every second, it is unlikely that a person can enter a room and pass through it without his entry being recorded.

Crime Scene Clues

A **pinhole lens** is literally a lens for a camera that is about the size of the tip of ballpoint pen. Not literally "pin" size, but close, it can be concealed quite easily, particularly in dropped ceilings, where the ceiling tiles have a rough texture. This size lens is also popular in Nanny Cams, where the hole for the lens can be concealed behind a small piece of plastic, such as you might find on radios or many other appliances. Pinhole lenses are frequently used when installing a camera in an air-conditioning vent.

A problem with all installations is that somebody needs to review the tapes. Whether you're using a Camera in the Bag or a professionally installed camera with a time-lapse recorder, you will have two hours of tape to review. Using a professional quality VCR that has *jog and shuttle* capability can shorten the reviewing time. These features allow the viewer to fast-forward through the tape, stop the tape when action is observed, and run the tape forward or backward, one frame at a time. Nevertheless, it still takes a keen eye to catch the action.

Another way to minimize how much tape you have to sort through every day is to set the installed camera up so that it records only when activated by a motion sensor. Most professional time-lapse recorders can be activated by passive, infrared motion sensors or, if a monitor is left on, video motion on the monitor can trigger the recorder.

Crime Scene Clues

Jog and shuttle are two functions of a videocassette recorder that allow an operator to play the tape backward and forward, one frame at a time, or in multiple-frame increments that are determined by the user. Generally, the jog-shuttle control is a wheel device on the VCR that the operator rotates forward or backward causing the VCR motors to rotate in sync with it forward and reverse, faster and slower.

Information obtained from hidden surveillance cameras can be used in a variety of ways, including the courtroom, as long as ethical and legal standards are followed.

The basic rule of thumb for the placing of covert or hidden cameras is: When does a person have a reasonable expectation of privacy? My firm will not place cameras in bedrooms or bathrooms where persons other than the client himself might be caught on tape. Obviously, if we're going to catch an underwear thief, then the camera will have to be in the bedroom. But the camera will not be turned on while that client is home. Again, in commercial buildings, we won't place cameras in restrooms. Somebody else may, but we won't, because most people would have an expectation of privacy there. The U.S. postal inspectors used to have cameras and peepholes in the employee restrooms at the post offices. Postal employees would sometimes steal items from the mail, retreat to the employee restrooms where they could close the door, open the package in secret (they thought), remove the valuables and hide it on their own person before returning to work. At lest that was the alleged reason why the Postal Inspectors said they needed to see what happened in the restrooms. Finally, the inspectors were forced to close the peepholes and remove the cameras to insure privacy in the restrooms.

Suzanne was facing a divorce. Her husband was the son of a prominent businessman. The husband's family owned a professional sports franchise in the western United States, and her husband helped manage the business. The soon-to-be ex-husband smoked marijuana heavily. This habit wore on the marriage until, finally, Suzanne had had enough of it. Obviously, his drug usage could prove embarrassing to the family because the team's management subjects the players to regular drug testing. It wouldn't look good for management to be hypocritical in the area of zero drug tolerance.

Proving her husband's drug usage would be difficult in court without some corroborating evidence. Otherwise, it would just be her testimony against his. Obviously, she expected him to deny the drug allegations. Who wouldn't? She didn't really want to create problems for him and the family, and she recognized that it was also in her best interest if the sports franchise continued to thrive. After all, her future alimony payments would depend upon it. Basically, she wanted to extract a fair settlement from the husband without damaging his reputation and the business.

Suzanne showed me her husband's stash of marijuana. He really had quite a bit. Multiple mason jars of it were hidden in different places throughout the house and in the garage. He certainly had more than enough to be arrested for possession with intent to distribute. She swore that he did not sell it, but only had it for his personal use.

This presented me with an ethical quandary. Private investigators frequently find themselves in situations that make them privy to what may be illegal activity. To some, it may appear black and white. There is marijuana in the house. It is illegal. Call the police.

On the other hand, the very key to the nature of private investigations is the fact that it is *private*. PIs are not officers of the court. Nor are they sworn law enforcement personnel. Clients usually call on private investigators because the issues involved are civil in nature as opposed to criminal. Or, if it is a borderline civil/criminal issue, the client doesn't want to involve law enforcement. Just as often, the local law enforcement officials refuse to become involved, even though they've been invited into the case such as runaway teenagers, parental kidnappings, a partner in a business who's violating his noncompete agreement, or an employee who's sleeping with a competitor and giving away company secrets, or members of a firm who are stealing company products. Banks, law firms, and high profile local companies are particularly hesitant to involve law enforcement and hence, the media, in embezzlements or other high-ranking employ-ee dishonesty matters where the institutions reputation might be tarnished. They'd much rather prove to their own satisfaction that the transgression has taken place and quietly have the guilty party leave the company.

Each private investigator has to address this type of situation with his own conscience, subject to his own standards, and draw the line where he will. A good private investigator uses discretion, tact, and an experienced hand. In Suzanne's case, we agreed to help her without involving any law enforcement.

We placed a pinhole-lens camera in an air duct located in the study where her husband smoked his marijuana. He usually smoked when she was not in the house because he knew she disapproved. We transmitted the video signal to a time-lapse recorder concealed in an attic crawl space. We set the VCR close to the opening where Suzanne could change the tapes daily.

Suzanne brought us the tapes every two or three days and one of my investigator interns reviewed them. At the end of a two-week period, we had a dozen instances of the husband rolling, lighting, and smoking joints while seated in his favorite chair. We made a compos-ite videotape with all of the smoking sequences on it. Our client received a generous alimony settlement shortly thereafter.

Some people might say that Suzanne blackmailed or extorted her soon-to-be ex-husband. This might sound cold, but I've worked this business too long not to know. The reality of divorce is that it involves emotional blackmail, extortion, exposure of illicit acts, and the fostering of guilt on the part of both parties. In this case, we just documented the facts. That is our job as private investigators. How the documented truths of a person's actions are later used in negotiations is beyond the control of the private investigator.

You've read this before in this book and you'll read it at least one more time before you turn the last page: The private investigator's job is to get the facts and reveal the truth to her client. Then she has to let the chips fall where they may.

Tapping Your Own Phone

It's Saturday morning and you're pushing the lawnmower around the yard, trying to get the grass cut before the temperature rises to 100°. The screen from your 14-year-old daughter's bedroom window is off the window and leaning against the house. That's funny. This makes the second time in a week you've put it back on.

An hour later, you've finished the grass and go to speak to your daughter. The door to her bedroom is locked, as usual. Well, girls need their privacy, right? Eventually, your daugh-ter opens the door. You ask her about the screen and she shrugs her shoulders. What do girls know about windows and screens? It's a dad's job to keep those things fixed.

Now it's midweek. You're up late, say 2 in the morning, working on a project. You step outside to get a breath of fresh air and clear your head. You walk around the house, admiring your begonias and there, darn it, is the screen standing against the house again. Then it hits you. If the screen were just falling off, it would be flat on the ground, not leaning against the house. Either your daughter has been climbing out or, worse, somebody unknown to you has been climbing in.

Knocking on your daughter's door brings no response. You find the little key that unlocks interior doors and go into her bedroom. It's empty. Where is she, what is she doing, and who is she with?

Three hours later, she finally comes home. You're thankful she's home safe, but this kind of behavior can't be tolerated. You threaten to ground her for life. She shrugs her shoulders, says fine, and still she refuses to tell you where's she's been or with whom. She's not going to talk about it. At least, not to you.

Teenagers, especially teenage girls, will talk at great length with their friends about exploits, problems with parents, and the general unfairness of life. There is probably no better way to find out what is happening in your teenager's life than to listen to her telephone conversations with her friends.

That being said, eavesdropping does have its downsides. It's an invasion of privacy. Some parents can't keep a secret and will have to pull the superior tone, telling the child that they know what she's up to. Once you let on to your child that you're listening in on her conversations, you can kiss that technique good-bye. She'll be much more guarded in her conversations on the telephone for quite a while. In addition, she'll claim no forgiveness for you in this life, or the next. The teenager may get really mad, and have to act out in some way to show you that you can't control her. The acting-out behavior could actually be worse than the sneaking out. And lastly, listening in on someone's phone conversations may be illegal in your state.

Legalities

The recording of telephone conversations is covered in most state statutes under the interception of wire communications. To record or intercept a telephone call without breaking the law, under federal statutes, one party to the conversation has to be aware of the fact that the telephonic conversation is being recorded. This means that under the federal law, I can record a telephone conversation I'm having with another person and not advise them that the call is being recorded. Why should I have to advise them? If I took shorthand, I could record the call on paper just as easily. This is called the one-party rule.

Some states have a narrower view of recording telephonic conversations than the federal government. These states insist that all parties to the telephone conversation be aware that the call is being recorded. This is called the two-party rule, or a two-party state. See

Appendix B for a list of one-party and two-party states. Note, two-party actually means all parties in the conversation.

Elementary, My Dear Watson

Remember Linda Tripp and her recording of her telephone conversations with Monica Lewinsky? After the President Clinton-Lewinsky fiasco, the state of Maryland brought charges against Linda Tripp for the illegal recording of those telephone calls. Why? Because Tripp was in Maryland, which is a two-party state, meaning that both parties are supposed to be notified that the phone conversation is being recorded. Tripp didn't tell Lewinsky she was recording the phone calls, so she was in violation of Maryland's interception of wire communication law. Eventually, the charges were dropped against Tripp, but it took awhile and probably some big-dollar attorney fees.

So how can you legally record your daughter's phone calls? Obviously, you don't want her, or her friends, to know that her calls are being recorded. If you live in a one-party state and your child is a minor, then basically, as her adult guardian, you can give consent for her to record her telephone calls. If she's over 18, however, that won't work.

I've had many clients complain that they're paying for the phone line so they should be able to record the calls on it if they want to. Let's talk real life here. The likelihood of a local district attorney prosecuting parents for listening to their own child's phone conversations is nil. The legal research hasn't been done in each state, but certainly, at someplace, at sometime, some parent has been prosecuted for recording his kid's calls. Just as certainly, there were some other exacerbating facts that warranted the prosecution. Perhaps there was parental abusive behavior or some other action on the part of the parent that required prosecution.

If my teenage daughter were sneaking out at night, you can bet that I'd be listening to the conversations between her and her friends, and I live in a two-party state. Traditionally, the courts give wide latitude to parents in how they raise and control their youth.

Technicalities

The simplest way to record a telephone conversation within your own home, without letting your teenager know about, it is to purchase a Multi-Phone Recording Control from Radio Shack. The product number is 430-1236. You can search the Radio Shack website at www.radioshack.com. Put that number in the search field, and you can read the specifications on the device. The normal retail price is $24.99, but it sometimes is on sale for $19.99.

Decide in advance where you want to locate the recording equipment. It should not be in your child's room. I suggest in your own bedroom or some room that your teenager doesn't normally use. You can put it in the garage if you have a phone extension out there.

In conjunction with the recording control device, you're going to need a cassette recorder with a remote switch input jack and a microphone jack. The recording control device has a telephone modular plug that will plug into a spare phone jack. If you don't have a spare phone jack, then also buy a modular duplex jack (Radio Shack catalog number 279-357.) This will allow you to plug both your phone and the control device into your phone line at the same time.

The easiest method to record telephone calls within your house.

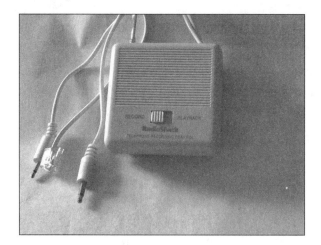

Plug the microphone jack into the microphone input on the recorder. Insert the remote switch plug into the remote switch jack on the recorder. Put a tape in the recorder. Set the cassette recorder's control Record/Playback switch to Record. Push down the Play and Record button on the tape recorder. Now take any phone on that line in the house off the hook, lifting up the telephone receiver. As soon as you do that, the recorder will start recording.

Anytime someone makes or receives a telephone call on that phone line, anywhere in the house, from any extension, it will be recorded, as long as there is a blank tape in the recorder and the recorder has power. It doesn't make any difference if the phone call is on a hardwired phone or a portable phone. It works just as well either way. It's that simple. The instructions that come with the device are very clear, and the help at Radio Shack is very good. You just have to hope that the guy who's helping you at the store isn't the one your daughter's sneaking out to see in the middle of the night.

The last step is to hide the recording equipment. Usually, shoving it under the bed and covering it with a towel will work. The devices make no noise and generate no heat, so they are pretty innocuous, as long as your kid doesn't stumble across it.

One problem that does occur is that teenagers sometimes spend hours on the phone. You may find that you need to record more than one 90-minute tape will allow. If that's likely to be the case, find an electronics specialty shop on the Internet and buy a cassette recorder that's been designed to slow down such that a 90-minute tape will last 12 to 24 hours. These recorders aren't that expensive—a couple of hundred dollars at most.

You'll have to spend some time listening to the tapes to find out what your daughter is up to, but this technique never fails for getting the facts. One recommendation is to be sure to get all of the facts before you confront the teenager. Don't jump to conclusions based on one phone call. Take your time, settle down, work out a game plan with your spouse that you both agree to, and then speak to your child. Remember, teenagers don't think of themselves as children. To put the whole situation into perspective, it might help to remember what antics you pulled as a teenager, including the ones where you never got caught. Now that's scary, isn't it? How you handle the situation after that is beyond the scope of this book, but tar and feathering would probably get you in trouble with the law, and Radio Shack doesn't carry those supplies, anyway.

Wireless Cameras

You're surfing the Internet and close the website you've been examining. A pop-up advertisement appears on your screen. The view through a window shows a well-endowed, scantily clad woman. Then the picture pans to an infant's crib. Finally, the advantages of a wireless camera are listed on the screen.

The reality is that you can make any camera wireless for about $100. Emerson makes a transmitter called Wavecom Senior that you can buy at consumer-electronics stores. If you can't find it there, then go to www.mjsales.net and buy the unit online. Retail price is about $230, but they sell it for $99. The Wavecom includes a video transmitter and a separate receiver. The units operate on a 2.4 GHz frequency, which avoids the more crowded lower bands like 900 MHz or the 400 MHz range, where you might get interference from portable telephones.

Typically, the maximum range of these units is about 300 feet. I've used them in installations to make employee theft cases. In one particular case, we broadcast several hundred feet through concrete walls, where we couldn't run cable, and still had a very acceptable picture.

If you need something smaller than the Wavecom, you'll have to switch to a battery-operated unit, and the price goes up. These units are good for short durations, but they'll top out at half a day or thereabouts. It simply depends on what your specific application requires from a wireless camera. You can find these online or from your local "spy shop." It pays to shop around for prices, and be sure and compare specs.

There are only so many manufacturers of camera equipment. The prices vary quite a bit for the same equipment, so if money is important to you, look for the best deal.

Elementary, My Dear Watson

The heart of any closed-circuit television (CCTV) system is the camera itself. To evaluate the camera, there are three major factors one must know: the price, the number of lines of resolution, and the lux. Lines of resolution will tell you how fine of an image you'll get from the camera under optimal conditions. The higher the number, the better the resolution, and the better the picture. The lux refers to the camera's video board's or video chip's sensitivity to light. Some cameras use charged coupled devices (CCD). For our purposes, consider them chips. Whatever they use, the lower the lux, the more sensitive the camera is to light, which is very helpful in indoor applications. Price speaks for itself. Be sure to compare all three features before buying a camera.

Catching the Peeping Tom

Seventy-year-old Mrs. Weinstein had her attorney call me. She lived alone in a fancy, high-end, nongated community. She alleged that teens would knock on her door and bedroom windows in the very early morning hours before daylight. The local sheriff's office had made numerous visits to her residence, but had been unsuccessful in capturing the culprits, and now refused to respond at all. Her attorney wanted to know if we could catch them so this elderly lady could get a good night's sleep.

There were no streetlights where she lived, which created a problem for our equipment. The first thing we did was install floodlights around her house, and then tied them to motion sensors. We adjusted the sensitivity of the motion sensors so the local raccoon population could go about their business of raiding the garbage cans, but anything the size of teenage boy should cause an illumination like the Fourth of July.

I also installed a CCTV camera and wired it to a recorder that would begin recording when the motion sensor turned on the lights.

A few days later, the attorney called and said our client had visitors but our lights hadn't worked. Not good for business. We checked out the lights and they seemed to be working fine for us, but since the motion sensor didn't activate the lights the previous night, the camera didn't come on either. After tweaking the lights a little, I set the camera to begin recording at midnight and to run until six in the morning, not relying on the motion sensor. I ran the recorder at *real time*, so we could record sound as well. I set the recorder to self-rewind when it reached the end of the tape so I didn't have to go out each day and replace the tape or rewind it.

Another few days passed. Again the attorney called and said our client's hooligans were back at it. I retrieved the tape and took it to my office to review. The sheriff's office received a call from her at 3:45 A.M., so I began my review at 3:30. At 3:38, I could hear her get out of bed and begin walking around. A light in the bedroom came on at the same time. The camera was inside the house looking out, but I could see her reflection in the window. There was no activity outside that I could see.

She padded out of the bedroom. I could hear the refrigerator door open and close. In a second, she was back in the bedroom. Again, I could see her quite clearly in the reflection. She poured a glass of wine, drank it, and dropped the empty wine bottle into a trashcan next to her bed.

She called the sheriff's office and complained that someone was pounding on her door right this very moment. She couldn't understand why the operator couldn't hear it. Of course, I didn't hear anything either. Then she said they'd moved to the window and were pounding on that. The tape was silent, except for her talking to the sheriff. In about 10 minutes, a sheriff's patrol car pulled onto the property. The floodlights came on, and I lost her reflection, but had a good view of the deputies. The lights worked perfectly.

The attorney and I went to Mrs. Weinstein's house and played the tape for her. While there, I snooped through her trashcan in the bedroom and found a plethora of empty wine bottles and prescription tranquilizers. The combination of the two was causing her to hallucinate, creating her midnight visitors.

To this day, Mrs. Weinstein believes somebody was knocking on her doors and windows, but all the rest of us now know better. It was a successful conclusion to the case, just not what we expected.

The Least You Need to Know

- Placing a hidden camera in the home can catch abusive babysitters, uninvited visitors, and illegal behavior by spouses or friends.

- Techniques for using hidden cameras include the Camera in a Bag, Nanny Cams, and Installed Cameras, which usually utilize pinhole lenses.

- Tapping your own phone is a valuable technique for obtaining information about family members.

- Tapping your own phone may be illegal in two-party states, or if the persons being recorded are not aware of the recording. In one-party states, you may give consent for your minor child's conversations to be recorded, making recording in those instances legal.

- Tapping your own phone is easily accomplished by purchasing equipment at Radio Shack.

- Wireless camera advertisements are frequently seen on the Internet. Shop around before purchasing, as prices vary greatly for the same piece of equipment.

- Camera specifications include price, lines of resolution, and lux. Lower price, higher lines of resolution, and lower lux are preferable.

- CCTV installations can be tied to motion sensors and can help catch intruders, vandals, and thieves.

Part 5

Advanced Techniques

Now that you've learned the basics, it's time for the heavy-duty cases. You should be up to the challenge; you've learned the techniques.

These chapters will show you how to find that teenager who's run off before she gets into real trouble. You'll learn how to check a phone line for wiretaps. We'll deal with investigating crime, including catching pickpockets, purse snatchers, car thieves, and even burglars. Handling the evidence and preparing your case for court is the next step. When the big moment finally arrives, you'll be ready to present your case in front of a judge and jury.

Chapter 20

Catching the Runaway Teenager

In This Chapter

- ◆ Making a to-do list
- ◆ Dealing with the police department
- ◆ Tracking the runaway down
- ◆ Determining if the ex-spouse is harboring
- ◆ Making other parents your ally
- ◆ Sending photos around the country
- ◆ Using the "credit" in credit and debit cards
- ◆ Taking advantage of cellular technology

The wall clock reads 2 in the morning, and your 15-year-old daughter, Billie, is not home. Acid churns in your stomach. One moment you're mad as hell at her for not being there, the next instant you're close to tears worrying about your baby girl.

You're afraid to call the parents of any of her friends because you don't want to wake them up at such an awful time in the morning, plus you're feeling a little ashamed. As a parent, you should have better control over your teenagers, shouldn't you? Boy, are you ever going to give it to her when she gets home. No dating until she's 21. No telephone for two years, and she can forget about ever, ever having a car.

You've dozed off in the chair for a little while. The first light of the day is creeping through the blinds. The clock reads 5 A.M. Now you know for certain that the reason she's not home is more than just a flat tire or an empty gas tank. In Billie's room, you notice her makeup bag is gone. But she carries that in her purse, no big deal. You can't tell if any clothes are missing, since she and her girlfriends trade clothes back and forth like they own a consignment clothing store. You don't know how they keep track of who bought what.

At 6 A.M. the phone rings. You and your husband both look and then simultaneously lunge for it. You get to it first. It's Missy, a good friend of Billie's. Missy is calling to relay a message. Billie just called her and asked her to tell you that she was all right and not to worry. Don't call the police because she was old enough to be on her own. Billie doesn't want to live at home anymore. She's tired of you making her go to school. She doesn't like school and school doesn't like her. She'll call you when she gets settled down someplace. She has a few dollars and she'll be okay. Not to worry. Yeah, right.

Evaluating the Situation

If the evidence is clear that your or your client's teenager has run away and has not been abducted, then the next step is to collect the facts at hand and make some hard decisions. Find out from your client why she ran away. Be probative in your questions and observant of your surroundings. You're not going to get the real answer at the beginning. Down the road, when you've located the missing girl and are ready to have her picked up, you have to be convinced that her home environment is better than whatever alternatives exist. While your contractual obligation is to your client, your moral obligation is to the child.

Is this the first time she's run away? When I get calls from clients about their runaway teenager, almost invariably it's not the first time the child has left for parts unknown. It's just the first time the parents haven't been able to find her.

Here are 10 things to accomplish that will get you started and help move the investigation along. For the questions, write the answers down on a piece of paper. Gather the other materials together. If you are the parent, you'll want to have this information handy when you go to the police or to a private investigator. If you're the investigator, you'll see how we'll use it later in the chapter.

◆ Find the most recent picture you have of her.

◆ What was she wearing when she left? Runaways don't change clothes very often, and she'll probably be wearing the same thing for several days.

◆ Does she have any tattoos, piercings, or other identifying marks?

◆ Where did she run to before?

◆ Is the same boy or friend involved? Get his or her address and phone number.

◆ How did she make her escape? Chances are somebody drove a car and waited for her down the street. If you find the driver, you'll find the teenager.

◆ If she has a car and it is gone, write down a description of the car and the license plate number.

◆ Does she have a cellular telephone or a pager? What are the numbers? Did she take them with her? Get the last month's bill for her cell phone.

◆ Does she have credit cards or ATM cards with her? What banks do they draw on? Write down the account numbers.

◆ Make a list of all her friends, even if there are 50. Include their names, telephone numbers, and addresses. If you don't know their addresses and complete names, write down their first names and who else might know the rest of the name and how to contact them.

Next, if you don't have Caller ID on your telephone lines, then call the telephone company and have it installed immediately. Usually, it only takes 30 minutes for the telephone company to add it to your service. Send somebody down to the store to buy a Caller ID unit. It's probable that when she calls home, she'll block the call, but you never know. You could get calls from her friends who may not think to block their calls.

Handling the Police Department

I always recommend reporting the runaway to your local police or sheriff's office as a runaway/missing person. The reality is that thousands and thousands of teenagers run away from home every year. Unless there is some sign of physical abduction, your local police department has bigger fish to fry than to look for your wayward daughter, so don't expect much help from them until you've done the legwork and have her located. There are several other reasons why you want to report her missing, though.

Elementary, My Dear Watson

If your teenager is a good kid and a reasonable student, and gets involved in some illegal activity, I never recommend calling the police unless you absolutely have to. Having your child arrested and subjected to our criminal justice system is one of the worst things you can do to your teenager. I know that goes counter to what some say, but having been involved in this business for 20-some years, trust me. I'd do everything necessary to keep my child out of our jails and court system.

Some well-intentioned fathers will say that a night in jail will be good for the kid. Wrong. Once you put a child in that system, your control of the situation is lost. You've abdicated your rights as parents and turned those rights and responsibilities over to society. The jails are nothing more than a school where delinquents can learn to be better delinquents. They'll learn how to steal, do drugs, and become con and scam artists. When they are released, they'll be heroes among their peer group, and you don't want their illegal actions to be glorified in that manner.

The only time I'd consider having my child arrested would be if a jail were a safer place than where he is now. If your child is endangering himself or others, then give up your rights as a parent and have him arrested. Otherwise, handle the problem yourself.

With runaways, we're not talking about arresting your child—just having her picked up and transported home. The police can, and you need to insist that they do, put your child's name, date of birth, and description into NCIC (the National Crime Information Center) as a runaway or missing person. Be sure to include any tattoos or other identifying marks. When kids are picked up, they'll deny their own identity. A good description of a tattoo, especially one with a name or word on it, is very helpful to the patrolman on the street if he thinks he has a runaway.

Reporting her missing to the police accomplishes three things:

- When the kid is picked up someplace for loitering or is stopped for whatever reason, and she is identified, the agency that stopped her will hold her, usually in a juvenile facility if it's in another city, until you can make arrangements to retrieve her.

- A timely reporting of the disappearance of the child shows that you are a caring and concerned parent. You'll have a lot less trouble with the police and the juvenile authorities if you've reported the child missing right away. If you wait three days before reporting it and she is finally picked up, you may have some explaining to do to the state family services department before they let her come home.

- While your child will huff and puff and pretend to be incensed that you've involved the police, she will secretly be pleased that you wanted her back.

Imagine how she will feel if she finds out she was gone for three whole days before you finally got around to reporting her missing. You think she'll want to stick around after that?

Sammy the Snitch

Police departments and juvenile workers will interview a runaway teenager prior to releasing her to the custody of her parents or guardian. They have a responsibility to assure themselves that they are not returning the child into a harmful environment. If she makes allegations of physical or sexual abuse from her parents, stepparents, or another person in the home, even though totally false, then a whole can of worms is opened that you may not want to open. It's not unusual for a teenage girl to make false accusations against her parents. Be prepared for it. This is her defense mechanism and a way to hurt those parents. And it works very well.

Unless you live in a small community, the police probably will not come to your residence to take a runaway child report. They may assign the case to one of their officers who handles juvenile offender cases. Find out who this person is and write her name and contact numbers down. If they don't have an officer who works juveniles, then ask who you can talk to in the future. You will want to make additional contact with this person if the child is not found within 48 hours.

Most runaway teenagers either return by their own choice or, if entered into NCIC, are picked up and returned to their parents (or reach some sort of accommodation with their parents) within 48 hours.

The bottom line with police departments in mid-sized to large cites: Don't expect any real investigation to happen based simply on the runaway report. If you know where the child is located at a given moment, you can call the police, and they will send a squad car to pick her up and return her to your home. Other than that, you're basically on your own, as far as tracking her down is concerned. That's another good reason to keep this book handy. It'll help when the cops can't.

Tracking 'Em Down

In the rest of this chapter we're going to get into the nuts and bolts of actually "running to ground" a missing teenager. I'm going to assume that you have unlimited financial resources. I know you don't, but I'm going to lay out here all the things you can do. Most of them don't require much in the way of money, anyway. Some will.

You can pick and choose what you can afford to do, and decide for yourself where the action may fall on the cost-benefit curve.

People are creatures of habit, even teenagers. If she's run away before, she may use the same support apparatus that she used last time. How did she make her escape last time? Contact whoever drove her away before, or whomever she stayed with before. That's the first place to look. If she used a boy before and he is long out of the picture, don't discount him. Even if he hasn't had any contact with her for a while, if he's in the area, he'll know who your daughter has the "hots" for and who has the "hots" for her. It could be a boy that she doesn't even like, but she'll use him as a vehicle to get away. The old boyfriend will likely know who that would be.

If she was missing overnight before, who put her up? She stayed somewhere with somebody, and she just might be there again. You have to be a little sneaky here. I wouldn't just call and ask for her. Even teenagers have more street smarts than to fall for that. If there are some parents there that you trust, you might call them at work. Keep in mind that your daughter may be hiding in the house and the adults might not even know it. Teenagers stick up for each other, so those parents might ask their children, who in turn will lie to "protect" your daughter.

There are two options in this case: Ask the parents to search their home after work and look for any signs that your daughter may have been there. Or, set up surveillance on the house or apartment and see if she shows up.

My client Ralph finally called me after his son, Jimmy, had been gone for three days. This was the second time I'd worked this runaway, the other being the year before. He's the same boy we talked about in Chapter 11 in the payphone section. You'll meet Jimmy again later in this chapter. Jimmy was a big 14 year old. He was bigger than his father and as tall as I was, and he's kept me pretty busy.

I had his father make the list as we talked about earlier in this chapter. In going over the list of friends, we evaluated the lifestyle in each kid's home. Remember, kids will hide each other and protect each other from their own parents. In a runaway situation, all adults are the enemy. One friend popped out. This friend figured prominently in the previous escape. He lived in an apartment complex with his single mother. The mother worked during the day, so the kids were free to come and go as they pleased.

We thought this living arrangement might provide an opportunity for Jimmy to have a place to hide out during the day without any adult supervision. We had listed Jimmy as a runaway with the local sheriff's office and we confirmed that his name had been placed into NCIC.

I tried to make contact with the *courtesy officer* at the apartments, but he was working on duty at the moment. I didn't want to contact the management of the apartments and create any grief for the friend's mother. Single working mothers have it hard enough, and my intention is almost always to try to calm situations down, not inflame them.

Crime Scene Clues

A **courtesy officer** is usually a local police patrol person or sheriff's deputy that is given some sort of discount in his rent at an apartment complex in exchange for parking a marked patrol unit on the grounds and handling disturbance complaints at the complex when he is present. This is usually considered a good deal for the apartment management and the law enforcement department, as it reduces crime and does not increase law enforcement costs.

In working surveillance at an apartment complex, it is normally a good idea to make contact with the courtesy officer, if there is one. Because apartment complexes have so many people coming and going, you can hide for several hours and usually the tenants won't be concerned over your presence when they do see you in the parking lot. However, employees of the apartment complex will notice you and will contact the courtesy officer to have you checked out. If you've already spoken with him, then you head off a confrontation, and he'll tell the management that you're okay.

We set up surveillance on the apartment where the friend lived. There were a number of kids coming and going, and I felt it would be beneficial to have another investigator on site so we could follow some of these other kids, as they might lead us to Jimmy. The client approved the second surveillance man. Just a few minutes after my second man arrived, a green Volvo showed up at the apartment. Jimmy hopped out of the back seat and ran into the building. In a few moments he was back and into the Volvo. It left the complex and we followed.

Jimmy's father had told me that Jimmy was using marijuana, and he hoped that when we had Jimmy picked up, we would find marijuana on him, because he wanted him to spend a week or two in a juvenile detoxification center.

We followed the Volvo around the beach area until it finally returned to the apartment. The car left a few minutes later, but Jimmy remained in the apartment. At that point, since we had Jimmy located and he was not on the move, we contacted the local sheriff's office. About this same time, the friend's mother came home from work. In a while, the courtesy officer showed up, and we explained what was happening.

We followed the courtesy officer to the apartment where we found Jimmy hiding underneath a bed. The mother didn't know he was there. Jimmy didn't have any marijuana in his possession, so the sheriff's office would not transport him to the detox center. The clients arrived and, with them in the front seat and myself and my other investigator on either side of Jimmy in the back seat, we took him to the detox center, where he spent the next two weeks.

> **CAUTION**
>
> ### Sammy the Snitch
>
> A word of warning here. Never pick up a runaway teenager yourself. Remember, PIs are not law enforcement and generally don't have the right to use force except as an ordinary citizen would in defense of himself or others. Also, unless you have a contract with the client/guardian that gives you temporary guardianship rights, you don't have parental rights either. You don't want the client suing you later when the teenager, especially a female, alleges that you hurt or abused her. The runaway is not going to be happy about being found, and she will lie about your actions as a form of revenge if she can. It is best to ensure that she is listed as a runaway in NCIC, and then have the local police department pick her up.
>
> If I were the parent of a runaway, I wouldn't pick up my own child, either. Suppose I go to a house where I know she is staying, and three 20-year-old males greet me at the front door holding baseball bats as they inform me she's not coming home. What do I do? It's best to have the police make the actual pickup and avoid any confrontations yourself.

Checking Out the Ex

Some divorces are friendly and some are not. With child custody thrown into the mix, divorces can get downright nasty. If your client has custody of the runaway and there is an ex-spouse in the picture, take a good look at the relationship. If the ex is talking and being helpful with your client, then the kid is probably not there. But if there is animosity between the two parents, it's not unheard of for the ex-spouse to hide the child from the custodial parent.

Remember, all the ex is hearing is the nasty stuff coming from the teenager, detailing the mistreatment and unfairness of living with the custodial parent. The ex, perhaps, doesn't have the true picture, or if he does, he maybe can use this as a method of causing some grief for your client. Childish, I know, but so is most of the bickering that goes on during and after divorces. Makes you wonder who the adults really are in this world.

In Jimmy's case, the third time he ran away he was 16. That time he hid out at his mom's place for a while. The dad, meanwhile, was spending big bucks with my firm trying to find him. Making her ex (my client) spend money unnecessarily was part of her retribution plan.

We actually never found Jimmy at the ex's place, even though we did stake it out that time. We talked to the maid who worked there and she told us the ex was expecting Jimmy to show up. She'd left instructions with the maid to let him use the guest bedroom when he arrived.

Be sure to consider that a runaway teenager may try to get to the ex's residence. If it is out of state or some distance away, that makes it even more attractive to the kid. In her mind, the more distance she can put between herself and "the problem," the better.

Likewise, if your client has a troubled relationship with other of his own children, especially older siblings of the runaway who are already living independently, be sure to consider them as possible hosts for the teenager. The siblings may harbor the runaway and not tell their parents for a while. It all depends upon the fundamentals involved in the relationships.

Rely on Other Parents

With all of the missing/runaway teenage cases I've worked, I've almost always gotten good cooperation talking to parents of other children. Parents seem to stick together in this type of case. Parents of teenagers seem to have this "us against them" mentality, just like their offspring.

When Jimmy was 17 he ran off for the fourth time. This time we thought he'd taken off with a bunch of other kids his age for a skateboarding tournament on the west coast of Florida. The young men and women who worked at a local surf shop verified he'd been in there earlier in the day, identified his picture, and told us how the boys were talking about who got the bed in the motel room and who had to sleep on the floor.

We tracked down the mother of a member of that group of boys. She worked as an early-morning waitress in a local breakfast eatery. I called on her at work the next morning, and she confirmed that her sons were headed to St. Petersburg, Fla., to participate in the tournament. She didn't know where they were staying but the kids had promised to call her when they found a room. She, in turn, promised to call us when she found out the motel and room number. That is just an example of the kind of cooperation you can expect from other parents.

As it happened, our client flew myself and another of my investigators down that same day to St. Petersburg to try and intercept Jimmy at the skateboard rink. Again, we received very good cooperation from the management at the arena, after we promised them there would be no trouble. Jimmy's friend, who was actually entered in the tournament, wasn't scheduled to skate until late afternoon.

When we arrived in St. Petersburg, I coordinated with the local sheriff's office, and they confirmed that Jimmy was listed in NCIC as a runaway. They agreed to pick him up once we had him located and identified. See the value of making sure the child is listed in NCIC? Wherever you go after he's in there, you will, to some degree at least, get local cooperation.

Identifying him was a problem. A lot of skaters maintain similar appearances. Even though I'd run him to ground twice in the past, I hadn't seen him for nearly a year. Fortunately, by this time, he'd tattooed his name on his shoulder, so once we got a look at his shoulder, we'd know if we had the right kid or not.

While we were waiting for Jimmy and his friends to make an appearance, the Daytona Beach Police Department called and said they'd picked him up in Daytona. Apparently, he wasn't in St. Petersburg at all. He'd had a change of heart, and instead of going to the skateboarding championship, he'd decided to catch a ride to Daytona with another friend.

My investigator and I hopped back on the plane and flew across the state to Daytona. Eventually, the Daytona authorities released him to us, and we returned him to his parents. How long do you think he stayed at home that time? Less than a week. I wasn't uncomfortable taking custody of him because there were two of us, a male and a female. It was unlikely he'd try to accuse us of anything in that situation.

The waitress mom, true to her word, called me later that evening and told me which motel the kids were staying in. Parents of other teenagers are usually willing to help in runaway cases. Don't hesitate to be honest with them and inform them about the case you're working on. You may get unexpected assistance from them. And, who knows, as a PI, you might end up getting a new customer, too, when it's her turn to deal with a runaway child.

Plaster the Country with Photographs

The fifth time Jimmy ran off, he was still 17 and not too far away from his 18th birthday. We didn't know for sure whether he had headed north or south. We did know that he was traveling with a guy who was about 22 years old, who we were able to identify. He was from a town in New Jersey, and had been involved in selling marijuana in the beaches area of northern Florida.

I prepared a one-page report on Jimmy, including his description, tattoos, the fact that he was a juvenile, and the name of the person we thought he was traveling with. I included five copies of Jimmy's picture plus a disk with his picture on it in *JPEG* and *GIF* format. I first called the police department in the New Jersey town where the parents of Jimmy's friend lived. I asked for the name of the officer who worked juvenile and runaway matters. I then directed the letter and photographs to his attention.

> ### Crime Scene Clues
>
> JPEG (pronounced *J-peg*) and **GIF** (pronounced the way it looks) are two common digital formats for graphic files such as photographs. If photographs are going to be transmitted to a police agency or another investigator electronically or via a computer disk, it is best to save them in either JPEG or GIF format, because most computer photo programs can open and work with those formats. Other formats are not as common, and the police department may not be able to open and print the photograph.

I did the same thing when we heard rumors that he was in Daytona and then again in West Palm Beach, Fla. It's amazing the different levels of cooperation I received.

In New Jersey, where I expected the least amount of cooperation, the police staked out the residence of the friend for a week and kept a close eye on the neighborhood for a long time after that. They'd call me every few days with an update.

In Daytona, they shrugged their shoulders and basically said, "So what?"

In West Palm Beach, we had a list of pay phones that his girlfriend was calling. Jimmy would call her from a pay phone, give her the number he was calling from, and she would turn around and call him right back at that pay phone, using her cellular phone.

Since the girlfriend was using her cellular phone to call the pay phones, I had my phone source retrieve a copy of all the calls she made to the appropriate area codes.

We tracked down the location of the pay phones he was using and marked each one on a map. They were all within a three-block radius. See Chapter 11 for a discussion of how to find the location of pay phones in this type of a case.

With the letter and photographs, I also sent to the West Palm Beach Police Department the list of pay phones he was using and their locations. They agreed to keep an eye out on the phones for us. If our client had really wanted the boy back, we could have staked out the phones ourselves, and in a few days we would have found him and had him picked up.

I think our client was about ready to give up trying to force his son to stay in school or to lead a productive life. If the police found him, fine. Otherwise, he'd just let him turn 18, and then there was nothing he could do anyway. And that's exactly what happened. Interestingly, after he turned 18, Jimmy came home all by himself. It figures, huh? I was half expecting to get a call from Jimmy, saying that the day after he'd come home, his dad had run away, and did I think I could find him.

Checking the Credit

If the runaway teen has a credit card or an ATM card that either belongs to the parents or for which the parents cosigned on the bank account with the teen, the parents should be able to have nearly immediate access to usage information.

You can check the usage of most credit cards online. Most credit card websites update daily. Depending upon how a transaction occurs, however, it may not post until several days after the transaction. You can try talking to the credit card company to see if they can tell you when authorizations on the card are received. Usually those are all done electronically, and the company itself may not know where the authorization comes from until the charge actually posts. In serious kidnapping matters, it's a different story. The information is there, but getting it out of the credit card company depends upon the stakes at hand.

CAUTION

Sammy the Snitch _____

A word of warning: Some parents are tempted to cancel the credit cards immediately, but unless it's a serious money factor, you should advise your client against that. Credit card charges can provide good leads to finding the runaway. If the child is under the influence of someone much older he'll probably max out the card pretty fast, the person of influence will take the cash or goods. If the card has a high credit limit you'll want to lower it ASAP. You have to balance the financial cost with the quality of the information you're receiving concerning your child's current whereabouts. There are no cut and dried answers on that one.

ATM transactions, even if used on an ATM machine that is not part of the bank network, usually post the same night that the transaction takes place. The next day, the client's banks should be able to tell which machine was used for the transaction. With that information in hand, you may only be hours away from the teen. Hours can transform into hundreds of miles, but then again, you may get a handle on the child's direction of travel. Many ATMs have video surveillance cameras. You should liaison with the bank-security folks to get photos from the surveillance tapes. You may also get lucky and obtain a photograph of whom the runaway is traveling with. That person might be easier to track than the runaway.

Tracking the Cell Phone

In this and previous chapters, we've talked about obtaining cellular phone records. Most good phone sources can't get those records until after the bill *has dropped*, so even if the teen is using a cell phone, as many as 30 days could pass between when a call was made and when you can get the record of it.

There is an aspect to cellular usage that is more immediate. Each cell phone has its own electronic serial number (ESN). When a cell phone is in the "on" position, it periodically broadcasts this ESN. This is how the cellular company knows where to route a call when one is received for any particular cell phone customer. The company computers keep track of where all the active cell phones are at any given minute.

Under the right circumstances, a cellular company might be convinced to alert you when the teen's cell phone is turned on. Again, this will take some pressure, and perhaps even some law enforcement intervention, to get the cell company to do this, but it's worth it. Why? Because when the cell company picks up the ESN signal, its computers will know that it's coming from a specific cellular site. This would pinpoint the location down to an area of no more than a few square miles or, in a down town area, to within a few blocks. None of the teenagers I've tracked down had ever had cell phones, but with the proliferation of cellular usage, more teens under the age of 18 have them than before, and the number is growing. Teens are rapidly moving from pagers to cell phones.

Crime Scene Clues

When a cell or telephone bill **has dropped,** it means that the billing cycle has ended, and the charges are en route to the consumer. Some phone sources cannot access the list of phone charges until the bill has entered the billing system's computer. Better phone sources can access the charges as they occur. With enough pressure, you might get the cellular company to give you the calls daily as they're made.

There may be no other case that carries with it so much emotion as a missing child or teenager. Some of us wish our teenagers were missing more often. (Just kidding.) More than one mother has said that she wouldn't sell her teenager for a million dollars, but some days she would flat give her away.

Except for the mother in the preceding paragraph, usually the parent of the missing youth will have her emotions run the gamut from worry, to fear, to anger, to hurt, to frustration, to desperation, and finally, to resignation.

When dealing with these clients, be sensitive to their needs. Keep the welfare of the child uppermost. Don't make promises you can't keep. Be the calming influence, the face of reason, and the beacon of hope.

The Least You Need to Know

- There are 10 items of information that should be gathered at the onset of any runaway investigation.

- Runaways should always be listed in NCIC by informing the local police departments. The police should be informed of the missing child as soon as possible as a sign of good faith on the part of the parents.

- Consider surveillance of possible locations or friends' residences where the teen may be hiding. Always ask the police to pick up the runaway once he's been located. Don't do it yourself.

- Ex-spouses have been known to harbor the runaway, hiding her from the other spouse.

- Parents of other teenagers usually will cooperate in a runway case. Use them.

- Send photographs of the teen to police departments in cities where it is likely the teen may be.

- Charges on credit cards, as well as ATM withdrawals, can provide timely information as to where the teenager is located or her direction of travel.

- A cellular phone in the "on" position transmits its serial number to the cellular company. With enough pressure, the cell company might tell you the location of the cell site on which it is receiving the signal.

Chapter 21

The Ins and Outs of Electronic Surveillance

In This Chapter

- ◆ Learning the differences between bugs and taps
- ◆ Who done it? Cops or robbers?
- ◆ Tapping the line
- ◆ Gathering the tools
- ◆ Finding the inside taps
- ◆ Catching the neighbor

The second-most common call received by a private investigative agency is a request for a countermeasure sweep. The caller doesn't use those words, but that's what she wants. Normally she'll say, "I think my phone is tapped." Or, "My husband and I are getting a divorce and I want to make sure he's not recording my telephone calls."

A countermeasure sweep is an active measure by an individual with the goal of finding or countering an aggressive action taken against him or her. Typically, the term is used in the sense of actively searching for and eliminating any electronic transmitters (bugs) or wiretaps that are directed toward locations or facilities where the target of the measure would likely be heard. A variation of the term is also used in respect to surveillance. A counter-surveillance is a surveillance initiated by an individual to determine if he is under surveillance by an outside group. If properly conducted, a counter-surveillance will identify the entity conducting the surveillance. So, you'll know who at the diner counter is watching you.

There are four aspects to conducting a complete countermeasure sweep:

- ◆ Evaluate the threat level
- ◆ Interception of wire communications: telephone sweeps
- ◆ Interception of oral communications: transmitters
- ◆ Video surveillance: hidden cameras

In this chapter, we're going to examine the first two. Hidden video cameras we've talked about to some degree in Chapter 19. Sweeping for concealed transmitters (bugs) is beyond the scope of this book. If you have a situation that calls for this type of action, contact a reputable PI firm that specializes in countermeasure sweeps.

Before we go into details, though, we have to understand exactly what we're looking for.

Bugged or Tapped: It's Terminology

I frequently receive telephone calls where the new client says, "I think somebody has bugged my phones." Is that possible? Sure. Is it likely? Not unless we're dealing with a bug or a phone tap instituted by law enforcement under a legal warrant. Can somebody bug your house? Sure, it happens all of the time. Can somebody other than law enforcement tap your phone line and record your conversations? Sure, we see it at least once a month. But bugging your phones is unlikely. Confused? That's because the general public doesn't make a distinction between a bug and a wiretap. It's a matter of terminology. To understand intercepts, we need to understand intercept technology and get the terms right.

What the caller probably means is that some privileged information that he told somebody on the telephone has leaked out. He didn't tell anybody else, and he's sure that other person didn't relate it to anybody either; hence, his phone must be tapped (not bugged).

A bug generally refers to a microphone-transmitter combination. The microphone picks up the conversation and the transmitter sends it out using radio frequency (RF) energy. There are other ways to get a conversation transmitted out of the room without using RF, but to read about it, you'll have to wait for the advanced version of this book.

Bugs—let's call them transmitters—are used to capture a conversation between two or more people within the same room. We're all familiar with the bug disguised as an olive in a martini glass. In that case, the olive is the microphone-transmitter and the toothpick is the antenna.

Having your phones tapped generally means that, at some point on your *landline telephone line*, an interception has been made, and the interceptor most likely is recording the conversations that transpire over your phone line.

Other forms of communication, such as cellular phones and portable handsets, can be compromised as well. If the conversation travels through the air, it can be intercepted.

Crime Scene Clues

A **landline telephone line** refers to a normal telephone line that has a physical demarcation point at a residence, business, or pay telephone. The phone call at least begins and ends its transmission along a pair of wires, regardless of whether transmission of the call includes microwave or satellite in between both ends. This is in contrast to a cellular phone, or any type of radio communication, which is considered wireless communication—literally, not connected to the ground at some point with wires.

Evaluating the Threat

Paranoia runs rampant in our society. We like to say in our business, just because you're paranoid doesn't mean someone hasn't tapped your phone. (It's a variation of the old axiom, "Just because you're paranoid doesn't mean that there is nobody following you" discussed in Chapter 18.) The real question you have to ask yourself, or the client, is whether there's anything you're saying on the phone that's so valuable to another person that they'd be willing to go to an awful lot of trouble and expense to listen to your conversations. It doesn't have to be illegal stuff. For example, is the client involved in big money deals? Then it may be worth the effort for the competition to listen in.

Is his wife fooling around on him and he wants to know for sure? Then he may consider tapping his own phone to listen to her conversations. Generally in most states, taping your home telephone to listen to your spouse's calls would be illegal. There are special circumstances that might make it legal to tap your own phone involving calls made my your minor children. Check Chapter 19 for the details on that.

If you're searching for a phone tap or a transmitter placed by your client's spouse, then chances are you can find it with the instructions from this chapter. Even if the spouse has big bucks, it's unlikely that he'll spend the tens of thousands of dollars it would take, assuming he knew the people who could do it, to tap the phone in such away as to make detection impossible.

If you think the FBI or U.S. Customs has tapped your phone and a PI offers to sweep the phone lines for $150, you have the wrong PI. When law enforcement executes a legal telephone tap, they basically have the phone company run an extension of your phone line into their offices. There is no physical connection made at your house or business. There is an electronic connection made at the telephone company's central switch to have your calls routed both to your phone at home and to the local FBI office. That puts a few chinks into some of those television movies, doesn't it?

There are some equipment manufacturers who claim their test equipment can alert the technician performing a countermeasure sweep that a legal tap is on the line. How? In a legal tap, the length of the telephone circuit has basically been extended to include the local FBI office. The manufacturer is selling you on the ability of their equipment to test for a change in the length of the circuit. If you really think your phone is tapped by law enforcement, that means it's been done with a warrant, and this chapter won't help you find it. And if that's what you're up against, don't buy the fancy testing equipment. Hire a good lawyer.

However, if you're thinking it's an illegal tap by a cowboy cop, then there is a good chance you'll find it. If the telephone tap threat is from your husband, next-door neighbor, or the guy who lives two floors below you in the same building, then $250 per line to check your phone lines is reasonable, because finding that sort of wiretap is not a high-tech search. Still, the person doing the sweeping has to know what he is looking for. Before this chapter is over, you'll be able to do it yourself.

Tapping telephones without the consent of the parties involved, or without having a warrant for the tap, is illegal in every state. That means you have to consider in advance what action you'll take if you discover that your telephone is tapped or your house is bugged.

Do you call the phone company? Call your lawyer? Call the police? The natural reaction is to want to nail the person responsible, but you need to stop and think it through. Do you really want the person responsible to go to jail? If the guilty party is a soon-to-be ex-husband, just remember that he won't be able to pay child support or alimony if he's in prison. You may have to go to court to testify, and that risks making everything part of the public record for anyone to read. Are you sure you want to do that? Think this through very carefully before you involve law enforcement, because once you start the legal system in motion, there's no turning back.

Know what you're going to do before you start looking, and then be prepared to photograph the tap for later evidence.

Tools of the Trade

Remember the old gangster movies of the 1940s? Neither do I, but I've seen a few remakes. In the old movies, when the guy wanted to tap a phone, he went down to the basement of the building and found the telephone junction box where all the phones in the building came together. Then he clipped on a couple of wires using alligator clips, ran those wires to another set of wires that went to an apartment in the same building, or maybe to a small room or closet in the basement. He could sit in the room with a headset on and listen to the phone calls all day. The PI would bring him coffee periodically throughout the day and ask if there was anything new. Ah, the good old days.

Well, surprise. The good old days are basically still here. Things haven't changed that much. You can find most local telephone taps with three tools: your eyes, a screwdriver, and a *butt set*.

Type "butt set" into any Internet search engine and you'll find lots of listings. You can spend over a thousand dollars if you want, or you can make your own for less than $20. Here are full instructions for making your own butt.

Take an old touchtone telephone or buy one from a local phone store. You don't need any special type of phone; the more plain the better. Buy a short phone extension cord, (cost $2.95) a couple of alligator clips (cost $2.00). Plug one end of the extension cord into the telephone. Cut off the other plug end from the cord. Strip the outside wire cover back about a foot. Strip the red and green inside wire covers back about two inches baring the copper wire. Assuming it's a two pair extension cord, clip off the yellow and black wires because you won't need them. Attach the alligator clips to the red and green bare ends.

There you have it. A homemade butt set for the cost of a telephone and $5.00 in parts.

> **Crime Scene Clues**
>
> A **butt set** is a handheld device that looks like a cordless phone, has a touchtone keypad, and is used by telephone and electronic service people to identify telephone lines. It will have a set of wires with alligator clips at the end. You can buy butt sets for less than a hundred dollars over the Internet or at Radio Shack.

The Inside Job

The easiest way to access your phone lines is from within your residence or the property in question. If your spouse, partner, or some other person who has regular, daily access to your home wants to tap your telephone line, it's probably being accomplished as an "inside" job.

A butt set is a tool used to identify phone lines.

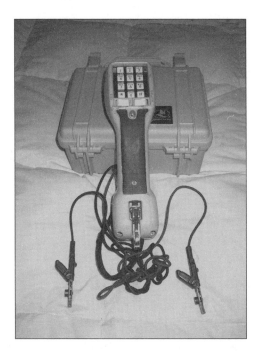

Look in Chapter 19 at the telephone recording control device from Radio Shack. That's what you're looking for. Search under every bed. Get a flashlight and look behind every piece of furniture. Using the light, search every wall in the house for a phone jack. If there are wires coming out of any phone jack, examine them to make sure they are only going to telephones and not to a control device or a tape recorder.

Physically run your hands along the wires from the phone jack and trace them back to the phones. Don't just eyeball it. A clever guy will splice the wires partway up the line and put the recorder and controls behind a piece of furniture. If you just look at the wall and at the phone, you'll say to yourself, "Okay, nothing there." So run your hand all the way down the line from the telephone to the wall jack.

Check under the beds and in your husband's office. Does he have a locked drawer or cabinet in his study? Are there any wires leading to that drawer or cabinet? Check the spare bedroom, too. You have to check every room, every wall, and every phone jack.

Still didn't find it, but you're sure it's there? Hit the garage. He's going to be sneaky, so you have to be as thorough as he is clever. Look in every closet. If your husband is the least bit technical, he can splice into the phone line in the attic and put the recorder up there. Or he can run a line from the splice in the attic to another location in or around the house.

Walk around the outside of the house. Are there any phone lines coming out of the crawl space that you can't identify? Most women, and men for that matter, won't know which lines are supposed to be on the outside of the house and which aren't. That's okay. Just follow them visually to see where they go. No need to run your hands on these wires. You might accidentally be following an electrical wire that is not grounded and fry yourself, so don't touch any wires outside of the house. It'll be pretty obvious if they go into a box that your husband has made to hold the tape recorder.

Husbands frequently hide the recorder and controls in a box under the porch or under a wooden deck, so get a flashlight and look there. If you don't want to be poking under the porch yourself, then find a PI who advertises countermeasure sweeps and get him to do it. But you can save the $250 by spending an hour and doing it yourself, since you know what to look for.

The Outside Job

In most areas of the country, it is fairly easy to tap a neighbor's telephone. I say *neighbor* because tapping the phone is also going to require that you be able to listen to or record the conversations. The further away the listening post is, the more problematic the exercise becomes. A method to circumvent the distance problem is to tap the phone outside the house or at the *junction box*, and hide a recorder in the bushes somewhere close by. This happens all of the time.

To find an outside wiretap, you must have a basic understanding of how telephones work. Phones require two wires. These two wires are referred to as one pair, just as two shoes equals one pair. If you have two pairs of shoes and only one pair of feet, like most of us, then you have an extra pair of shoes. If you have two pairs of wires and only have one phone line (one active phone number, not to be confused with extensions with the same phone number), then you have an extra pair. Almost every house in America that is wired for phone service has at least two pairs of phone wires in the house. Many newly constructed houses will have three or four pairs of wires so you can have three or four different telephone numbers at the same location.

All of these pairs of wires run throughout your house and lead from your building to the telephone interface, and then to the junction box.

> **Crime Scene Clues** _____
>
> A **junction box** is a piece of telephone company equipment where several customers' telephone lines are housed and connected to a phone company cable. Typically, these junction boxes house from two to two dozen connections. There is normally 1 on every block, or 1 for every 10 to 12 subscribers.

Typically, the active pair of wires are the red and green wires, known as tip and ring. The other pair is usually yellow and black but can be blue and blue/white, or orange and orange/white, or any other two colors.

Your telephone wires from the inside of your house will interface or connect with the phone company's wires. Do not confuse this telephone interface with the telephone junction box.

The telephone interface attached to your garage or outside of your house is usually a gray box divided into two sections. Your side can be opened by a flat-bladed screwdriver. The other side belongs to the telephone company and normally requires a special tool to open it. You don't really need access to the telephone company side of the interface anyway.

A typical Bell System junction box.

A telephone interface joins the lines you own with the lines owned by the phone company.

Locating the Junction Box

Now you need to locate the junction box. How will you recognize one when you see it? The junction box is usually a $2^1/_2$-foot-tall, cylindrical, green metal post or cabinet. It'll be located on the ground and you may find it in the middle or at the end of a block, or any logical place where phone lines come together.

Our client, Heidi, asked us to check her lines for taps. She was suspicious of a neighbor who lived across the alley from her. He'd been insinuating that he was listening to her telephone calls after she'd ended their relationship. He wasn't stalking her, but he clearly pined for her. He also had occasional access to her apartment, feeding her dogs for her when she was out of town. Consequently, we did the inside checks as we've talked about and then went outside. The figure of a typical junction box was actually Heidi's junction box exactly the way we found it. It is not unusual to find them falling open or with the covers askew. It certainly makes getting into them easier.

Cable television junction boxes are similar and frequently are shorter and more round. However, just to mix you up, some cable boxes are larger and more square. Walk up and down the street or around your subdivision and you'll see the phone junction box. It probably has a phone company logo or sticker on it, but sometimes it may be weathered off. The cable boxes usually say "cable TV" on them.

The junction box is easily opened by a flat-bladed screwdriver. Some phone companies have recently begun utilizing security screws, which require a special tool. Don't let that stop you. Most of those boxes are left unsecured by careless telephone serviceman anyway, as was Heidi's. Often, they've been run over by cars or backed over by trucks, and that usually leaves them open as well.

On the older models, the front cover will lift up and then slide forward. There should be no need to completely remove the cover. Newer editions are totally round and the cover lifts completely off.

Finding Your Phone Line

In order to tell if your phone line has been compromised, you have to find your terminals inside that junction box. When you open the junction box, it may look daunting, but it's really not that difficult. Sometimes, the telephone numbers are written on paper or plastic tags attached to the wires. I hope you're one of the lucky ones, but don't count on it.

The inside of the junction box will look similar to the one in the following figure. In this box, the servicemen had written one of the phone numbers and the address inside the box for us. I like that guy.

Telephone wires carry about 52 volts of direct current. That's why your phones still work even if the electricity to your house is shut off, unless you have only cordless phones, which require the base station to be plugged into the AC current. There is not enough amperage to really hurt you, but you can get shocked, so don't be messing around in the junction box in the rain. The trick here is to find your lines and make sure that nobody has jumpered them to another pair like we talked about with the old gangster movies. That's exactly what we're looking for.

Inside a telephone junction box.

So, you opened the junction box and none of the phone lines are tagged or labeled. How do you figure out which one is yours? You'll need your butt set, and something called an *ANAC* number that will work in your area.

Every telephone company has a local phone number you can dial that is hooked to a computer that will repeat back to you the number from which you are calling. You might try dialing 211 or 311 (or any number between 205 and 220). That works in a lot of areas. If that doesn't work, then the easiest way to get this callback number is to ask a telephone service repairman. When you see one working on the street, just stop and ask him. You may have to ask two or three before you find one who will give it to you, if he knows it.

Surprisingly enough, many repairmen don't know it themselves. Some phone companies will give it to you if you ask for it. Try calling the repair department and asking.

> **Crime Scene Clues**
>
> **Automatic Number Announcement Circuit (ANAC)** is a telephone number that, when dialed, will announce back to you the number you are calling from. These numbers vary within area codes and sometimes vary within switches in the same city.

Take your butt set, homemade or purchased, and attach the alligator clips to the first pair of terminals in the junction box. You should hear a dial tone. If you don't, it's not an active pair.

Disconnect the clips and move down to the next one. Make sure the clips don't touch each other while you do this. It's not dangerous, but you won't get a dial tone if the alligator clips are touching. At each dial tone, use the touchtone keypad on the butt set, dial the ANAC number, and it will tell you the telephone number for the phone line you are connected to. If you connect to a line and hear voices, you are listening in on your neighbor's conversation in progress. Simply disconnect and move to the next one, or else you will now be the one who is illegally tapping another's line. Even though it's accidental, it's still not nice. Sure, it could be interesting, but don't be nosy and certainly *don't talk*, because if you do they will hear you, just as if you had picked up an extension in their home.

Sherlock's Secrets

Here are some 800 numbers you can use that belong to MCI if you want to find out the phone number for the phone line you are using. You may have to navigate through a set of menus to get the number repeated back to you. Press option one and then one again. 1-800-444-4444, 1-800-444-3333, and 1-800-727-5207 will all give you that number. Here is another 800 number, but you can only call it twice a day from the same number: 1-888-324-8686.

Eventually, you will find your phone line. Examine it closely. Is there anything out of the ordinary? Anything different from the other lines and terminals in the junction box? I suggest you mark the terminals with a felt marker so you'll be able to identify your lines in the future. If there is a set of jumpers from your line to another, then yes, your telephone is tapped. Mark both sets, photograph the inside of the junction box and replace the cover.

If by the time you read this the 800 ANAC numbers given in this chapter do not work, and you can't find ANAC numbers for your area, there is still another way to determine which pair of wires in the junction belong to you.

Have a friend sit in your house and make a phone call to anybody. Have them continue talking while you're at the junction box, methodically plugging into one pair of wires and then the next, until you eventually hear your friends discussing your paranoia. Voilà.

As I mentioned earlier, if your line is tapped, you have to decide what action to take.

In Heidi's case, I checked the junction box. The cover was half off the box as you see in the photograph. I opened the junction box and easily found Heidi's phone lines. How? Because I could see that one set of terminals had a pair of wires running to another set of terminals further down the box. I checked the phone number for the first set of suspicious terminals by using my butt set and dialing the ANAC. These were Heidi's lines, all right.

I then went over to the telephone interface, the gray box where the phone lines entered the subject's apartment, and checked there. Yep, he'd basically run an extension of Heidi's phone to his place.

Heidi didn't want to involve the police. After photographing it, I disconnected the tap and closed the box. One of the investigators who works for me is about 6 feet 4 inches tall and 260 pounds. When I walk down dark alleys, he's the one I take with me. I usually let him lead the way. He and I went and had a little talk with the neighbor who'd tapped Heidi's phone. She hasn't had any trouble with him since.

Tapping a phone by jumpering wires has its dangers. It's possible that an alert phone company service man will discover the tap while he is in that junction box working on someone else's line. The phone company may then report it to the police.

I don't advocate tapping phones. I get asked to do it all the time but refuse to do so. It's illegal and I won't do anything illegal because it's not worth losing my license for a few thousand dollars. However, let me emphasize that it is not illegal to find out if your own phone line has been tapped.

The Least You Need to Know

- The term "bug" refer to a microphone-transmitter combination that transmits room conversations to another location. "Tap" refers to an interception of wire communications.

- The threat level must be assessed. If the suspected source of the bugging or tapping is the FBI, then more sophisticated equipment will be needed to determine if both the room and the phone lines are secure. If the threat is a soon-to-be ex-husband, other, less sophisticated techniques are probably adequate.

- Tapping telephones without consent of the parties involved or without having a warrant for the tap is illegal in every state. Upon discovering an illegal tap, evaluate if you want to involve law enforcement. If the guilty party will be paying your alimony, you may not want him in jail.

- Most illegal telephone taps can be located with your eyes, a screwdriver, and a butt set. You can make a butt set at home or buy one for less than $100.

- Thoroughly check every phone jack and every conceivable hiding place in the house for a tape recorder and a telephone remote control device. Also check in the garage, the attic, and the bushes outside of the house.

- To find an outside telephone tap, locate the junction box and examine the appropriate pair of wires.

- When dialed, Automatic Number Announcement Circuits (ANAC) will announce the number calling them.

22

You've Been Robbed

In This Chapter

- ◆ Learning the ropes of personal crime
- ◆ Finding help from unlikely sources
- ◆ Hot sheeting the stolen cars
- ◆ Solving the burglary
- ◆ Detailing the pawnshop detail
- ◆ Crime scenes and dumpster diving
- ◆ Owner-applied numbers and NCIC

Crime in America is a fact of life. In the year 2000, the FBI Uniform Crime Report indicates there were over 2 million reported burglaries in the United States. To help you put that number into perspective, it means that just under 1 person out of 100 was a victim of a burglary. Want to get personal? Boil it down to households, and it means about 1 in every 35 homes was burglarized. Makes you want to step outside and look up and down the street and count how many houses there are. The amazing thing is that the figures are down about 2.4 percent from the year before.

If you add burglary to other property crimes, including larceny-theft, theft of motor vehicles, and arson, the number of reported crimes for the year 2000 was over 10 million. That means that just over three out of every hundred persons, or every eighth household, was a victim of property crime. Uh-oh. Better step outside and recount your street.

In this chapter, we're going to talk about what to do when you're at the shopping mall and your purse is snatched. Then, you go out to the parking lot, and your car has been stolen, and after a cab ride home, you find your house has been burglarized. That's going to be a bummer of day, huh?

There's Never a Cop Around When You Want One

In many larger metropolitan areas, the police do not respond to smaller property crimes. They'll take the report over the telephone and give you a report number for insurance purposes, but you'll never see a detective and no investigation is ever done on the crime. Makes you wonder who's winning the war on crime.

Even though the police may not respond, there are other avenues. Private investigators don't often get called to investigate purse snatchings. The criminal and the evidence are both long gone before a PI could get to the scene. Don't give up. There are steps that you, a do-it-yourself PI, can take when something like that happens.

You're in the mall, walking through a store, and a lady bumps into you. She may actually apologize to you for her carelessness. Still, you'd better check your wallet, your watch, and your bracelet. Anytime you are jostled or bumped by another person, inventory the valuables you're carrying on your body and the contents of your purse, if you're carrying one. You may have been the victim of one of the most common pickpocketing techniques.

If your wallet is lifted while you're in a crowded place such as a mall or a large store, look around quickly. Whoever that person is, she will now be walking quickly away. Memorize what she looks like, what she's wearing, and, if she spoke, how she sounded. For example, did she have an accent? The pickpocket's next move is usually to hand the stolen item over to a third person. If you're quick, you can see her walk close and almost brush by her cohort, who will be approaching from another direction. If you think you see that, even if you're not sure, again, do your best to memorize what they are wearing.

The next step is the most important one, and you have to make a quick decision. There are three good options that follow. Each requires an action on your part. Choose one. The worst option is to do nothing.

- You can chase after the person who stole your wallet and confront her. Remember, it's likely she will no longer have the stolen goods, so even with a confrontation that brings the store security running, it's your word against hers. However, not all pickpocket and purse thieves work with an accomplice. If you don't see a handoff, and the thief hasn't had the opportunity to ditch the billfold anyplace, she might still have possession of it. Purse snatchers, in particular, seem to work by themselves and don't hand off the goods to a buddy. They'll just grab the purse and run. But are you up to a physical confrontation? If you haven't been running 30 miles a week, lifting weights, and keeping current on your karate lessons, I wouldn't recommend it. Confronting a thief is a personal decision and a decision you should probably analyze and make before the critical moment ever occurs.

- Make a scene. Call out that you've been robbed and point toward the person walking away from you. You may get immediate help from people around you. We'll talk more about this in a minute.

- If making a scene is too embarrassing for you, then at least immediately ask a salesperson to call the store security and mall security. Don't be polite about it. Don't wait until the salesperson finishes ringing up the sale she's working on. Tell her to stop what she's doing and make the call right now! Time is of the essence here. Major retailers have plainclothes security people on the sales floors during most of their open hours. There might be one right next to you and you wouldn't know it.

Regardless of which course of action you choose, a security person will eventually arrive. Tell him briefly what happened and give him the description of the thief. Shopping malls generally have very sophisticated closed-circuit television camera setups and can track any particular individual's movements throughout the building.

By acting fast and giving security a good description, there is a good chance the pickpocket and her cohort can be spotted and apprehended.

Several years ago, I was with the FBI, working in the downtown Loop area of Chicago just prior to Christmas. I witnessed a young man snatch a briefcase from an older gentlemen. The snatcher took off running. I gave chase. He was younger than I was, a little bit faster on his feet, had a good head start, and certainly had more motivation to run than I did.

I chased him down the street where I spotted another FBI agent I knew. I yelled at him and he joined with me. We ran into the Palmer House Hotel, the thief just 15 yards ahead of us. We entered the hotel from one street and ran clear through and came out on another street. In the process, we passed two house detectives in the lobby of the hotel. They also gave chase.

The pursuit continued across the street and up the block, where the perpetrator entered what was then a Montgomery Ward department store. Being just before Christmas, the store was incredibly crowded. People and tables of sale items went flying in all directions. Two plainclothes store detectives heard the commotion, saw us coming, and tackled the thief. I was huffing and puffing, but at least the thief hadn't been able to increase his lead any, so I felt good about that.

The briefcase belonged to a jewelry repairman who was making his rounds. It was full of watches and jewelry.

On another occasion, in New York City, a would-be bank robber had a bad day. He was in a teller line, waiting until it was his turn so he could rob the bank. He didn't know it was payday and the local FBI office was just up the street. When it was finally his turn, he slipped a note to the teller, instructing her to put all of her money in the bag that he passed to her.

An alert FBI agent standing behind the robber noticed something strange was happening. The agent said, "What's going on here?"

"Nothing," the bank robber said, turning to the agent. "Mind your own business. I'm robbing this bank." He returned his attention to the business at hand.

At least, he did, until the agent drew his weapon, stuck the barrel to the back of the robber's head, and said, "Like hell you are."

Instead of getting a large cash withdrawal, the would-be robber got bagged and tagged as the evidence.

The point is that even though a uniformed policeman may not be standing by to assist you, there are many security and undercover police folks around. You may be standing next to one and not know it. When your purse is snatched or your wallet lifted, don't just bemoan your bad luck and go home. Take some immediate action and you might actually get your belongings back. Even if your property is lost forever, at least you've waged your own little war on crime.

Flag Me a Cab, My Car's Been Stolen

In the year 2000, there were over 1 million reported thefts or attempted *motor vehicle thefts* in the United States, and that number is climbing every year. There is no more bewildering experience than to come out of a store and not be able to find your car, only to eventually realize it's been stolen. I know, it's happened to me three times.

Again, time is the important factor here. If you can get the report made and have the reporting officer call it in so that the vehicle's description and tag number are reported over the air, there is chance the car will be seen and recovered.

My car was stolen the first time in San Juan, Puerto Rico. We'd parked on a busy street late one evening after the office Christmas party and visited with some friends living in a condominium on the beach. We'd only been in their place about 45 minutes. When my wife and I returned to the street, the car was gone. Unbelievable.

Crime Scene Clues

For the purposes of the FBI's Uniform Crime Report, **motor vehicle theft** is defined as the theft of automobiles, trucks, buses, motorcycles, motor scooters, snowmobiles, etc. This does not include the taking of a vehicle for temporary purposes by those having lawful access.

We went back upstairs and called it in. Then, using my friend's car, we drove home, halfway to the east end of the island, an hour away. It was now about 2 in the morning. The telephone rang. It was the Police of Puerto Rico. A patrolman had been driving down an unpaved road through the jungle, in a place about an hour west of San Juan. He saw a group of men stripping a car—my car. As he approached with his blue lights on, the men took a couple of shots at him and then fled.

When it was safe, he called a tow truck and had the car towed back to the police impound lot. They wanted me to come and get the car right then. I suggested we wait until daylight, but they insisted I retrieve it while it was still there. They couldn't guarantee it'd be there the next day.

Theoretically, the vehicle was drivable. All of the tires had been taken off but the tow truck operator put them back on. Everything in the interior had been taken out except for the steering wheel and pedals. The dash was removed, as were all of the seats, interior lights, everything. The patrolman and tow truck driver had gathered up all of the parts they could find and tossed them into what was the backseat area and the trunk. Only now it was just one large open cockpit.

The thieves had broken the ignition switch, but you could start the car with a screwdriver instead of a key. I drove it the two-hour drive back to my residence and spent the next week putting it back together. Every part was there, with the exception of a few screws. The only part I had to buy was a new ignition switch.

I was very lucky. The car wasn't insured and I would have eaten the entire loss. You never know when your stolen car might be spotted by the police. That's why it's best to get the report in as quickly as possible. Had I not reported it until the next day, it would have been too late. The police would have eventually found it, but the vehicle would have been totally stripped to its bones, and we would have needed the car's dental records to make a positive identification.

If your, or your client's, car is stolen, report it immediately. Police departments will usually broadcast the stolen report to the entire department on the chance that somebody may see it. Also, departments produce a *hot sheet* that is reviewed by each new shift. As the patrols prowl around the city streets, they are always on the lookout for any vehicle on the hot sheet.

Crime Scene Clues

A **hot sheet** is a current list of recently stolen vehicles. Police departments, of course, have hundreds of patrol cars driving around their jurisdiction all day long. Patrolmen are on the lookout for any car that may be on the hot sheet. Many police department patrol cars are now in communication with their headquarters by computer, and they access the hot sheet list on the computer rather than a physical printed list, as in smaller departments.

Now, as a PI, you'll sometimes get calls about stolen vehicles. Usually, the victim will have some ideas or some clues as to who might have stolen it. We have recovered stolen cars for clients that the police never got around to looking for. One client owned a franchise for a major tune-up shop. He had four locations in the city. He called me one day, frantic because a customer's car had been stolen from one of his shops. It had been missing three days and the police didn't appear to be actively looking for it. His customer wanted his car back, and he was running out of excuses. He'd lost other cars, and if he lost one more, his insurance company was going to cancel his policy. He was getting desperate.

His 25-year-old store manager, Robert, had taken the car home, along with the bag containing $3,000 of the day's receipts in credit card charge slips and checks. During the evening, Robert partied at several bars and, while traveling to the next bar, picked up a hitchhiker named Jason. Robert's impaired driving ability didn't go unnoticed. Eventually, he was stopped and arrested for driving while under the influence. A search under the front seat of the car led to an additional charge of possession of cocaine. Robert passed the car keys to Jason, and that's the last anybody had seen of the vehicle. The police report did have the name and alleged address of Jason, the hitchhiker.

Robert's parents bailed him out of jail the next morning and whisked him away to a drug rehab facility. They would not tell me, or anybody else, where he was, and I had no way of locating him. Most drug and alcohol rehab facilities will not respond to any questions about whether a certain person is or is not a patient.

My next move was to attempt to locate the hitchhiker, Jason. I talked to the detective assigned to the case. He told me the address for Jason was fictitious. I went to the address given on the police report, 2872 Magnolia Circle South, anyway. The detective was correct, there was no such address, but there was a Magnolia Circle South. Just no 2872. Magnolia Circle was an unpaved, heavily rutted sand road that led back into the woods. The mailboxes were clustered together on the shoulder of the main paved highway.

I did what any good investigator would do, just as we discussed in Chapter 13; I started knocking on doors. At the third door, a neighbor told me which house Jason lived in.

As I approached the house, a kid, about 13, was fooling around in the street. I asked him if Jason lived where I'd been told he did. "Oh, yeah. He lives there. But he's not there right now. He's at work."

I knocked on the door anyway. Nobody answered.

"See, I told ya. I bet you're here about that car, ain't ya?"

That got my attention. The kid wanted $100 to show me where the car was. I negotiated him down to $40. In a few minutes, he'd led me down a sand trail about one fourth of a mile away.

He got his money and I called a tow truck to haul the car out of the sand, where it was stuck.

From start to finish, it took about four hours to locate the stolen car and have it towed back to my client's shop. I'd called the client to let him know it was on the way. With a spare set of keys from the owner, we opened the trunk, and the bag with the $3,000 in charge slips and checks was in it. The client thought I was a genius, and to this day he continues to refer business to me.

My genius abilities aside, the reality was that the police detective assigned to the case could have done the same thing, but he stopped at the first roadblock, the nonexistent address. Persistence and the neighborhood investigation are two of the best tools an investigator has. Don't forget to use them both.

The Home Burglary

Do you live in a suburban neighborhood? Drive around your block. Odds are that one of the houses on your block will be *burglarized* this year, and one was last year as well.

If your house has been burglarized once, the odds of it being burglarized again are higher. Doesn't that just make your day? This chapter is not designed to talk about preventive measures, but you should know that simply having a burglar alarm system in the home will reduce your chances of being burglarized by 90 percent.

Crime Scene Clues

The Uniform Crime Report defines **burglary** as the unlawful entry of a structure to commit a felony or a theft. The use of force to gain entry is not required to classify an offense as a burglary.

You've had a long day. Your purse was snatched at the mall. Your car was stolen from the mall's parking lot. And now, as you enter your home, your place of sanctity where you can isolate yourself from the world, you realize that burglars have been hard at work while you were gone. The feeling of violation that occurs with the discovery of a burglary is tremendous. Strangers have been in your bedroom, pawed through your clothing, and taken your personal belongings.

Burglaries are particularly hard cases to solve. Nationally, the police solve just over 12 percent of cases involving forcible entry, whereas they solve nearly 50 percent of rapes and sometimes over 60 percent of aggravated assaults. But you can see why. With rapes and assaults, the victim has seen the perpetrator. With most burglaries, the perpetrators are never seen, so there are no eyewitness.

Typically, private investigators get calls to solve burglaries for two reasons:

1. The police don't investigate because the dollar amount of the loss is not sufficient enough to warrant the manpower.

2. The police responded but haven't solved it.

In either case, chances are you won't be called until several days after the fact. Any evidence that was there is now probably destroyed, with the exception of fingerprints. Remember, fingerprints can stay on surfaces for years. Hopefully, your client has read this book and followed the instructions in Chapter 17.

The bottom line on a burglary is you're not going to solve it unless your neighborhood investigation turns up something or your client has a suspect already in mind. Most victims of burglaries know the burglar; they just don't realize it. Sure, some burglaries are committed at random. But usually, the burglar has been in the house before, either on a pretext, as a salesperson, or perhaps a relative of the cleaning staff. Don't overlook friends of the victim's teenaged children. You'd be surprised how often property crimes are committed by teenagers who know the victims and who associate with their children.

Elementary, My Dear Watson

Contrary to popular belief, the crime scene unit (CSU) is not normally the first to respond to a burglary. Most police departments start by sending a patrol car to the site. Some departments have what's called a minimum-loss policy, where they won't send a CSU for a loss that's less than or equal to $5,000, for example. The responding officer will get an estimate of the loss from the victim. If that estimate exceeds the policy's minimum amount, he will call for the CSU to process the scene for fingerprints and other evidence. Other departments, however, don't have a minimum-loss policy, and leave the decision about involving the CSU to the discretion of the responding officer. As a consumer, you might want to find out what your local police force's policy is so you can be prepared to gather your own evidence, should your loss not qualify for a crime scene unit.

If you're a do-it-yourself PI, go over the list of people who might have committed the burglary. The perpetrators probably don't go to church with you, but consider who else has been in your home in the last 90 days. Delivery men, movers, installers, employees? House cleaners are almost always suspected, but I've found they're almost always innocent. However, their boyfriends certainly should be suspected. The house cleaner might not even know for sure, but she probably suspects her boyfriend and doesn't really want to know the truth, because then she'd have to choose between her boyfriend and her customer.

Hopefully, a neighbor will have a description of someone, or the perpetrator will have left some evidence behind—a cigarette butt, maybe. Thorough interviewing of your client and a careful neighborhood investigation will sometimes turn up the culprit.

Remember Chapter 12 when Luke Smith burglarized his parents' house, removing the safe and the $40,000 that it contained? The sheriff's office had come out and done a mediocre crime scene investigation. They had not done a neighborhood investigation, or a detailed interview of the parents. They even neglected to ask the parents if they had any suspicions about who was responsible.

In just a few hours, I had their money back and the crime solved. It can be done, but you have to be smarter than the criminal (usually not too difficult) and more motivated than the police department (again, usually not too difficult).

If it's a random burglary committed by a crack head looking for some quick bucks for his next piece of rock cocaine, you're probably not going to solve it. However, the next two sections detail some other steps to take to cover all of the bases. Only by covering each possibility will you have any chance of recovering the stolen property and seeing the burglar in jail.

The Pawnshop Detail

Most local law enforcement agencies maintain some sort of a pawnshop detail. Pawnshops are required to inventory each item they purchase or take in on pawn. They send, sometimes weekly, sometimes daily, a ticket to the local police department with the description of the item received, including a serial number, if there is one.

This is usually not a voluntary system. In order to keep their licenses, the pawnshops have to comply. The police pawnshop detail will also make periodic, unannounced visits to each pawnshop, checking their inventory against the pawn tickets it's submitted.

Likewise, the detective or officer in charge of the pawnshop detail will check the pawn tickets against lists of stolen property already entered into NCIC. Matching descriptions of jewelry or electronics sometimes will result in the pawnshop detail confiscating the stolen property from the pawnshop operator.

> **Elementary, My Dear Watson**
>
> Police departments that have moved into the twenty-first century require the pawnshops to upload this information daily in electronic form to the police departments' computer server. In these departments, the paper tickets are a thing of the last century, but not all departments are so computerized.

Therefore, if your, or your client's, property is stolen, be sure that an accurate and detailed description is given to the police department. If it is an item that might show up at a pawnshop, request the description be given to the pawnshop detail unit. This doesn't always happen automatically. Usually, it is up to the investigating detective to compare the items stolen with the information provided by the pawnshops. There is nothing wrong with calling the pawnshop detail directly.

Working the Crime Scene

If a crime scene investigation was not performed by the responding police department, then do it yourself. In Chapter 17, you'll find full instructions on how to conduct a crime scene investigation.

One aspect to crime scene investigation that we didn't talk about there is checking the dumpsters and trash cans in the local area. If your wallet is lifted, purse snatched, jewelry box stolen from your house, or briefcase and camera taken from the trunk of your car, search the dumpsters and trashcans in the immediate area.

In the mall, look through the trashcans within 200 to 300 yards of where the crime occurred. Purse snatchers and pickpockets will rifle through the purse and billfolds they've lifted, remove the credit cards and cash, and then toss the stolen item into the nearest garbage can. Even though the money is gone, the driver's license and other identity cards may still be recoverable.

Sammy the Snitch

Most dumpsters are dived every day. If you want to dispose of something and you don't want anybody to ever find it, don't put it in a dumpster thinking it will be co-mingled with the other trash. In all likelihood, somebody will find it. Even if the garbage truck picks it up, there are people at the garbage dump going through the trash.

I have one investigator, Bob, who has worked for me for 15 years. Bob regularly dives dumpsters for fun and profit. He and another investigator were working a workers' compensation surveillance and saw our subject throw something into a dumpster. Bob went diving. The subject was just discarding trash, but Bob also found a couple of purses that had been snatched, complete with driver's licenses and other identity cards. He turned them over to the local police department. He's found unopened envelopes with valid credit cards. Diving the dumpster behind the Internal Revenue Service office, he found boxes and boxes of unused, perfectly good red pens imprinted with "U.S. Government" on them. Now that's government waste. Maybe the bureaucrats thought that if they got rid of all the red ink, they'd get rid of the deficit. Don't I wish. Bob brought them into the office, and we didn't have to buy any red pens for years.

When burglars break into your home and only take small items like jewelry boxes and important papers, they'll toss the material that can't be converted into quick cash into a dumpster. They want as little incriminating evidence on themselves as possible, because they never know when they'll get stopped by the police. Individual pieces of jewelry are a lot easier to hide than the entire box.

Also, after a burglary, be sure to walk around the premises. If there is a wooded area nearby, search it. I can't tell you how many times we've recovered stolen items that were stashed close to the crime scene by the thieves for later retrieval. You just never know, so you have to cover all of the bases.

NCIC

We've mentioned NCIC elsewhere in this book. The National Crime Information Center is a huge computer database run by the FBI. Within this database, there is a stolen articles

Sherlock's Secrets

NCIC allows not only for manufacturers' serial numbers, but also for "owner applied numbers." If your client had the foresight to engrave his or her social security or driver's license number on items that were stolen, be sure to get them into NCIC as well.

section. Stolen items that can be uniquely described or have unique serial numbers can be entered into this database.

NCIC has different files, or sections, for different types of stolen property, such as vehicles, license plates, boats, guns, articles, and securities (stocks, bonds, and bills).

> **CAUTION**
>
> **Sammy the Snitch**
>
> If you're a fugitive and warrants have been issued for your arrest, don't get your hopes up, thinking your name will be purged from NCIC after four years as if you were a car or a boat. No such luck. Your name will remain there until you're caught, or until the charges are dropped.

If your client has the serial numbers of any items that were stolen, be it a motor vehicle or television, be sure that this information is relayed to the police department. It, in turn, will have the items entered into NCIC.

Stolen items remain in the NCIC computer for a certain length of time. Unrecovered stolen articles will be in the computer for the balance of the year they are entered, plus one additional year. If for any reason during that time, an officer gets suspicious about a certain item, he can run it in NCIC. If it's stolen, a match will be made, and eventually the item will be returned to you.

Unrecovered motor vehicles remain in the NCIC computer for the year of theft plus four more, as do stolen boats.

The Least You Need to Know

- If random crime strikes, make a scene. Help is frequently available from undercover or plain-clothed security people.

- Stolen cars are located faster if the report of the theft is made quickly. Police departments have hot sheets that are reviewed by each shift.

- Victims of burglaries usually know the burglar. It is somebody they've met, or somebody who has been in their house recently.

- Police agencies have pawnshop details that compare items pawned with lists of stolen items.

- After a burglary or other property crime, the investigator or victim should always look in the nearby trashcans and dumpsters. Thieves dump billfolds and purses into the trash after removing the money.

- NCIC maintains lists of stolen articles for up to two years from the date of theft. Stolen vehicles and boats can remain for up to five years. Wanted persons, missing persons, and fugitives are listed until found or removed by the listing agency.

Chapter 23

Curtain Call

In This Chapter

+ Using the evidence to make a case

+ Understanding recorded and signed statements

+ Handling the evidence

+ The FBI FD 302

+ Feeding the secretary

Reporting the results of your investigation to your client is, in some sense, just as important, if not more so, than the investigation itself. After all, no matter how well executed the investigation, no matter how valuable the information is to the client and how sure the victory in court looks, it won't mean squat if the PI fails to submit a report detailing his findings, or if his reporting skills are inadequate, or the report is so faulty that it's unusable.

I've known investigative firms that sent investigators into the field. The investigators shot good video on workers' compensation claims and verbally reported the results to their clients. The firm sends the tape and a bill to the client, but no detailed report, no documentation of their investigation. Three years later, the case goes to court. The attorney for the insurance company wants to use the tape to prove that the claimant wasn't really hurt, and needs the investigator to testify. Nobody in the firm can remember who shot the tape. Do you think they have a little problem?

In almost every investigation, there comes a juncture when the investigator has to step back and analyze the direction of the case and how the investigator's efforts are directed. We deal with that in this chapter. Then we take a look at how to wrap up the case and present it to the client in a professionally formatted report.

Sifting Through the Evidence

The general rule of evidence is, naturally, that somebody collected it and, logically, that same somebody needs to be present to introduce it into court. We discussed in Chapter 17 the need to maintain the chain of custody on the evidence. That is true not only for evidence collected at the crime scene, but also for anything of evidentiary value, including videotapes.

In surveillance matters, the videotape is really not the primary piece of evidence. Actually, the investigator's testimony is what counts. Videotape just corroborates what the investigator saw, and can do it in a very dramatic way. Remember, we've relied on eyewitness testimony long before videotape was ever invented.

I can testify that I saw a workers' compensation claimant with an alleged neck injury standing on his head on a surfboard while surfing. That's good testimony. But let me play the tape, and the jury is totally convinced. You can tell when they laugh at the claimant that you've made your case.

Workers' compensation evidence is fairly straightforward. Either you catch the claimant engaged in activities he says he can't perform, or you don't. In other types of cases, the evidence is not so clear, and we have to sift through it to see what we've got.

An 18-year-old boy, Darby, is employed at a restaurant as a server. The drinking age in the state is 21. One July evening after his shift is over, Darby leaves the restaurant in his pickup truck and prevails upon his older buddy to buy some beer. They start club hopping, drinking the beers in his pickup truck on the drives between clubs. Darby claims he only had two beers. Later, near closing time, Darby returns to the restaurant where he works, enters through the back door to the kitchen, and proceeds to the bar area. At the bar, the bartender, according to Darby, gives him three free drinks made with an expensive brand of whiskey. Darby leaves the restaurant and, while driving home, drives off the road, hits a tree, and is now paralyzed from the neck down for the rest of his life.

Darby and his parents sue the restaurant/bar for serving Darby because he is underage and then allowing him to leave the bar and drive while under the influence. It's a terrible tragedy. Now you be the judge and tell me who's at fault.

Two years later, the attorney representing Darby asks us to investigate the circumstances of that night in July. He wants a blow-by-blow account of what transpired in the restaurant and the bar. And, oh yeah, the restaurant/bar went out of business over a year before he decided to take the case.

We have to track down the former employees and interview them, then sift through and evaluate what they can remember about that night. While that night was momentous in Darby's life, to everyone else it was just another night. Can you remember where you were on July 23, two years ago? Neither can I.

We obtained the police reports and rescue reports detailing the accident investigation. No question about it. Eighteen-year-old, underaged Darby was drunk. His blood alcohol level was more than twice the legal limit.

The bar records from that night were examined. There is a log of the drinks served and at about the time, 11 P.M., when Darby says he was served, the log shows three double drinks of that same expensive liquor being rung up as complimentary drinks.

A pattern emerged from the interviews of the former employees: The young owners of the restaurant allowed their underaged employees to drink alcohol on the premises. They were "cool." They sponsored several employee parties after work and provided the booze, allowing everyone there, regardless of age, to imbibe. They even had an employee meeting to discuss the subject of underage employees drinking, and the owners seemed to think that, even though 21 was the statutory drinking age, their employees could pretty well do whatever they wanted, as long as "it didn't get out of hand."

Not everybody that we talked to was so forthcoming. Some, in an effort to protect the owners, said they never saw anybody underage drinking. Others maybe never did. They came to work, did their job, and went home. Some seemed to hang around after hours until the lights were turned off.

As for the bartender who'd actually served Darby the drinks, all we had was a fairly common first name. No last name, no social security number, nothing we could use to help us locate him. Since we represented the plaintiff, we didn't have access to all of the employee records.

We also had not talked to any employee who could say definitively that Darby had been drinking at the bar. We had employees who saw Darby return to the restaurant. One of the cooks in the kitchen said when Darby came in he was carrying a beer can, and the cook told him he couldn't bring outside beer into the restaurant.

Everyone in my office worked the case pretty hard for two weeks, locating and interviewing the former employees. Some only worked at the restaurant for a month, others worked the entire two years it was open. Some of the former employees were never found. But let's sift through what we've got.

Positive for the plaintiff Darby:

- Darby worked at the restaurant.

- Testimony as to a clear pattern of underage employees being allowed to drink inside the restaurant.

- Testimony that the owners knew underage employees were drinking and almost implicitly encouraged it.

- The bar tab shows three doubles of the same liquor being served as complimentary beverages at about the time Darby says he was served.

- Darby was drunk when he hit the tree, and he'd just left the restaurant.

- While there were beer cans in the bed of the pickup truck, nobody could say how long they'd been there.

Positive for the defendants (the restaurant):

- At the accident scene, there were numerous beer cans in the back of Darby's pickup truck.

- Some employees never saw any underage drinking.

- Darby left the restaurant sober after his shift was over.

- Darby returned to the restaurant with a beer can in his hand.

- No one witnessed Darby drinking at the bar the night of the accident.

Does Darby have a case? We don't want to get into a discussion here about personal responsibility, and a good PI must learn to compartmentalize such things from the hard-core legal issues of any case he's working. Legally, the bar will have liability if Darby was served alcohol and had a traffic accident afterwards. True, nobody poured the liquor down his throat, but it shouldn't have been offered to him. Even though the bar was now out of business, the bar owners and their insurance company would still be on the hook if the case went to trial and Darby prevailed.

Our client, Darby's attorney, called and informed us that the next day they were to have a pretrial settlement hearing. What have we got? I synopsized for him all of the statements we've taken and couriered them over to his office. We'll talk later in this chapter about how to do recorded statements. The attorney wanted to know where the bartender was and why hadn't we found him. We were looking for him as hard as we could.

Periodically, while working a case, a good investigator will take a step back and evaluate the evidence he's collected so far. He'll know what the attorney needs to make the case, and so he'll adjust his investigative efforts, shift the focus or the direction he's going to meet those needs.

Late that afternoon, I contacted another employee who used to room with the bartender. We got lucky. He gave me the bartender's complete name. He'd moved to another state, but we tracked him down on the West Coast, and the time there is three hours earlier. The bartender finally arrived home after midnight our time. I got a recorded statement from him saying yes, he did serve Darby three drinks and his recollection was that the liquor was that particular brand which Darby said it was. His memory was pretty clear about it because the next day at work all the buzz was about Darby's wreck and he knew he'd served him some drinks.

I called the attorney at home and woke him up. After I related what I'd just gotten, he was elated and said we'd just found the Holy Grail. The next morning, I faxed the attorney's office a synopsis of the bartender's statement. During the pretrial settlement hearing, he read the synopsis to a representative of the insurance company and the attorney representing the restaurant. After a few minutes of private consultation, the company agreed to settle for the policy limit, which was $1 million. Our client agreed to the settlement and, right or wrong, it was done.

Taking Recorded and Signed Statements

Private investigators need to know how to take *recorded* and *signed statements*. A written statement, signed and sworn to by the person signing it, is a very good piece of testimonial evidence. Recorded interviews are very beneficial as well.

You may recollect the law concerning the recording of communications from Chapter 19. In that case, we talked about one-party and two-party states. There is a list in Appendix B of which states are one-party consent states and

> **Crime Scene Clues**
>
> A **recorded statement** is a voice tape recording made by a witness concerning facts and/or the witness's recollection of the pertinent incident. A recorded statement can be taken either over the telephone or in person. A **signed statement** is a written declaration made by a witness concerning facts and/or the witness's recollection of the pertinent incident that is signed by the witness.

which states require all parties to consent to being recorded. Those rules apply to the interception of telephone calls. There are separate rules that apply to the interception of oral communications not conducted over a wire.

When a telephone call crosses state boundaries ... beware. The recording of the telephone conversation may be legal in one of those states but not in the other. Take the case of Linda Tripp and Monica Lewinsky. Lewinsky was in the District of Columbia, which follows the federal guidelines and is a one party state. No problem there. However, Tripp, was in Maryland which is a two (or all) party state. It was Maryland that decided to prosecute Tripp for violation of its two party rule, even though the other party resided in a one party state.

Many states make it illegal to record a conversation, other than telephonic, between two or more people, unless all parties agree to the recording. Therefore, if you're going to take a recorded statement from a witness to an accident, be sure the witness affirms verbally on the tape recording that he is aware he is being recorded and you, the private investigator, have his permission to do so.

Why would you want to record a witness? Remember, sometimes a case may not go to trial for three or more years after an accident. Witnesses may forget what they saw, or at least what they told you they saw. There is nothing better to help refresh a witness's recollection of the incident than to let him listen to his own voice telling you what he witnessed.

As a PI, it's important to understand that the witness's sympathy might really be with the plaintiff. If your client is the defendant, that means you're asking for a statement from "the opposition." By getting the witness's statement on tape, you're protected, so that when the witness's wife berates him for "helping" the wrong side, and all of sudden he can't remember exactly what he saw, it won't matter. It's on the tape. This happens all of the time.

Crime Scene Clues

Impeaching a witness's testimony means to call into question the reliability or truthfulness of the testimony being given.

As I've noted over and over again, a good investigator just gathers the facts and lets the evidence chips fall where they may, but witnesses often have their own agenda and flexible standards to suit it. A recording of the witness's statement, therefore, can be used to *impeach* her testimony in court if she has a sudden change of heart and testifies to something other than what she originally said.

When a witness changes his testimony, the courtroom dialogue would go something like this ...

Attorney: Mr. Witness, didn't you tell our investigator that you witnessed the blue car run the red light and strike the white car?

Witness: No, I don't believe so. The light was green when the blue car entered the intersection. I have a very good recollection of that.

The attorney plays the tape with the witness telling the PI that the light was definitely red and the blue car ran the red light.

Witness (looking at his wife and shrugging): I guess it must have been red. It's been so long, I got confused.

That's how impeachment works in a courtroom. You want the tape so the egg ends up on the witness's face and not yours.

Raymond was in a custody battle with his wife, my client, Sheila. Part of the court order was that Raymond, an alcoholic, would not drink. Raymond was about 28 years old, a tall, lanky, good-looking fellow who happened to own a very popular restaurant. Our client needed to prove that Raymond was still drinking and carousing.

I followed Raymond on numerous occasions. I photographed him using the drive-through window of a liquor store. There was an exchange of funds and the clerk passed a brown paper bag with his purchases to him.

Raymond also frequented topless bars. While in the bars, he drank a lot of beer. I documented how many beers he drank and what brand they were. When the case was ready to go to court, I interviewed the waitresses at these topless bars. I found one good witness who remembered Raymond and what she served him. The waitress remembered the brand of beer he preferred, how he tipped, and how many beers he usually drank while he was there. He was a regular and would come in about three times a week.

We subpoenaed her the next day for the trial. In court, she testified that she never told me Raymond drank beers, that when he came in, he always ordered a soft drink. She didn't ever serve him beer or any other alcohol, always a cola drink. Do you think Raymond got to her? You can bet on it. I wished I'd had a recorded statement from her, but I didn't get one. What I did get was egg in my face in front of the jury. Took me a couple of hours to wash it all off.

People lie in court. It always amazes me that they will perjure themselves, but it happens everyday. Oh, and what did Raymond say about the drive-through liquor store? He claimed he bought a two-liter bottle of cola. Right.

The Format for the Recorded Statement

A recorded statement should begin like this: "This is investigator [enter your name] and today's date is [enter the date]. I am speaking with [enter the witness's name]. Mr. [witness], you are aware that I am recording this conversation, is that correct?"

Make sure the witness says yes. A nod of the head can't be heard later.

"And I have your permission to record this, is that also correct?" Again, make sure you get a verbal yes.

"Now, Mr. [witness], for the record, please state your name and your address." Then make sure you get his telephone number, his date of birth, and his social security number.

Next, ask where he is employed and what hours he works. Why? You want all that detail, because if it takes a couple of years for the case to go to court, that might be the only way you can track him down.

After the introduction, ask him to tell you what he witnessed. Let him talk. In addition to the recording, take good notes. I try not to interrupt the witness. When he has finished I go back, using my notes, and ask appropriate questions for clarification purposes, or to elicit more details or facts that the witness didn't give the first time through.

If there is something you want to ask the witness, you need a potty break, or you need to talk about something that is not relevant to the case, it is permissible to turn off the tape recorder and deal with whatever it is. Before turning the recorder off, state what time it is and that you are turning the recorder off. When you go back on the record, be sure to state the current time and get the witness's permission again to record the conversation.

You'll know you've exhausted the interview when you can't get another fact out of the witness. To officially conclude the recording, state the time, that the interview is finished, and that you're turning the recorder off.

It never fails. After we've recorded the interview, as I'm walking out the door, the witness remembers something very important and just blurts it out. You should stop and discuss it in detail. Then sit back down, turn the recorder back on, reconfirm the person's identity and permission to record the conversation, and have the witness repeat that last tidbit of detail for the recording.

Do all recorded statements have to be done in person? No. Most of the recorded statements my firm takes are done over the telephone. We use the same Radio Shack device mentioned in Chapter 19. We follow the same rules as laid out here in the preceding paragraphs. The format is the same; you just don't have the eye contact with the witness. Remember the bartender from Darby's case? He was in California, I was in Florida. The settlement hearing was to begin in less than 12 hours. There wasn't even time to have a local investigator go to his house and take a statement. A telephonic recorded statement is just as valid as one done face–to–face.

To be successful at interviewing, you have to build a relationship with the interviewee. That's harder to do over the telephone, but it can be done. I prefer all interviews be performed face-to-face, but that's not always possible. Frequently, budget and time don't allow it, so you have to settle for a telephonic interview. If you utilize the techniques in Chapter 12, you can accomplish a successful telephonic interview and obtain a recorded statement that will hold up in court all the same.

Formatting the Signed Statement

Signed statements are a pain to do. The reason is the private investigator usually has to sit and handwrite the statement for the witness. And the statement might be several pages of handwritten material. I usually try to get a recorded statement. Then, if necessary, I type up what we need in the signed statement, go back to the witness, and have her sign it. If your client is an attorney, she'll want to have some input into what's included in a signed statement, and she may draft it herself.

Why take a signed statement instead of, or in addition to, a recorded statement? An attorney can take the signed statement into court and present it as evidence. It's easily readable, is concise and, if it is properly notarized, the person who signed it probably won't have to appear in court.

A signed statement should begin with:

"I, [name of witness], reside at [insert residence address]. My date of birth is [insert DOB] and my social security number is [insert *SSAN*]. I am making the following voluntary signed statement: ...." Then proceed with the statement.

At the end of the statement, the following sentence should appear:

"I swear that the above statement consisting of this and [insert the number of other pages in the statement] is true to the best of my recollection." (If the statement is a total of three pages long, that sentence would read, "consisting of this and two additional pages.")

Crime Scene Clues

SSAN is the standard abbreviation in most federal law enforcement circles for Social Security Account Number.

Then have it signed by the witness. If you are not a notary, take one with you and have her notarize the statement. You'll have to pay the notary for her time, but you can charge that to the client anyway and add a markup on it to increase your bottom line at the end of the month. PIs notarize lots of odd things at odd hours in odd places, so find yourself an adventurous one or become one yourself. In my firm, one of my investigators or secretaries always keeps her notary status current. When she goes with us into the field we charge her time to the client at our investigative rate.

The requirements to become a notary are different in the different states. The National Notary Association's website www.nationalnotary.org lists all fifty states and the District of Columbia and each state's respective requirements.

Originals and Duplicates

As a private investigator, you're maintaining evidence in your office. You've shot some videotape. You have recorded interviews and you have signed statements. What do you do with all of that evidence? How do you store it?

Most importantly, when you send your report and your bill to your insurance client, you also want them to see the videotape you're so proud of. Send them only a duplicate of the videotape and not the original. The original should be labeled, signed or initialed, and dated by the investigator who took it. The labeling, initialing, and dating should occur the minute the investigator takes the tape out of the camera or the tape recorder, if it's a voice recording. The last thing you want to do is mix up the original with a copy.

It took my firm a long time to educate the insurance companies not to ask for the original videotape. Insurance adjusters come and go. Companies merge, reorganize, and close offices. If the original tape is in their possession, it will most likely get lost or misplaced. In addition, the investigator who shot the video is going to have to testify in court and introduce the video into evidence, not the insurance adjuster.

We've talked before about maintaining chain of custody on the evidence. Here's the first thing one of the attorneys will ask you: "Is this tape you're introducing an original?" The second question will be: "Has the tape been in your care, custody, and control since it was made, and has it been tampered with in any way?" If the tape has not been in your control the entire time, then you can't answer yes. You don't know if it's been tampered with or not, do you?

We had an insurance company client for which we worked a lot of liability cases, such as slip and falls in grocery stores. We took a lot of recorded statements. The insurance company representatives insisted that we provide them the original of the recorded statement. We refused, to a point, but they were paying the bills, so finally we agreed. We did make them sign a release saying that they had the original tape and would not hold us responsible in the future for the safety of the tape. I can't tell you how many times they would call us a year or two down the road, asking us where the tape was. We'd fax them a copy of the release and tell them happy hunting.

As far as recorded statements are concerned, we rarely transcribe them. If the client wants it done, we quote him our secretarial rate for the service. If I'm paying a secretary $12.50 an hour, we charge the client at least $18 an hour for tape transcription. If they want a transcription, it's usually so one attorney can send it to the other, hopefully encouraging him to settle the case.

What usually satisfies the client is a synopsis of the witness's recorded statement that the investigator dictates into a handheld recorder. Our secretary types the synopsis, which is included in the full report to the client, and that way, the report of the interview is full and complete.

Sherlock's Secrets

If you're the PI, charge the dictation and the time spent writing the report at the same rate as your normal hourly rate. If you don't, you'll be losing money.

Superior Reports Are the Mark of the Professional PI

A competent private investigator should produce a clear and concise report, written in good, grammatical English. If the report has a lot of misspellings and grammatical errors in it, do you think the clients will be excited about you representing them on the witness stand? Or will they be embarrassed that they hired you?

If spelling is not your bag and you don't know the difference between *your* and *you're*, or *billed* and *build*, then hire somebody who has mastered proper English to do your paperwork. A talented secretary can even make a bozo look good.

Police departments are notorious for producing poorly written reports. They don't get much in the way of report-writing instruction in the police academies. Having had several years to cement some bad writing habits, an officer retires or leaves the force and starts his own private investigative agency. How is the quality of the reports he writes then? About the same as what he did on the force. The same mistakes and the same poor formatting, because that's what he's done for 20 years.

A proper PI report should look very much like an FBI report. Why? What's the big deal? Because every law school graduate is familiar with *FD 302s*. One way or another, the whole purpose of most private investigations is to win a case in a court of law. Certainly, not every case you work will go to court, but the PI should prepare each and every one of his cases as if it will. The bureau's been writing reports for a long time, and its reports are clear and unambiguous.

The following is a typical example of the wording at the beginning of an FD 302, or, in your case, a good investigative report ...

> The following investigation was conducted by Steven K. Brown, of Millennial Investigative Services, on May 15, 2002, at Jacksonville, Florida:
>
> On this date Mary Jane Doe, date of birth 10/20/1947, SSAN 261-00-0000, was interviewed at her residence of 1234 Any Street, Jacksonville, Florida, and provided the following information:
>
> Doe advised that she witnessed an accident between ....

In the reporting of this type of interview, the investigator's name, agency, and date the interview took place are laid out at the beginning. Once that's done, the reader knows who did the interview, as well as when and where it was conducted. The investigator's name doesn't have to be repeated again anywhere else on the page, nor does the investigator refer to himself as "the writer," which is so often the case in police reports. By following this format, your reports will be plain, clear, easily read, straightforward, and done in a style that all attorneys are familiar with. If you tell your client up front that your reports are similar to FD 302s, they'll make you for a professional from the beginning.

Crime Scene Clues

An **FD 302** is a federal form number used by the FBI for part of its report. Specifically, it reports the results of interviews conducted by FBI agents. All interviews are reported in a standard format and are typed or printed onto FD 302s. Law school students learn this early in their schooling, and the forms are referred to throughout judicial opinions.

If you produce good reports, you will earn your client's respect and, most importantly, his repeat business. Remember, you can be the best investigator in the world, but your client only sees two things from you: the quality of your report and the quality of the evidence you collect, be it videotape or photographs. You can have a lousy car and a rotten pair of binoculars, but your client will never see those. If your reports and tapes are superior, then he'll figure you for a superior investigator. This is the best way to produce a professional image. Talk is cheap. What's left on your client's desk when you leave his office is what counts.

Show Me the Money

In the business of running a private investigative firm, there are a couple of cardinal rules you must follow for the business to thrive:

1) You have to get paid.

2) You have to get paid soon.

The best way to get paid is to collect a retainer before beginning a case. Always do this, without exception, in domestic cases, or when your client is an individual as opposed to a corporation. View this as the acid test. If she can't scrape the money together to pay you the retainer, what makes you think she'll have any more money when you hand her the final bill?

Work the case up to the amount of the retainer you have, and then inform her that you'll need more money if she wants more work. Don't let her get into your pockets, and don't be shy about asking for money. If you don't ask, you won't get it.

If there is any piece of advice I can give you that will help you succeed in the PI business, this is it. Always present a bill with the report. We always put the bill on top so the client sees it first thing. And try to collect the money due right then. If you hide the bill on the bottom of the report, it'll get overlooked, and you'll be begging for your money six months after the case is completed.

Sherlock's Secrets

I'm about to share a company secret with you that we've never shared with any other PI, ever. It's something I came up with after a few years in business and several different attempts at building our secretary's time into our investigative rate. She has to be paid. She told me so. That means I have to charge for it, and so do you. Just ask your secretary, I'll bet she says the same thing. The problem is, if you bump up your hourly rate to include her time, then you might price yourself right out of the market. Your competition's rate will look much lower.

I came up with a solution that has worked for 15 years. In all that time, I've never had a complaint or even a question about it from a client.

On the invoice, under Expenses, we include a charge for Secretarial and Administrative Charges. We look at the total fees billed on a case and multiply that amount by 8.25 percent. That is our secretarial charge. This spreads our administrative costs over all of our cases and doesn't increase our quoted hourly rate. Other PIs have adopted this practice, but as far as I know, I originated it.

It's best to keep the client apprised of the tab he's incurring as the case progresses. Nobody wants any surprises at the end of case. He may be thinking he's only spending a few hundred dollars. Imagine his surprise when he receives a bill for a few thousand. And, likewise, you're not going to be happy when he refuses to pay. It's best to keep a running tally and give him the current total periodically.

Being a professional investigator requires performing superior investigations, properly maintaining the evidence, and reporting the results of your investigative efforts in such a manner as to distinguish your firm apart from the competition.

In the nearly 20 years I've been running a PI business, I can count on one hand the number of times I've been "stiffed" by a client. Two were attorneys, one of whom was out of state. One was a client whose retainer check bounced but we didn't know it until the work was completed. She filed bankruptcy. The other was a large out of state corporation that left me on the hook for over $50,000. They filed bankruptcy right after we completed the work. That's why a retainer is so important. I should have gotten one from that corporation but they had several thousand employees and I figured they were good for it. I haven't made that mistake again.

The Least You Need to Know

- During the middle of a complex case, a good investigator will step back, look at the direction of the case, and shift the focus, if need be, to obtain what will be important in making the case in court.

- Recorded and signed statements are valuable items of evidence and can be used to impeach a witness's testimony should the witness change her story during a trial. There are specific formats and certain verbiage that should be used in recorded and signed statements.

- Original videotapes and recorded tapes should always be held in the investigator's control until needed for trial. Each tape should be labeled, initialed by the investigator who took the tape, and dated as soon as the tape comes out of the recorder.

- A superior method of report formatting is to follow the FBI's use of FD 302s. This is a clear, concise method of reporting, and is a standard that all attorneys learn in law school. It will set your firm apart from the competition.

- Always submit a bill with each report. Getting paid is necessary to running a successful PI business. Always charge for report writing and secretarial time.

Chapter 24

The Judges' Chambers

In This Chapter

- Ghostwriting from jail
- Time to testify
- Swearing under oath
- Understanding the privileges
- The secrets to the secret grand jury
- Putting your best foot forward
- Directing and redirecting in the courtroom

As private investigators, we deal with facts. I use the term "we" because if you've read this entire book, then you're pretty close to being an investigator, and "we" means you and me.

All of an investigator's effort comes to fruition when the case goes to court. In this chapter we'll talk about how to accept a subpoena. Once the investigator has been subpoenaed she has to be ready to testify. Her testimony may come in the form of a deposition, or even an appearance before a Grand Jury.

You'll learn first about legal privileges, such as work product rules. Also how to charge your client different rates for testifying and waiting to testify. And finally, how to testify in court and maintain your professional "cool" while under cross-examination. Going to court is the "final exam." You should be ready for it.

Just the Facts, Ma'am

Most of the cases that a PI works will have something to do with the law. Divorces, traffic accidents, nursing home abuse, child custody, asset location, slip and falls, criminal defense, and witness locating all start out headed toward court. Few of those cases actually end up in court. Ninety out of one hundred will settle before reaching the trial date. The private investigator must prepare his case in such a manner that the evidence is admissible in a court of law. The investigator must present his findings in such a manner that the judge, jury, and opposing attorney will be able to recognize him as a nonpartial professional investigator.

If you learn nothing else by reading this book, learn that you must not only *appear* to be impartial in your investigation, but also, in fact, you must *be* impartial. You should have this next statement memorized by now, since I've repeated it and similar statements through out this book. It is the cardinal rule of private investigation. Say it out loud with me:

> *The professional private investigator searches for all the facts.*

There. You got it. The best PI in the business seeks the truth and reports his findings to his client accurately and uncolored by the position his client has taken.

Unfortunately, there are many PIs who don't follow that standard. They report only the facts their clients want to hear. Some even deliberately misstate witnesses' statements in order to please their client. Others even practice what is labeled in the industry as *ghost-writing*.

Thomas, an investigator I subcontracted with, worked in the Orlando, Fla., area. When Thomas began working for me, he usually shot some pretty decent video on the insurance claimant cases. After a few months, I noticed that he no longer seemed to shoot any videotape whatsoever.

Crime Scene Clues

Ghost-writing, in PI terms, refers to an investigator who makes up reports or details of reports. Often it is practiced by a dishonest investigator, who rather than do the work, just writes a report indicating he performed the investigation but actually spent the day at the beach.

On one particular case, Thomas had been out on surveillance on a lady named Sarah. He submitted his report and, again, there was no accompanying videotape. The report showed absolutely no activity on Sarah's part on one particular day, June 22. I thought this highly unusual and, noting Thomas's lack of productivity, I reassigned the case to another investigator, Camille.

Camille went to check out Sarah's residence and discovered that Sarah no longer lived where we thought she had. I called Sarah on a pretext and chatted with her. In the conversation, I verified her new address and asked her when she'd moved. "Oh, it was June 22 I moved. I had my two nephews there and the three of us spent all day moving my stuff down those stairs and into that pickup truck. We must have filled that pickup truck at least a dozen times, making runs back and forth to the new place, before we emptied everything out of that apartment. Why, I never knew I had so much stuff."

Amazed, I asked Camille to go to the apartment manager and verify the move-out date. She did. June 22. Do you think I ever subcontracted with Thomas again? Now think how embarrassed Thomas would have been if he'd gone to court to testify to the "facts" in his report. Sarah would have stood up and said, "That's not true. I was moving on June 22." And my firm's credibility would have suffered more than just embarrassment. It would have cost us some business and some bad word of mouth.

I know of another investigative firm that actually was criminally prosecuted for ghostwriting reports. The principals of the firm apparently just made up reports, like Thomas did, and went ahead and billed the insurance company for work that was totally fictional. Eventually, the Florida Department of Insurance found out about it and prosecuted the owners of the company for insurance fraud. They were fined and spent time in jail.

Do your job. Do it professionally. Gather all the facts, good or bad, for your client. Present them to your client in a professional manner. Then let the chips fall where they may.

Accepting the Subpoena

As an investigator, you will be receiving *subpoenas* for court appearances or depositions. We'll cover depositions in the next section. Sometimes, even your own client will send you a subpoena. Attorneys are strange that way. Even though they hire you, they still feel the need to subpoena you. I recommend telling your client there is no need to subpoena you, just let you know when and where they need you, and you'll be there. Save the client the $50 it will cost them to have you subpoenaed.

Don't play hide and seek with the subpoena service agent. Be professional about it. If your client doesn't want you to be served, then don't call up the opposing counsel and give him your schedule, but don't hide or try to evade the service, either. As much as you'd like to accommodate your client's desires, you are a professional, and you should conduct yourself as such. If you are served, the subpoena is an order from the court

> **Crime Scene Clues**
>
> A **subpoena** is a command from the judge of a court requiring that the person or representative of an institution named in the subpoena appear in court or at another specified location on a specific day at a certain time.

for you to appear. If you don't appear, then you're in contempt of that court. Better to have your client mad at you than to be held in contempt.

If you don't respond to the subpoena and you're held in contempt you could be fined and will be required to testify anyway. The reality of the business is such that if you fail to respond to the subpoena and your client wanted you there, you'd lose a client. If the stakes are high and the opposing counsel issued the subpoena, you might find the sheriff on your doorstep with his handcuffs out.

If you are subpoenaed as a witness for trial, you're eligible for a witness fee. The witness fee, big deal that it is, usually amounts to about $20 or less.

Getting paid for your time is another good reason to have a contract with your client. I always bill my own client, even if I am subpoenaed by the opposing counsel. I am there because of my client's needs, and I expect her to pay for my time and mileage. You'll note that the contract specifies a minimum amount that will be paid for courtroom appearances. The contract can, of course, be modified any way you desire. Change it to suit your own needs. There is a sample contract in Appendix B.

Usually, the subpoena you receive will be for you to appear at the trial at the courthouse. Other times, you'll get subpoenaed for depositions, which usually take place at one of the attorney's offices or at the office of the court reporter.

Most of your testimony will be given in your county, but not always. We routinely get subpoenaed for areas all around our state, and sometimes across the country. If your client is an insurance company, a large business, or an attorney, they know the standard is for you to be paid for your time, including travel, and to reimburse your travel expenses.

CAUTION

Sammy the Snitch _____

Don't take the report you sent to your client with you to court or to a deposition. If you need notes to refresh your memory, then take notes. There could be facts in your report that your client doesn't want the other side to know. If you refer to your report during your testimony, then the other side has a right to a copy of it. And you certainly don't want them seeing your bill. The last thing your client, the insurance company, wants is the claimant's attorney announcing to the jury that the company paid you $4,000 to sneak around and spy on that little old lady claimant, instead of paying her doctor's bills with that money.

If your client is an individual, get your travel expenses and anticipated hourly rate up front in the form of an additional retainer. It's always easier to get money from your client before you perform the service than it is afterward.

I usually bill my clients one rate for waiting time in the courthouse and another, higher rate, for time spent testifying. Time spent waiting to testify at trial might go as long as several days. The attorney will usually have a good idea on what day she'll need you, but sometimes she will guess wrong. You've set everything in your schedule aside for this trial when you could be out working other cases. The attorney's office owes you for that time.

In order to speed the legal process along, I tell my secretaries that they have my authority to accept a subpoena on my behalf, as long as I am in town. If I am out of town on an extended trip, then they ought not to accept the subpoena. Why? I might not be back in time to testify on the date desired, and I don't want to be held in contempt of court. Normally you'll be given several weeks notice, but I've been subpoenaed one day for testimony the next.

Everything You Wanted to Know About Depositions

A *deposition* is the meat between the bread in the legal sandwich of our jurisprudence system.

Private investigators are deposed by the opposing counsel all of the time. There would be no need for your own client to depose you. Since you are working for him, he already has your reports.

Typically, a court reporter is present and makes an official record of the deposition. Your client, or your client's attorney, will be there, as well as the opposing attorney. The court reporter will have you raise your right hand and swear under oath what you are about to say is true.

With all that high-priced talent in one place, you can just hear the cash-register cha-chinging, can't you? There's the court reporter, both attorneys billing their clients for their time, and you, the PI, billing your client for your time. Conducting a deposition can be expensive. And that is the precise reason why private investigators are in business.

By having the private investigator first go out and interview potential witnesses, attorneys can make a decision as to which witnesses to depose. There is no need to go to the expense of deposing someone if they have no recollection of the incident or

Crime Scene Clues

A **deposition** is a statement made under oath by a witness, usually written or recorded, that may be used in court at a later time. If there is the likelihood that the deponent will not be available later—for instance, due to illness—it is not uncommon for the deposition to be videotaped. The **deponent** is the witness being deposed.

matter at hand, or never even saw, for instance, the traffic accident you're investigating. It's a lot cheaper to pay the PI his hourly rate than to orchestrate a deposition that will be totally nonproductive.

Another reason for deposing someone is if they are a *reluctant witness*.

> ### Sherlock's Secrets
>
> A PI should give his client a progress report every few days. It can be as simple as a phone call or an e-mail. This regular updating has two very beneficial purposes. First, your client will appreciate knowing how the case is moving along. Second, it's not unusual for your client to assign you additional work, either on the current case or on a new assignment. Just talking to your client makes him think about other cases he has where your services could be useful. And more work means more billable hours and a better bottom line for your business.

Leslie was an emergency room nurse working in a local hospital. Our client, Hugh, had been a resident in a nursing home. The rules of common care in nursing homes require that patients be bathed daily. In addition, any sores or open wounds should be noted on their files, and a nurse specializing in wound care is supposed to tend to these sores.

The attendants, or certified nursing assistants, at these nursing homes are also supposed to make notes as to whether or not the residents are eating their meals. If the residents don't eat, their health can quickly fail. Nursing homes have nutritionists on staff who can help residents with eating disorders.

Hugh was already in delicate health due to his age and some other exacerbating physical conditions. He apparently hadn't been eating any of his meals, but it was not noted in his file.

> ### Crime Scene Clues
>
> A **reluctant witness** is an individual who may have considerable knowledge of the incident that is in question, but will not discuss her knowledge of this incident unless she is forced to by a court.

Finally, one day, a nurse noticed that Hugh was having difficulty breathing. She called for an ambulance, and Hugh was transported to the emergency room where Leslie was on duty.

In making a preliminary examination of Hugh, Leslie discovered many open sores and wounds on the lower portion of his body, including not only his legs, but also his groin and genitals.

Leslie made note that the wounds were infected. She saw maggots crawling throughout the open sores. She cleaned the wounds and admitted Hugh to the hospital because he was severely malnourished.

One of the witnesses that Hugh's attorney wanted me to interview was Leslie. I tracked Leslie down and one day dropped by her house unannounced. Leslie was cordial, but insisted on calling the legal department of her hospital before talking to me. Note that the hospital was not being sued. In this case, the nursing home, a totally different institution altogether, was the defendant.

I had several discussions with the legal department at that hospital before they finally agreed to let Leslie talk to me—if she wanted to. The discussion had to be limited to Leslie's original observations when Hugh was admitted. We could not discuss his treatment while at the hospital. That was fine, because all we wanted was her testimony as to the neglectful physical condition Hugh was in when he arrived at the hospital.

Sherlock's Secrets _____

Generally speaking, it's better to talk to witnesses without first making an appointment to see them. If the witness knows you're coming and he really doesn't want to talk to you, he won't be there when you arrive at the appointed time. Also, the witness's sympathies may lie with the other party, and if he knows you're coming, he'll call the other party, who probably will tell him not to talk to you. Then, when you arrive for your appointment, you will have wasted your driving time because the guy's not going to give you a statement.

True, an investigator can waste a lot of driving time making repeated trips to the witness's home, trying to catch him there without an appointment. An investigator has to weigh the time involved with the lost opportunity of surprise.

Overall, a private investigator will get better witness statements if he just shows up unannounced, but that's not always possible.

Leslie still refused to be interviewed. She wouldn't tell me why she wouldn't talk to me. Consequently, my client, the attorney for Hugh, set her deposition. Once she was under oath and compelled to talk, she testified to what she'd seen that day when Hugh was admitted. Leslie was a reluctant witness. A witness will have her own reasons for not wanting to testify. It might be inconvenient for them. It may be company policy that employees don't testify unless compelled to or she may harbor fears that her own actions, and in this case, the quality of the way she treated this particular patient, might come into question.

Work Product from the Attorney's Office

There is a general rule of law that says that work performed or originated by one attorney is not discoverable by the opposing attorney, unless it is violated by the attorney and given to other parties. This is called the *work product* rule.

In a case headed for trial, each attorney is under the obligation to present, to the opposing side, a list of the witnesses he intends to use during the trial. The opposing counsel can then interview or depose these witnesses and discover what the nature of their testimony is going to be or what evidence the witness will introduce. This is called discovery.

Crime Scene Clues

Work product is described as the attorney's notes and research materials and other documents or matters that the attorney makes, prepares, or uses as he works up the case. The reports of a private investigator, hired directly by the attorney or working out of the attorney's office, are also considered work product. A **privilege**, under law, is a special right that someone enjoys that the public at large does not enjoy. For instance, the marital privilege asserts that a wife cannot be forced to testify against her husband, or vice versa. The clergy privilege declares that communications between a clergyman and his parishioner are considered privileged.

If the attorney voluntarily gives a particular piece of work product to the opposing counsel then he has violated the work product privilege for that item and that work product no longer enjoys the privilege. It can be used by the opposing counsel, even if the attorney who originated the material has changed his mind and does not want it to appear in the court record.

For instance, if your client, the attorney, shares a copy of your report with the opposing attorney, your report will no longer enjoy the work product privilege.

As most of us know, anything you discuss with your attorney is confidential and cannot be disclosed to another attorney, law enforcement officer, or the court without your permission. This is called the attorney-client *privilege*.

Why do private investigators care about work product and privileges? Many private investigators are "in-house" investigators and work directly for attorneys.

Most private investigators hopefully have a broad range of clients, including attorneys. If a PI is contacted directly by an attorney to perform an investigation, then the results of that investigation are usually considered work product from the attorney's office, and are not discoverable.

Mary Ellen was 69 years old. For her birthday, she took a week-long cruise, departing from Fort Lauderdale and touring islands in the Caribbean. The cruise ship had an elevator to carry passengers between decks. Mary Ellen had the misfortune to be on the elevator when it broke down. She was trapped inside that small cubicle for about three hours.

Eventually, a mechanic managed to free the elevator but couldn't get it to stop exactly on the next floor. The elevator stopped about two-and-one-half feet above the landing. To get out of the elevator, Mary Ellen was forced to jump down to the deck. In doing so, she fell and fractured her hip. She sued the cruise ship line and the manufacturer of the elevator.

> ### Elementary, My Dear Watson
>
> In some states, investigators who work solely for one law firm do not have to meet the licensing requirements of the state and do not have to have a private investigator's license.

Our assignment was to put Mary Ellen under surveillance to determine her lifestyle and range of motion. We videotaped Mary Ellen over several successive days as she drove to the grocery store and ran other normal errands.

She definitely walked with a limp and used her cane occasionally. The evidence we collected basically was noncommittal. It pretty much showed a 69-year-old woman who'd undergone hip surgery.

Our client, the attorney for the cruise line, did not want to use the videotape or any of our reports in the trial, not because there was anything damaging to his case, but because he was afraid that the jury would be incensed that the insurance company had hired private investigators to snoop on this nice little old lady.

Sherlock's Secrets

When an individual, not an attorney, first calls to discuss a new matter, the PI should ask if the client is represented by an attorney. In order to protect the work product rule, the case needs to come from an attorney. It is also suggested that the report and invoice be directed to the attorney and the attorney should pay the invoice out of his own firm's funds. In this manner, the investigator can answer truthfully that his client is the attorney and not the individual.

If the caller has no attorney, don't refuse the case. Just be aware that later, your reports will be discoverable by the opposing side, and the individual who called you will be your client, not his attorney.

The other attorney figured that there was probably a video of his client and he wanted to play the "big bad insurance company" card at trial with the jury. He subpoenaed me for deposition. At the deposition, I refused to testify on the grounds that my work was work product from an attorney's office.

This case went to trial and the attorneys argued before the judge, out of the presence of the jury, about the admissibility of the videotapes. My client, who'd paid for the tapes, didn't want them admitted. Mary Ellen's attorney did.

Finally, again, out of the presence of the jury, I was called in and I showed the video-tapes to the judge. He agreed that there was nothing significant on the tapes that would help either case and declined to let the jury know that the tapes or the investigation even existed.

If the insurance company had hired me directly, then there would have been no work product privilege, and the tapes and my testimony would have been admitted. Mary Ellen's attorney would have made a big deal about the insurance company stooping so low as to spy on this nice little old lady, and the jury's sympathy might have been swayed toward Mary Ellen more than it otherwise had been.

In this case, Mary Ellen was awarded several hundred thousand dollars for her injury. At least her award was not prejudiced by the fact that the insurance company hired a PI to check her out. Right or wrong? You be the judge.

Elementary, My Dear Watson

The rules covering privileged communications are usually found in the state statutes concerning the rules of civil evidence or the rules of criminal evidence. Some states vary in what privileges they allow.

There is a general misconception that there is a privilege between a doctor and his patient in criminal matters. Most states recognize no privilege in that relationship with reference to a criminal matter.

However, in civil matters, there is a doctor-patient privilege that applies to the doctor's treatment or diagnosis of any condition of the patient. But, if the patient confides a matter to the doctor that is not related to the patient's medical condition, there is no privilege.

The Grand Jury

It's not often that a private investigator is called to testify before a *grand jury*, but it does happen. In testifying before a grand jury, the private investigator should present herself just as if she were in a regular trial before a judge and jury. She should, in other words, be her usual professional self.

The grand jury is usually composed of 12 to 18 people who meet on a regular basis, usually once a week. These people are called to be members of this grand jury for the duration of the jury. The jury duration might run from 6 to 18 months, depending on the jurisdiction in which it is called.

A grand jury has no judge sitting with the jury while it is in session. The district attorney (or one of his assistants) or, in federal matters, the U.S. Attorney (or one of his assistants) runs the grand jury. The assistant district attorney in charge of the grand jury presents evidence and calls witnesses pertaining to a crime under investigation. After the evidence has been presented and the witnesses have testified, the grand jury takes a vote to determine if there is probable cause that the crime occurred and that a particular individual committed the crime. The grand jury will either return a *true bill* (probable cause) or a *no bill* (insufficient evidence).

Unlike a regular jury trial, in a grand jury, the members can ask questions of the witnesses and of the assistant district attorney. Also unlike a regular jury trial, no attorneys are allowed into the grand jury proceedings. Only the members of the jury, the assistant district attorney in charge, and the witness testifying are in the room.

> **Crime Scene Clues**
>
> A **grand jury** is a jury or group of men and women, usually culled from the voter's registration rolls, that hears evidence and determines if there is probable cause to believe a crime has been committed and that a particular person committed that crime.

> **Crime Scene Clues**
>
> The grand jury will return a **true bill** if it finds probable cause or a **no bill** if there is not sufficient evidence to find probable cause that a crime has been committed and that a particular person committed that crime.

The testimony being given a grand jury is usually considered secret. However, the names of the witnesses called to testify are not confidential. If a witness refuses to testify, the assistant district attorney will ask a judge to order the witness to testify. If the witness continues to refuse to testify, the judge will hold the witness in contempt and put him in jail until he does testify, or until the grand jury has disbanded.

Presenting the Evidence at Trial

Unless the private investigator is called to testify as an expert witness, the judge and jury are not interested in his opinions. They want only the facts that he uncovered. Your client's attorney should meet with you, the PI, and go over what questions he will be asking when you eventually sit in front of the jury. Answer all the questions truthfully. If your client's attorney wants you to answer a question in a less-than-truthful manner, don't do it. Instead, simply tell the attorney not to ask that question.

The jury will be able to tell if you're hedging on a question, so if you're having any doubts about anything, work them out with the client's attorney before the trial ever starts.

If you, as the investigator, are presenting physical evidence, the evidence should be properly bagged and tagged as per Chapter 17. You did read that one twice, didn't you? If I put you on trial for being a PI, would I have enough evidence to convict you?

If the evidence consists of surveillance videotapes, the tapes should have been initialed and dated on the day they were made. If the original videotape to be presented is hours and hours long, I suggest that a duplicate tape be made, using only the highlights of the original tape.

The opposing attorney and the judge will normally resist the investigator's suggestion to show the highlight tape. But after about 30 minutes of a slow-moving, nothing-much-happening tape being shown, the jury will be getting antsy, and the judge will start looking at his watch. At this point, the judge will reconsider your offer to show an edited version, i.e., the highlight tape. Even the opposing attorney usually agrees, because he doesn't want to waste anymore of his time, either.

In nearly 20 years of showing videotapes to judges and juries, I've never had a judge fail to ask for the highlight copy after the first 30 minutes, if there are hours and hours of tape available. The judge will ask the investigator if this represents a true and accurate portrayal of what the investigator witnessed. Answer that in the positive and then pop the duplicate highlight tape into the VCR.

> **Sherlock's Secrets**
>
> If you, as the PI, are expected to show videotapes during the trial, you should check with the attorney or the court to see what equipment is available and make sure that it is reserved for the day that you are to testify. Alternatively, bring your own VCR and television, just in case.

The Cross-Examination

On the witness stand, you'll be sworn to tell the truth. The attorney for your client will ask you the questions that she's prepared you for, and you'll give truthful answers.

Next, the opposing counsel will ask you questions. Answer his questions straightforwardly and truthfully, even if you think the answers will hurt your client's case. The judge and/or the jury are not stupid. You are only one part of the case. Be professional and answer assuredly. Don't hesitate while trying to phrase your answer in the best light possible. Just answer it.

After the opposing counsel asks you his questions, your client's attorney will have another chance to redirect questions to you. It's her job to clear up any doubts that the questions from the other attorney may have raised, not yours.

The job of a private investigator is the search for truth, the facts that surround every accident and every lawsuit. Let the attorneys present only the evidence that is beneficial to their cases.

Their job is to take all of the facts that the investigator gathers, sift through them, and present the evidence in an order that will substantiate their case. The attorneys may omit facts. That's okay. There is no law or rule that says they have to present all of the facts. There is a rule that says the PI must present all of the evidence to his client or his client's attorney. After that, the job of the private investigator is done, and it's on to the next case.

The Least You Need to Know

- Some investigators are guilty of ghostwriting reports. This is illegal and is a prosecutable offense.

- Subpoenas command the investigator to appear for trial or depositions. Not responding places the investigator in jeopardy of being held in contempt of court.

- Depositions are held to make a record of a witness's testimony. They can be recorded by a court reporter, or videotaped for viewing at a later trial if the deponent's health is unstable.

- Privileged communications exist between attorneys and their clients. Also, if the circumstances are right, an investigator's work may be considered work product of an attorney's office, making it not discoverable by the opposing counsel.

- Private investigators occasionally are called to testify before a grand jury. The testimony is secret and, except for the assistant district attorney in charge, there are no attorneys allowed in the grand jury room.

- Investigators should present their evidence in court in a professional manner. A highlight videotape may be made, showing a shortened version of the original. Most judges will desire this tape be used instead of wasting hours watching the original.

- Testimony in court by the private investigator should be straightforward and honest. It is the attorney's job to rectify any misleading impressions caused by the opposing counsel's questions.

- The job of the private investigator is the search for truth. He must present to his client all of the evidence that he gathered.

Glossary

ANAC Automatic Number Announcement Circuit is a telephone number that, when dialed, will announce back to you the number you are calling from. These numbers vary within area codes and sometimes vary within switches in the same city.

arbitration Arbitration refers to a process where the plaintiff and the defendant in a civil lawsuit meet with a third party, known as a professional arbitrator. This arbitrator is skilled in negotiating, and it is his or her responsibility to help the two different sides come to an agreement. This process reduces the number of cases going to trial and helps clear the court calendar for cases that cannot be settled.

being made Being made means that a covert operation like a surveillance has been exposed and its presence made known to the subject of the operation. It's a clue you've been made when the person you're following gives you the finger.

binding arbitration Binding arbitration means that a settlement must be reached during arbitration. If the parties cannot decide upon a settlement considered fair by all, then the arbitrator, after being fully informed of the facts, will reach what he considers a fair conclusion. His determination is binding on both parties.

breaking squelch The squelch is the point where a radio receiver is tuned to its most sensitive setting. If tuned beyond this point the squelch is "broken" and the radio makes a loud, piercing sound similar to a screeching parrot.

burglary   The FBI's Uniform Crime Report defines burglary as the unlawful entry of a structure to commit a felony or a theft. The use of force to gain entry is not required to classify an offense as a burglary.

burned   Getting burned has the same meaning as "being made." The subject has become aware of the surveillance.

butt set   A butt set is a handheld device that looks like a cordless phone, has a touch-tone keypad, and is used by telephone and electronic service people to identify telephone lines. It will have a set of wires with alligator clips at the end. You can buy butt sets for less than a hundred dollars over the Internet or at Radio Shack.

center-weighted average   Many single-lens reflex cameras have built in light-metering capability that automatically adjusts the f-stop and the shutter speed. A good photographer will know if his or her light meter averages the measurement of the light over the entire surface of the lens or center weights the average, giving more importance to the amount of light coming through the center of the lens, where presumably the important image is located.

city directories   Sometimes called reverse directories or criss-cross directories, these books are privately published, frequently by Cole, Polk, Donnelly, and other publishers. These directories sort their listings by name, address, and telephone number. You can take a telephone number, check it in the "reverse" listing, and find the subscriber information. Likewise, you can take an address within the city, search the directory by address, and it will give you the person living there and his or her phone number.

countermeasure sweep   A countermeasure sweep is an active measure by an individual with the goal of finding or countering an aggressive action taken against him or her. Typically, the term is used in the sense of actively searching for and eliminating any electronic transmitters (bugs) or wiretaps that are directed toward locations or facilities where the target of the measure would likely be heard. A variation of the term is also used in respect to surveillance.

countersurveillance   This is a surveillance initiated by an individual to determine if he or she is under surveillance by an outside group. If properly conducted, a counter-surveillance will identify the entity conducting the surveillance. So, you'll know who at the diner counter is watching you.

courtesy officer   A courtesy officer is usually a local police patrol person or sheriff's deputy who is given some sort of discount in his rent at an apartment complex in exchange for parking a marked patrol unit on the grounds and handling disturbance complaints at the complex when he is present. This is usually considered a good deal for the apartment management and the law enforcement department, as it reduces crime and does not increase law enforcement costs.

crime scene investigation Conducting a crime scene investigation entails the collection of evidence or possible evidence toward the goal of placing suspects at the scene of the crime. The evidence must be collected according to the rules of evidence, which have been established by law and judicial precedence.

criss-cross Sometimes called reverse directories or city directories, these books are privately published, frequently by Cole, Polk, Donnelly, and other publishers. These directories sort their listings by name, address, and telephone number. You can take a telephone number, check it in the "reverse" listing, and find the subscriber information. Likewise, you can take an address within the city, search the directory by address, and it will give you the person living there and his or her phone number.

data brokers Also known as information brokers, these are individuals or companies that have access to specialized sources of information or use advanced techniques to gather information and then resell it to the private investigator. An example of this would be asking an information broker to obtain a nonpublished telephone number, or a list of credit card charges that the PI couldn't get himself.

defendant Legal actions require a minimum of two parties. The plaintiff is the party who initiates the action or lawsuit. The defendant is the person on the receiving end of the action.

deponent The deponent is the witness being deposed.

deposition A deposition is a statement under oath, usually written or recorded, that may be used in court at a later time. If there is the likelihood that the deponent will not be available later—for instance, due to illness—it is not uncommon for the deposition to be videotaped.

depth of field Depth of field refers to the apparent range of focus in a photograph. In portrait photography, the background and the foreground may be intentionally blurred and out of focus while the subject, in the center of the photograph, is in focus.

drive by A drive by is performed by private investigators to make a casual check of a subject's residence to see if he or she is home or to observe what activities are taking place at a particular location during a specific time.

dropped When a cell or telephone bill has dropped, it means that the billing cycle has ended, and the charges are en route to the consumer. Some phone sources cannot access the list of phone charges until the bill has entered the billing system's computer. Better phone sources can access the charges as they occur. With enough pressure you might get the cellular company to give you the calls daily as they're made.

due diligence A due diligence search can be a check of an individual, but more often of a company's reputation, ability to perform under contract, and verification that there are no liens or judgments filed against the company. A good due diligence search will also encompass any lawsuits, pending or potential, or other current or potential areas of liability, such as a pending bankruptcy.

f-stop   F-stop refers to the setting on an adjustable single-lens reflex camera. F-stops are numbers and indicate to what degree the iris of the lens is opened or closed. The f-stop setting is one factor in determining the amount of light that passes through the lens and exposes the film. As the f-stop number increases, the iris is then "stopped down" to a smaller aperture and less light is allowed through the lens. Larger numbers equal less light, all other factors remaining the same.

FD 302   The FD 302 is a federal form used by the FBI that reports the results of interviews conducted by FBI agents. All interviews are reported in a standard format and are typed or printed onto FD 302s. Law school students learn this early in their schooling, and the forms are referred to throughout judicial opinions.

felonies   Criminal offenses are categorized according to the severity of the offense. Crimes that are punishable by one year jail time or longer are called felonies.

field identification   A field identification card is a card used by patrol officers when questioning persons who may have been acting suspiciously. It will contain the subject's identifying data, the date and location of the incident, and a short synopsis of why the subject was questioned.

grand jury   A group of men and women, usually culled from the voter's registration rolls, that hears evidence and determines if there is probable cause to believe a crime has been committed and that a particular person committed that crime, is called a grand jury.

hot sheet   A hot sheet is a current list of recently stolen vehicles. Police departments, of course, potentially have hundreds of patrol cars driving around their jurisdiction all day long. Patrolmen are on the lookout for any car that may be on the hot sheet. Many police department patrol cars are now in communication with their headquarters by computer, and they access the hot sheet list on the computer rather than a physical printed list, as in smaller departments.

hyperlink   A hyperlink is an area, picture, word, or phrase on a web page that you can select with your cursor in order for your browser to take you to another page or website whose content is linked in some manner.

impeaching   Impeaching a witness's testimony means to call into question the reliability or truthfulness of the testimony being given.

informant   An informant is an individual who cooperates, usually without the knowledge of others involved in the case, by providing information during an investigation.

He or she may or may not be a witness or a participant in the particular case under investigation. Frequently, an informant may receive compensation, or other benefit, for this information, whereas a witness never should.

information brokers   Also known as data brokers, information brokers are individuals or companies that have access to specialized sources of information or use advanced techniques to gather information and then resell it to the private investigator. An example of this would be asking an information broker to obtain a non-published telephone number, or a list of credit card charges that the PI couldn't get himself.

jog and shuttle   Jog and shuttle are two functions of a videocassette recorder that allow an operator to play the tape backward and forward, one frame at a time, or in multiple frame increments that are determined by the user. Generally, the jog-shuttle control is a wheel device on the VCR that the operator rotates forward or backward, causing the VCR motors to rotate in sync with it forward and reverse, faster and slower.

junction box   A junction box is a piece of telephone company equipment where several customers' telephone lines are housed and connected to a phone company cable. Typically, these junction boxes house from two to two dozen connections. There is normally one on every block, or one for every 10 to 12 subscribers.

landline telephone line   This refers to a normal telephone line that has a physical demarcation point at a residence, business, or pay telephone. The phone call at least begins and ends its transmission along a pair of wires, regardless of whether transmission of the call includes microwave or satellite in between both ends. This is in contrast to a cellular phone, or any type of radio communication, which is considered wireless communication—literally, not connected to the ground at some point with wires.

latent fingerprint   A latent fingerprint is a print that is not immediately apparent to the naked eye, but can be made visible by dusting, or fuming with chemicals. Latent prints can then be compared to inked prints of suspects. An inked print is a fingerprint taken in a controlled environment where the pads of a suspect's fingers are covered with ink and rolled onto a fingerprint card.

light-meter averages   Many single-lens reflex cameras have built-in light-metering capability that automatically adjust the f-stop and the shutter speed. A good photographer will know if his light meter averages the measurement of the light over the entire surfaces of the lens or center weights the average, giving more importance to the amount of light coming through the center of the lens where presumably the important image is located.

lines of resolution   This will tell you how fine of an image you'll get from the camera under optimal conditions. The higher the number, the better the resolution, and the better the picture.

lux   This refers to the camera's video board's or video chip's sensitivity to light. Some cameras use charged coupled devices (CCD). For our purposes, consider them chips. Whatever they use, the lower the lux, the more sensitive the camera is to light, which is very helpful in indoor applications.

misdemeanors   Criminal offenses are categorized according to the severity of the offense. Less serious crimes, those typically involving a potential penalty of less than one year, are called misdemeanors.

motor vehicle theft   For the purposes of the FBI's Uniform Crime Report, motor vehicle theft is defined as the theft of automobiles, trucks, buses, motorcycles, motor scooters, snowmobiles, etc. This does not include the taking of a vehicle for temporary purposes by those having lawful access.

NCIC   This stands for the National Crime Information Center. Among other things, NCIC maintains a huge database, run by the FBI, where subjects with outstanding arrest warrants are listed. Also listed are stolen properties and missing persons.

no bill   The grand jury will return a no bill if it finds there is not sufficient evidence of probable cause that a crime as been committed or that a particular person committed that crime.

optical zoom   On camera lenses; refers to the focal length achieved by physically moving the lens further apart from each other thereby achieving a greater focal length (hence the term zooming out with a zoom lens) and increasing the relative size of the image as it appears on the film or recording media.

PACER   An acronym for Public Access to Court Electronic Records.

parole   Parole means an individual was sentenced to and actually spent time in jail, but was released earlier than the original sentence called for. He also must behave himself for a specified period of time.

phreaking   Telephone phreaking is similar to computer hacking, only it involves the telephone system. A phreak is someone who wants to learn about the telephone system. Some phreaks take this knowledge and use it to make free calls from pay telephones, and to circumvent paying long distance charges on private phones. Both are clearly illegal, constitute theft of services, and might land you in jail.

pinhole lens   A pinhole lens is literally a lens for a camera that is about the size of the tip of ballpoint pen. It's not literally "pin" size, but close. It can be concealed quite easily, particularly in dropped ceilings, where the ceiling tiles have a rough texture. This size lens is also popular in Nanny Cams where the hole for the lens can be concealed behind a small piece of plastic, such as you might find on radios or many other appliances. They are frequently used when installing a camera in an air-conditioning vent.

plaintiff   Legal actions require a minimum of two parties. The plaintiff is the party that initiates the action or lawsuit. The defendant is the person on the receiving end of the action.

plead down   This means that the prosecuting attorney's office, in order to expedite the flow of cases and reduce his or her load and the burden on the court, reduces charges from higher offenses to lesser offenses. He or she does this if the defendant agrees to plead guilty to the lesser offenses.

point man   A point man on a surveillance is the investigator who actually has "the eyeball" or has physical sight of the subject.

premise liability   A premise liability case involves the allegation that a property owner was negligent by not curing some default in the premise or real property owned or managed by the defendant, and this negligence led to the harm of the plaintiff. An example of this could be the plaintiff alleging that the defendant failed to provide adequate exterior lighting, and the ensuing darkness was responsible for the rape or assault inflicted upon the plaintiff.

pretext   A pretext is a subterfuge or a ploy used by private investigators to encourage an individual to reveal information about himself or herself or another party, without being aware of the true reason for the conversation. In the course of responding to what appears to be a normal everyday query, the individual unsuspectingly releases the information the investigator actually is seeking.

privilege   A privilege, under law, is a special right which someone enjoys that the public at large does not enjoy. For instance, the marital privilege states that a wife cannot be forced to testify against her husband, or vice versa. According to the clergy privilege, communications between a clergyman and his parishioner are considered privileged.

probation   Probation indicates that a person was convicted of a crime, but rather than receiving a jail term, he is given probation to see if he can behave himself over a specified time period.

random access memory   RAM is an acronym for random access memory. It is the memory that the computer accesses when it processes information and runs computer programs. If there is not enough RAM in a computer, then the information being processed is swapped back and forth to the hard drive, which slows down the processing speed and leads to more rapid hard-drive failure and computer program lockups and crashes.

real property Real property is described as anything that is not personal property. Real property is anything that is a part of the earth or attached thereto which cannot be easily moved. Think dirt.

recorded statement A recorded statement is a voice tape recording made by a witness concerning facts and/or the witness's recollection of the pertinent incident.

registered agent An individual who agrees to be available to accept service, subpoenas, or other legal documents for a corporation is its registered agent. In the event you need to sue a corporation, your attorney will need to have it served with the lawsuit. The registered agent is the person who will accept notice of the suit on behalf of the corporation.

reluctant witness An individual may have considerable knowledge of the pertinent incident relevant to the matter under suit, but will not discuss his or her knowledge of this incident unless compelled to by a court.

repeater A radio tower that receives the signal from a mobile radio, such as a walkie-talkie, and repeats the broadcast signal over a larger area than a five-watt walkie-talkie could cover. The signal may bounce from one repeater to another to another, and possibly could be received over an entire state. This is common with the FBI radios. An agent in the field should be able to reach his division headquarters from almost anyplace within the geographical boundaries of his division's area. Most commercial repeaters, set up for business purposes, do not have such a broad area of coverage.

results billing Results billing is the practice of charging more than a standard hourly rate if the results achieved justify a higher bill or a higher hourly rate.

retainer Money paid by the client at the beginning of an investigation. Frequently a small portion of the retainer is nonrefundable if the case is canceled. Typically the investigator bills his time against the retainer on hand. Once the retainer is used up, the investigator will ask for additional funds before preceding any further on the case.

reverse directories Sometimes called criss-cross or city directories, these books are privately published, frequently by Cole, Polk, Donnelly, and other publishers. These directories sort their listings by name, address, and telephone number. You can take a telephone number, check it in the "reverse" listing, and find the subscriber information. Likewise, you can take an address within the city and search the directory by address, and it will give you the person living there and his or her phone number.

safe phone A safe phone is a telephone that is not traceable back to the user. It does not reveal its number to the Caller ID services on outgoing calls, but it has Caller ID service for incoming calls. It is set up in such a way that it can be answered in any manner necessary and is used for only one case at a time. As a good PI, you should always have one of these phone lines available in your office at all times.

search engines   Internet sites that allow a user to input a search criteria are called search engines. The engine then searches its own database of researched Internet sites and provides you a list of sites that most closely meet your criteria.

signed statement   A signed statement is a written declaration made by a witness concerning facts and/or the witness's recollection of the pertinent incident, and is signed by the witness.

single-lens reflex   A single-lens reflex (SLR) camera is a camera where the light (the image) passes through the lens and is reflected by a mirror to the viewfinder where it is viewed by the photographer. When the shutter button is depressed, the mirror flips out of the way and the image passes directly to the film. The advantage of SLR cameras over other cameras is that the photographer sees the exact image that will appear on the film. Also, with most SLR cameras the photographer has a wide range of lenses from which he or she can choose.

skip tracing   Originally referring to collection agencies' attempts to locate a debtor who'd "skipped out" on his obligation, skip tracing generally now refers to anyone that a private investigator is trying to find. Perhaps this person is intentionally eluding creditors or is merely a witness whose address is not currently known, but is sought by attorneys for an interview or a deposition. Universally, however, a person who is eluding his creditors is referred to in the business as "a skip."

SSAN   The standard abbreviation in most federal law enforcement circles for Social Security Account Number.

subpoena   In a subpoena, the judge of a court requires that a specific person or representative of an institution appear in court or at another specified location on a specific day at a certain time.

subpoena deuces tecum   A subpoena deuces tecum is a subpoena that requires the individual or institution to provide documents to the clerk of the court as outlined in the subpoena. Or, a subpoena could require both an appearance and the retrieval of documents.

suspect   An individual who may have committed or aided the commission of a crime that is under investigation is a suspect.

telephone break   A telephone break is the process of taking a telephone number, with no other identifying information, and obtaining the subscriber information, including the subscriber's name, the service address if it's a landline, or the mailing address if the number rings to a cellular telephone or a pager.

true bill   The grand jury will return a true bill if there is sufficient evidence to find probable cause that a crime has been committed and that a particular person committed that crime.

web browser   A web browser is the software program you use to "surf" on the Internet. Most likely it is Microsoft Internet Explorer, Netscape, or AOL's browser.

wild card   A wild card allows the use of only partial names in searches. This is accomplished by inserting an asterisk after the beginning of a name. For instance, if you're not sure if a person's name is Rick or really Richard, you can input "Ric*" (without the quotation marks) and the search will return Rick, Richard, Ricky, and Ricardo.

witness   A witness is an individual who may have testimony pertinent to an investigation.

work product   Work product is described as the attorney's notes and research materials and other documents or matters that he or she makes or uses while working up the case. The reports of a private investigator hired directly by the attorney or working out of the attorney's office are also considered work product.

writ of execution   A writ of execution is an order from a judge of competent jurisdiction commanding that certain actions be taken or cease to occur. A custodial writ would command the person having custody to relinquish custody to the person named in the writ.

Resources

Recording of Telephonic Conversations by State (Interception of Wire Communications)

Federal law allows one party to a telephonic conversation to tape record the conversation without notifying other parties participating in the conversation that the recording is taking place. Violators of the federal statute can be imprisoned up to five years and fined $10,000 (Title 18, Sec. 2511 (4)).

Thirty-eight states and the District of Columbia follow the federal precedent. Twelve states insist that all parties to the conversation should be notified and be made aware that the conversation is being recorded.

Also, different states have some peculiarities that don't apply to all states. Arizona, for example, may allow the subscriber to the telephone line (the person who pays the bill) to record conversations on that line with no party consent. Some states require tones or beeps be placed on the line every 15 seconds during recording. If you have questions, check the statutes in your state. Don't relay solely on this list.

Search the list by state to determine what the law allows in your state.

One-Party and All-Party States

California	All Party
Connecticut	All Party
Delaware	All Party
Florida	All Party
Illinois	All Party
Maryland	All Party
Massachusetts	All Party
Michigan	All Party
Montana	All Party
New Hampshire	All Party
Pennsylvania	All Party
Washington	All Party

All others not on this list are One Party States.

Sample Client Retainer Contract

The following is a sample contract between a client and an investigative agency. It was provided by and is used with permission of Vicki Childs of Blazer Investigative in Charleston, S.C. It is also used by the author's agency.

INVESTIGATIVE AGREEMENT

This hourly rate investigator-client fee agreement is between **ABC INVESTIGATIVE AGENCY,** a licensed Florida investigative agency and _____ client. The general nature of the case is _____

_____

This case will begin on or about the date below and continue for 90 days or until client withdraws.

Client employs and ABC INVESTIGATIVE AGENCY will accept employment to perform investigative services in connection with Client's case regardless of the disposition of this case. The Client agrees to fully cooperate with ABC INVESTIGATIVE AGENCY and provide accurate information as a basis for this investigation.

ABC INVESTIGATIVE AGENCY is not responsible for results of inaccurate information or leads provided by Client. Client understands that ABC INVESTIGATIVE may withdraw from this contact if Client should fail to pay all fees and costs set forth below.

Reports, video/photos will be provided within 10 days of a request by the Client, but may be withheld until payment is received.

FEES AND RETAINER

ABC INVESTIGATIVE AGENCY shall be compensated for all services rendered Client at the hourly rate of $ _____ per hour and $ _____ per mile. Client agrees to pay the sum of $ _____ as a retainer fee. ABC INVESTIGATIVE will bill hourly against the retainer fee. Client further agrees to pay for any other expenses incurred during the investigation, including but not limited to hotel bills, videotapes, photos, etc. If travel is anticipated, a fee of $ _____ will be applied toward costs and expenses incurred in the pursuit of this matter. Once any investigative effort is initiated in this case, a minimum of $200.00 of the retainer will be withheld should Client decide to end the investigation. Any other balance will be refunded to the Client upon request.

COURT APPEARANCES

If any agent of ABC INVESTIGATIVE AGENCY is called as a witness for deposition or Court, the cost will be a minimum of $250.00. If the Court appearance or deposition requires more than 4 hours time, the Client will be charged the hourly and mileage rate set forth above.

CLIENT AGREES THAT NO AGENT OF ABC INVESTIGATIVE AGENCY, INC. HAS MADE ANY PROMISE OR GUARANTEE REGARDING THE OUTCOME OF THEIR CASE OR FACTS GATHERED DURING THE INVESTIGATION PERFORMED BY ABC INVESTIGATIVE AGENCY, INC.

Client does hereby bind his/her heirs, executors, and legal representatives to the terms of this contract as set forth herein.

I HAVE READ THIS CONTRACT AND AGREE TO ITS TERMS AND CONDITIONS.

_____   _____
CLIENT   ABC INVESTIGATIVE AGENCY
Date: _____

Index

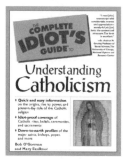

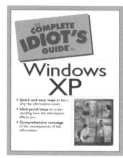